WILL WILLIMON'S

LECTIONARY SERMON RESOURCE

WILL WILLIMON'S

YEAR

A

PART 1

LECTIONARY

SERMON

RESOURCE

 Abingdon Press™

Nashville

WILL WILLIMON'S LECTIONARY SERMON RESOURCE,
YEAR A PART 1

Copyright © 2019 by Abingdon Press

ISBN 978-1-5018-4750-9

19 20 21 22 23 24 25 26 27 28—10 9 8 7 6 5 4 3 2 1

MANUFACTURED IN THE UNITED STATES OF AMERICA

Contents

LENT

EASTER

Introduction

For over three decades *Pulpit Resource* has been helping preachers prepare to preach. Now, in this volume, some of the most helpful resources have been brought together to help you faithfully preach your way through the first half (Advent through Easter) of Year A of the Common Lectionary. This *Lectionary Sermon Resource* doesn't claim to be the sole resource needed for engaging, faithful biblical preaching, but it does give you, the pastor who preaches, accessible, easy-to-use help on your way to a sermon.

No sermon is a solo production. Every preacher relies on inherited models, mentors in the preacher's past, commentaries on biblical texts by people who have given their lives to such study, comments received from members of the congregation, last week's news headlines, and all the other ways that a sermon is communal. Using this resource is equivalent to sitting down with a trusted clergy friend over a cup of coffee and asking, "What will you preach next Sunday?"

In the sermons that follow, I give you just what you need to begin the journey toward a sermon. I hope that this *Lectionary Sermon Resource* stokes, funds, and fuels your imagination. Rarely do I give you a full sermon in the Proclamation section that can be preached verbatim. I've left plenty of room to insert your own illustrations, to make connections that work within your congregational context, and to speak the word in your distinctive voice. Sermons are occasional: God's word spoken in a particular time and place to a particular people. Only you can speak God's word in your distinctive voice to your distinctive context. All I try to do in this volume is to give you my insights and ideas related to a specific biblical text and then leave you free to allow the Holy Spirit to work within you and your particular congregation.

From what pastors have told me, the value of this guide is its simplicity, its unvarying format. Every Sunday you are given the following sections: *Theme* (I still think the time-honored practice of using a theme sentence to begin sermon preparation is a good practice, enabling the sermon to have coherence and unity); *Introduction to the readings* (that can be used as preparation for listening to the texts read in corporate worship); and *Prayer* (because every sermon is a gift of the Holy Spirit). The sections *Encountering the text* (listening to the biblical text, engagement with its particular message, is the first essential step on the way to a faithful sermon), *Proclaiming the text* (my sketch of ideas and movements for developing what I hear in the assigned text), and *Relating the text* (copious illustrative material that helps the sermon hit home) are given on different Sundays.

I'm honored that you have invited me to be a partner in your preaching. It's a demanding, challenging, joyful vocation to which God has called us. Let's work together to make sure God's word is offered in a lively, engaging way to God's people. Onward in the great adventure of preaching!

—WILL WILLIMON

First Sunday of Advent

Isaiah 2:1-5

Psalm 122

Romans 13:11-14

Matthew 24:36-44

Have You Got the Time?

Selected reading

Romans 13:11-14

Theme

Christians are those who have been let in on an open secret: our time is not our own. In Jesus Christ, God has decisively intruded into our time, taken our time as God's own. Behind all the events of the moment, behind the headlines of today's newspaper, God is busy, God has come to us. Knowing what time it is provokes in us a question: How then should we live? Christians are those who keep time with the gospel—the good news that God has taken our time.

Introduction to the readings

Isaiah 2:1-5

Isaiah the prophet speaks of a coming time when God "will judge between the nations" (v. 4).

Romans 13:11-14

"You know what time it is," Paul writes to the church at Rome. "Salvation is nearer than when we first had faith" (v. 11).

Matthew 24:36-44

Jesus warns his disciples that the time is short, saying that the Lord comes like a thief in the night. Wake up! Be ready for God's advent.

Prayer

Almighty God, you have allotted us time to live in your good creation. The days of our lives slip past us; each day brings us closer to our end. Sometimes our short days grow wearisome and dull. We plod along in old patterns and accustomed ruts.

And yet, at times, our time becomes your time. You intrude among us, reveal yourself to us. You show up among us, surprise us, and redeem our dull days, making our time into your time.

May we be ever watchful, ever eager for your advent among us, anticipating your coming to us, standing with you in all our days. Amen.

Encountering the text

"Wake up! Do you know what time it is?" That is the underlying theme in today's second lesson from the thirteenth chapter of Paul's letter to the Romans. Christians, according to Paul, are those who have been given the gift to know what's really going on in the present moment. The coming of Jesus Christ is a claim about the significance of the present age. "Wake up. Your salvation is nearer now than when you first believed," says Paul.

From this sweeping claim about the present hour, Paul moves immediately to ethics. How then should we live, now that we know the time? Paul says that we ought to live as those who are members of a new age. In Advent we are preparing for the coming of Christ. Christ has come, is come, will come—that is the complex Christian view of time. Our time has been commandeered, overtaken, subsumed by a living, seeking God.

Today's scripture from Paul's letter to the Romans is therefore an opportunity to proclaim that the gospel is an assertion about time. It is also an opportunity to say to those of us who have become easy and restful with that gospel, "Wake up!"

Proclaiming the text

Paul writes to a waiting church. It had been perhaps only about four or so decades since Jesus was crucified and had been raised from the dead when Paul wrote this letter. The days right after the resurrection must have been exciting with the risen Christ appearing here and there, miraculously intruding.

But with time, the excitement may have cooled somewhat. Many Christians thought that when Jesus said, "I'm coming again for you," he meant he was coming in just a few years. But now many years had passed. Jesus had not returned soon.

Paul writes to the church reminding them that God doesn't do time the way we do time: "Our salvation is nearer than when we first had faith" (Rom 13:11).

It doesn't take one long, when you become a Christian, to realize that the church doesn't keep time as the world keeps time. We live much of our lives under the world's calendar.

The church invites us to live under another calendar—this is Sunday, the first Sunday of Advent. The church changes our worldview—our sense of what's going on in the world—by changing our sense of time.

Have you ever noted the peculiar tendency of the Gospel stories to locate themselves in a particular geography, constantly mentioning place, names, and specific geographic locations that no one has ever heard of or is likely to hear of again? The incarnation—God coming among us as Jesus Christ—is thus demonstrated by Judea, Bethlehem, and Galilee as typical of a God who locates.

But this Sunday I want you to note how the Gospels also take pains to state that Jesus occurred not only in place but also in time. Think of how often Gospel writers will say things like, "The next day...."; "It was about the third hour...."; "Immediately...."; "On the Sabbath...."; "It was night...."; I believe this is the Bible's way of saying that in Jesus Christ, God takes time, our time.

From Jews, Christians got the notion that time begins and ends in God's own good time. Christians claim that God became flesh, entered time, and died. Then God raised Jesus from the dead and thereby broke time's sovereignty, disarmed *chronos* (the Greek god of time). That victory is known as resurrection—old time's defeat. In the resurrection our comfortable normality was exposed and time ceased to be what we humans make of it; time became what God makes of it. In resurrection, God gave us human beings something that we could never have through our own efforts—a beyond.

And yet, what was the first act of the two apostles after they witnessed the aftermath of resurrection? They went back home (John 20:10). They attempted to get back to normal. Whenever the culture's official, predictable, accustomed time is disrupted, immediately we move into action and try to "get back to normal." Time disrupted and eventful is Jesus's time; time under the illusion of normalcy and eternality is the world's time. *Homeostasis*—that is, static time, uneventful time—tends to be the goal of most every human undertaking, including the church. We so want things to be predictable, tied down, fixed.

Against our deadly accommodation to the world's time in the life, death, and resurrection of Jesus Christ, death was disarmed and time was taken by God. We thought we had time—that is, we were managing time, taking time for our own ends—then time got commandeered by God. It is of the nature of the Trinity to disrupt time. Time in the Gospels seems compressed, heated, fast-paced (and not only in the Gospel of Mark, whose favorite chronological word is *immediately, euthys*).

- 4 -

One of the reasons we read the Gospels in church is to read ourselves into this peculiar, heated Gospel time. God is taking our time and making it God's time.

In exile, with no future, Israel had her end named as her beginning: "Don't remember the prior things...Look! I'm doing a new thing" (Isa 43:18-19). God is taking back time. It is so tempting to believe that the present social order is more real, more normal, and more eternal than the reign of God.

One of the things that the modern world did, in order to get going, was to banish God from time. That is, many modern views of God render God into a detached, serene, distant deity who is said to care about us but never actually shows up anywhere, never actually intrudes into our time.

I suppose we got this sort of God because we wanted, in the modern world, to have time as our time, time that was sealed off and safe from the periodic intrusions (and disruptions) of God. Is it not the nature of the miraculous to seem a shocking disruption of the orderly, predictable flow of things? Is that why many of us modern people are so perturbed by the miracles that are reported in scripture? We are disturbed that our time might not really be our time.

In Advent we focus upon, prepare for, and explore the significance of a God who not only loves us but also showed up among us, as one of us, as Jesus the Christ. In other words, Advent is a time when God disrupted our time and took it over as God's time.

When Jesus Christ was born among us in Bethlehem, we realized that something was afoot that was considerably beyond our conceptions of just what can and can't be. We realized that we were not left on our own, not as alone as much as we had been led to believe. God with us, God in our time, is Emmanuel.

So perhaps Advent is a yearly reminder that at any moment, your time could become God's time. The time that you thought was your own, to live as you please, is in reality God's.

Perhaps that's one reason why we come to church on Sunday. Here, in worship, our sense of God's presence often becomes particularly vivid and undeniable. Perhaps worship here on Sunday is preparation for God's presence to become particularly real and vivid to you on Monday.

You know his "Amazing Grace," but do you know this hymn by John Newton?

> How tedious and tasteless the hours
> When Jesus no longer I see
> Sweet prospects, sweet birds, and sweet flowers
> have all lost their sweetness to me
>
> The midsummer sun shines but dim
> The fields strive in vain to look gay
> But when I am happy with Him
> December's as pleasant as May.
>
> —John Newton, "How Tedious and Tasteless the Hours," (1779).

There we were, thinking we were just going through another humdrum, dull day and then Jesus shows up. Our time is transformed.

A man in my congregation had dangerous open-heart surgery. He was told by the doctor he had no more than a 50 percent chance of survival during the surgery. But he did survive. When I visited him afterward the surgery, I said, "You did survive after all! Isn't that wonderful?"

He said, "No preacher, I didn't just survive. I did more than survive; I was born again. I'm not the same person I have been for the past fifty years. It's like God reached into my life and, through this illness, made me somebody better than ever I was before. I've been given a second chance and I'm going to be different, better than before."

Once again, God in Christ had made an advent into a life and, just by showing up, just by intruding into the time, had transformed time.

In Advent we sing hymns like "O Come, O Come, Emmanuel." And what do we do when that prayer is answered and God comes, God shows up, and God makes our time into God's time?

So here is my Advent word to you (and I hope it's heard as "good news"): God has a way of taking time, taking time from you, taking time for you. In your life, it's not just the same darn thing again and again, because all that happens in time is not left up to us.

The time of your life, be it good or bad, painful or not, is not completely in your hands. Christians believe that our time can begin and end, can be disrupted, and can be transformed because time is not left up to us. God takes time. Emmanuel.

Relating the text

But when the fulfillment of the time came, God sent his Son, born through a woman, and born under the Law. This was so he could redeem those under the Law so that we could be adopted.... Therefore, you are no longer a slave but a son or daughter, and if you are his child, then you are also an heir through God. (Gal 4:4-5, 7)

We are not redeemed away from time, but as Paul says here in Galatians, God moves into time, adopts our time, redeems us from bondage to time's ravages, and generates "the fullness of time." That's the main reason why the church attempts to help us take time in the name of Jesus by demanding that we follow the church year. The church teaches us to mark time according to Epiphany, Lent, and Easter rather than as Fourth of July, Thanksgiving, and Mother's Day. We are thereby encouraged not to escape time, but rather to live in time as those who know what time it really is.

The Greek philosophers marveled that time was full of pattern, recurrence, and the eternal return. The first historian, Thucydides, said that the task of the historian was to sort through the flux of time and place, the confusing, odd particularities of human events and find universally recurring patterns. Armed with knowledge of these patterns, the historian could rise above the seeming senselessness of contemporary events and, because one had uncovered the eternally recurring patterns of human history, one could predict how future events would go. Nietzsche's "myth of eternal return" was something similar—this world is finite, closed, bearing within it only a limited number of possible combinations. True newness is impossible. What appears to us as "new" is only the cyclical recurrence of every finite situation an infinite number of times, said Nietzsche. There's nothing new under the sun.

Søren Kierkegaard was among the first (I presume) to note that the Jewish and Christian views of time are different from the pagan. In Christianity, the believer seeks not to rise above time or to escape time, but rather to hear the command of God in time, like Abraham heard God calling him on a starry night. Is that why the Synoptic Gospels begin with relinquishment, with Jesus's demand to let go of jobs, to abandon marriage and family, and to follow Jesus into an unknown, never predefined destination? Time flows along normally until Jesus sets foot on the scene.

Theologian Robert Jenson shows that Jews and Christians have a very peculiar idea of what it means when we claim that God is "eternal":

"The biblical God's eternity is his temporal infinity.... What [God] transcends is any limit imposed on what can be by what has been, except the limit of his personal self-identity, and any limit imposed on his action by the availability of time. The true God is not eternal because he lacks time, but because he takes time... [God] is not eternal in that he secures himself from time, but in that he is faithful to his commitments within time. At the great turning, Israel's God is eternal in that he is faithful to the death, and then yet again faithful. God's eternity is temporal infinity."

—Robert Jenson, *Systematic Theology,* vol. 1 (New York: Oxford University Press, 1977), 217–18

Perhaps it's because of my advanced age (I've clearly got more yesterdays on my account than tomorrows), but I find that I wake up each morning surprised, grateful even, just to be waking up in the morning! I find myself saying to myself, "So, you have one more day. What a surprise. What a gift. So, what will I do with today?" The time before me is a gift and an assignment, grace, and judgment. What will we do, and what will God do with the time?

Odd that we tend to think of the story of Jesus as something that happened in time past. Odd, if you consider the resurrection to be true. If the resurrection of Jesus really happened, as we believe it did, then we have more future with Jesus than past, more tomorrows than yesterdays.

Jesus is more of our present and future than our past.

Second Sunday of Advent

Isaiah 11:1-10

Psalm 72:1-7, 18-19

Romans 15:4-13

Matthew 3:1-12

The Word in the Words

Selected reading

Romans 15:4-13

Theme

Scripture is a gift of God that offers contemporary Christians encouragement and hope. Christians are those who align their lives to the demands of these ancient inspired texts. To be a Christian is to be guided by a higher standard of judgment than your own conscience. If we are humble and obedient, the Bible speaks to us today, giving us guidance and sustenance in our contemporary discipleship.

Introduction to the readings

Isaiah 11:1-10

Isaiah predicts the advent of the messianic king who will deliver Israel. The spirit of the Lord will rest on him. He will rule with wisdom, understanding, and might. His reign will be good news for the poor and meek and will inaugurate a change in the whole created order—wolves and leopards living side by side with lambs, lions eating straw like an ox, and babies playing alongside cobras.

Romans 15:4-13
Paul reminds the Romans that the things written in the scriptures were written to give them encouragement and hope. Thus Paul commends scripture as a guide to assist in the controversy about the inclusion of Gentiles into the faith.

Matthew 3:1-12
Fiery John the Baptist—the voice, the one preparing the way of the Messiah—preaches his message of repentance. Matthew remembers the words of the prophet who foretold the coming of the Messiah.

Prayer

Lord Jesus, Word of God incarnate, this day, in the reading and proclamation of scripture, open to us the riches of your revelation. Speak to us that which we could never speak to ourselves. Show us your glory and reveal to us your way so that we, having heard you, might understand you, and in understanding you we might follow you. Amen.

Encountering the text

During Advent we prepare to welcome Emmanuel, God with us. How? By doing what we attempt every Sunday. By submitting ourselves to scripture. The church is sustained, encouraged, and at the same time severely criticized and challenged by the very same scripture that the church produced. We meet Christ in scripture in a way that is singular and fecund. In our encounters with scripture we believe we hear the voice, see the ways, and receive the guidance of the living God.

Scripture was produced by communities of faith who had experienced God's presence and interaction in vivid ways. Something undeniable and real had happened to them and they wanted to tell everyone the news. Not that all their testimony was uniform or rendered in the same way. In fact, some of the diversity of the testimony is for me a sort of proof that the events they were trying to relate were so mind-boggling and boundary-breaking that they were very difficult to put into speech. We are the beneficiaries of their testimony; we are the result of the encounter that their testimony provokes in each succeeding generation. We'll probably read these words here in our church on Christmas: "What we have seen and heard, we also announce it to you so that you can have fellowship with us. Our fellowship is with the Father and with his Son, Jesus Christ. We are writing these things so that our joy can be complete" (1 John 1:3-4).

Proclaiming the text

We gather here at church, not primarily to hear what I've got on my mind this week, or even what you may have on your mind. Christian thought arises from and is answerable to scripture. The ancient Articles of Religion of the Anglican Church enunciate the great Reformation principle that the Bible "containeth all things necessary to salvation." I hope you are reassured by this belief that everything anyone really needs to know in order to be with God is graciously given in the Bible. We need not rummage around elsewhere for our ideas about God. It's all here, more than we'll ever be able to process in a lifetime of sermons, all that we need to know of God and more.

Today, when popular novels and movies come forth claiming to have exposed some secret knowledge, a story of some sinister church plot that has now been revealed, it's good to know that, while such claims make for a good story, the church loves us enough to reassure us that there are not two classes of Christians—those who have been let in on the secret knowledge and those benighted souls who have yet to find the hidden key. All struggling believers are reassured: God's revelation is not rare, arcane, and obtuse. What God is doing for us and what God promises us and what God expects of us is all fully revealed in scripture.

Of course, saying that the Bible contains "all things necessary to salvation" does not mean that Christian theology, based upon God's revelation that comes through scripture, is thereby simple or self-evident. One reason why you are listening to this sermon is that you know that God's word in scripture requires humble listening, informed discernment, and prayerful searching.

We are modern people who have been taught by our culture to believe that we are privileged to stand upon the very summit of human development. From our serene contemporary perch we stand in judgment upon everyone who got here before us. We have progressed. We are making progress. We know so much more than they. To affirm that scripture, both Old and New Testaments, is a reliable, unsubstitutable guide for our salvation, our future with God, is to go against modern prejudice. We look for God and listen for God with these ancient witnesses who have gone before us. We do our best to allow the various voices within the canon of scripture to share their distinctive testimonies with us. Fortunately, we need not "reinvent the wheel" in regard to Christian discipleship. If we will dare listen, the saints will show us the way.

To say that scripture ought to be read as a whole puts to rest the unfortunate stereotype that has demeaned the Old Testament, playing it off against the New Testament with slogans like, "the Old Testament is a collection of laws and judgment; the New Testament contains books of love and grace." There is love and grace to be found in all of scripture. Can there be any more gracious words than this Sunday's gospel from Isaiah? No wonder that Matthew thought of those words when he introduced John the Baptist. And no wonder that we recall these gracious words as we prepare for the birth of Christ.

Because we believe that all scripture is revelatory of the truth about God, we believe that it is wrong to lift out of context some single passage of scripture, attempting to read that passage isolated from other relevant passages. Scripture interprets scripture and cumulatively points toward God's love and care.

"Proof texting," searching for one passage that proves your pet doctrine or disproves your neighbor's pet doctrine, is an abuse of scripture's unity and overall message. All passages of scripture must be read in the context of the whole story that God is telling us. Martin Luther was fond of saying that the Bible is like the swaddling clothes that were wrapped around the baby Jesus and the manger in which Christ was laid. We don't worship the Bible; we worship the savior to whom all scripture—in diverse ways—testifies. All scripture, Old Testament and New, points to and is to be evaluated by the supreme revelation of God, the incarnate Word—Jesus Christ. As Jesus told some of his critics: "You search the scriptures because you think that in them you have eternal life; and it is they that testify on my behalf. Yet you refuse to come to me to have life" (John 5:39-40 NRSV).

On the Easter evening walk to the village of Emmaus, the incognito risen Christ attempts to "open the scriptures" to two dull disciples (Luke 24). Christ engages in a sweeping Bible study that begins "with Moses and all the prophets" (Luke 24:27). Note that the risen Christ interprets the miracle of the resurrection by reference to the ancient Hebrew Scriptures. And yet, despite Jesus himself doing the scripture instruction, the disciples understand nothing about the scriptures until Jesus, with them "at the table" (24:30), blesses, breaks, and gives the bread. Only then are their eyes opened, and they see that the stranger is none other than their Lord and savior.

This leads me to assert another principle of good Bible reading and interpretation: we need the presence of Christ to understand scripture. All scripture ultimately points to the Christ and must finally answer to the revelation of God in Jesus Christ, the one whose birth we prepare for, whose near presence we anticipate by opening up his word and by submitting ourselves to what he has to say to us.

This is the second Sunday of Advent, our second week of preparation for the birth of Christ among us. In a sense, this grand mystery for which we prepare, the incarnation of the living God with us, isn't so strangely a miracle. It's experienced every time we open up the Bible and dare to listen, and in daring to listen hear God's word for our lives.

Thanks be to God.

Relating the text

John Wesley, founder of Methodism, listed "searching the scriptures" as one of the primary instituted means of grace, right up there with other sacramental means of grace like the Eucharist and baptism. Against all fuzzy notions of grace in the contemporary church, Wesley's searching of scripture as a means of grace gives grace content, substance, and intellectual clout. As a lifelong student of scripture, Wesley boasted of being "a man of one book," reading the Bible in the original languages, showing a deep knowledge of both Hebrew and Greek in his notes on the Bible.

The expression "means of grace" indicates that true understanding of the riches of scripture requires the loving intervention of God—you can't read scripture by yourself at home or even in a college Bible class; you need the Holy Spirit to enlighten and enliven the word from the printed page. Reading and comprehending the Bible is an act of prayer.

Yet "searching the scriptures" is an expression that also denotes the need for active, earnest work in wrestling with the ancient text until it blesses us with revelation. Scripture reading and understanding require the gift of God's revelation coupled with our determined, intellectually responsible and responsive work.

Scripture is not to be read alone, not only in the sense that we need the descent of the Holy Spirit to make scripture work, to enable scripture to speak, but we also need help from our friends who have spent their lives working with scripture, ferreting out meanings from the ancient text, putting the text in context, and who now share their insights with the rest of us, challenging any of our merely personal, idiosyncratic, and uninformed interpretations.

The Bible is a thoroughly human, sometimes fallible and limited human product that is at the same time an utterly divine book, a living, breathing testimony to a God who refuses to be silent. Scripture itself is a wonderful demonstration of the truth of the incarnation.

To be perfectly honest, to modern readers, accustomed to rather linear, flat narratives that fit neatly into our limited definitions of reality, the Bible can come across to us as a mess. To be sure, one comes upon inconsistencies and contradictions, to say nothing of downright bad ideas in the Bible.

But we can take heart that the Bible contains within its own witness the ability to challenge and sometimes even to correct its own witness. Scripture has a marvelous way of arguing with itself, correcting itself—one witness giving counter testimony to another. Scripture is a record of a people's determination to hear God truthfully and then to follow God faithfully. The record is in the form of a journey through many centuries. Scripture is the account of the adventure of a journey, not a report on having arrived at a destination. Might I also point out that we ourselves are a mess of inconsistencies, contradictions, and bad ideas? Most of the time it's much easier to see the cultural and historical limitations of the people in the Bible rather than in ourselves. We are still on the journey. It's not a simple song that the Bible wants to teach us to sing. It is a grand symphony that must be heard together with all of its highs and lows and its seemingly dissonant notes, which all somehow come together and move in a definite direction.

It is of the nature of the Holy Spirit to reveal, to speak to us intimately and personally in the depths of our hearts, and to address us publicly, principally through preaching. Thus whenever we read scripture in our worship, it is typical to pray a prayer for illumination that calls upon God to "open our hearts and minds by the power of your Holy Spirit so that as the word is read and proclaimed we may hear what you have to say to us today."

Because the Holy Spirit is a member of the Trinity—that is, God—the Holy Spirit enables us truly to encounter Christ in our reading of scripture. The Holy Spirit produces scripture, enlightens our reading and hearing of scripture, and enables us to perform scripture. Miraculously, when we read scripture, Christ stands among us, present through our reading and hearing of mere words.

The Gospels, and indeed all of scripture, were born in a culture in which people passed information along orally, were careful to repeat things often, told only what was important, and looked for help from eyewitnesses to verify accuracy. The writers of the Gospels collected the stories about Jesus that had been circulated orally and wove them into careful and distinctive accounts of what he said and did—and why that matters. Generations of Christians have found these writings to truly reveal God in singular and life-changing ways. Besides, we're justified in giving particular weight to the testimony of those who paid for their friendship with Jesus by their blood.

But Jesus is more than his words remembered; he is interesting not only because of what he said but also for who he is. We should therefore also talk about Jesus through the medium of his friends. Paul (whose writings are older than the Gospels) never met Jesus until the risen Christ accosted him on the Damascus road. Yet Paul may know as much about Jesus as those who walked next to him down the Jerusalem road. Paul seemed neither to know nor to care about most of the teachings of Jesus or details of his life before the cross and resurrection, yet Paul's wildly adventurous life after meeting Jesus shows that Paul really knew Jesus. We are right to trust descriptions of Jesus given by those most disrupted by Jesus. Some people around Jesus looked at him and wanted to follow him, patterned their lives after his, and told everybody about him. The majority of people who met Jesus apparently thought he was nuts and wanted him dead. Sometimes, the burning sun is best viewed by watching those upon whom it shines.

Third Sunday of Advent

Psalm 146:5-10 or Luke 1:47-55

James 5:7-10

Matthew 11:2-11

Expectation and Reality

Selected reading

Matthew 11:2-11

Theme

In Advent, we are awaiting the Messiah, expecting the advent of the Christ. When Christ comes, when expectation becomes reality, sometimes he is not the messiah we expected. Christ comes to us, rearranging our conceptions of God, our expectations for the way a messiah ought to act. Can we risk encounter with the Christ? Can we accept him as he is rather than as we would have him to be?

Introduction to the readings

Isaiah 35:1-10

Isaiah foretells that blessed time when "the desert shall rejoice and blossom" as all of humanity beholds "the majesty of our God" (v. 2 NRSV).

James 5:7-10

The Letter of James urges patience as the church awaits the coming reign of God.

Matthew 11:2-11

John, in prison, sends his disciples to inquire whether or not Jesus is the long-awaited Messiah.

Prayer

Lord Jesus, give us the eyes to see you when you come among us. It would be a terrible thing to be praying so fervently for your advent, that we miss you when you come.

Give us courageous spirits, willing to risk your presence, willing to endure your judgments, able to receive mercy, able to walk down the road that you invite us to walk.

Come, Lord, come quickly. Amen.

Encountering the text

On this Sunday in Advent we are back with John the Baptist, but in a quite different context than last Sunday. In prison, John sends messengers to Jesus, asking a deeply troubling question: "Are you the one who is to come, or should we look for another?" (Matt 11:3).

We wonder what is the cause of John's question. John had been the outspoken forerunner of Jesus. Now he appears to be the chief questioner of Jesus.

When seeking a source of John's uncertainty, we first consider that John is in jail. His fierce preaching has at last caught up with him. Herod has had enough of John's criticism of his royal ways (14:1-5). Now silenced, alone, and in jail, John asks a troubling question of Jesus.

Perhaps the source of John's question lies in John hearing "what the Messiah was doing." John, in his sermons about the Messiah, had predicted a rather more dramatic and fire-filled ministry for Jesus. We heard John's predictions for Jesus's ministry last Sunday. John predicted a messiah who would come and separate the true from the false, the good from the bad. In Jesus, there is the Messiah who heals, who works among the poor, and who preaches good, rather than bad, news.

Jesus uses language from Isaiah (35:5-6; 29:18-19) to respond to John's question. While the ministry of Jesus does not fulfill John's expectations, it does fulfill some of the prophetic hopes of Israel. Jesus thus seems to desire to move John to a different understanding of what a messiah is all about. Many in Israel (perhaps John was one of them), observing the words and work of Jesus, took offense at him (Matt 11:6). He did not meet conventional messianic expectation. They wanted someone who would move in with power, with undeniable works of majesty and glory. They got the one who healed, who loved the poor, who preached good news.

Jesus, before he is done responding to John, turns to the crowds. "When you went out to hear John, what did you see?" he asks them, perhaps underscoring that our religious expectations are rarely fulfilled by God's appointed prophets. What we want out of God is not always what we get.

Thus today's sermon, building on the question of John the Baptist to Jesus, is a good opportunity to reflect upon the gap between our expectations for the Messiah and the reality of the Messiah. I remember a sermon by Fred Craddock some years ago that reflected on the gap between our expectation of Jesus and the reality of Jesus, interpreting John the Baptist as the embodiment of that gap in expectation. I am sure that Fred's sermon helped me in my thoughts for this exposition of John the Baptist and his question, "Are you the one or should we look for another?"

Proclaiming the text

We always encounter John the baptizer during Advent. In these Sundays of anticipation, John is a great preacher of promise. He is the forerunner, the one who comes preaching such stirring sermons, a man full of fire and fierce preaching.

John's message is searingly direct: Get ready, the Messiah is coming. God's kingdom is upon us. He is greater than I. He is a man of fire, unquenchable fire, coming to burn away all of the impurities in Israel.

John was a courageous prophet who attracted many hearers. People came out from the cities, from all over, to hear his strong preaching. Yet John said there is one coming, one so great I am unworthy even to stoop down and loosen his sandals.

But that great prophetic voice of John has now fallen silent. Our text begins with John in prison.

Remember that scene in the movie *The Apostle* in which the apostle, who had done so much good for so many and built a little Pentecostal church up from nothing, is arrested? They are having an evening service, full of the Spirit, then the police come and take the apostle away.

That happened to John.

John was arrested because he mixed religion with politics. Herod Antipas took his niece, who was already married to his brother, and married her.

John the Baptist was of the old school. He did not, like some powerful preachers do, snuggle up to the powerful and flatter them. No. John named it for what it was. He condemned Herod, and Herod took offense. Politicians don't like preachers accusing them of incest and adultery!

That once-powerful voice languished in jail. Earlier, John had touched many hearts. At the end of his sermons, great numbers of people said, "What then should we do?" And John told them. Repent! Turn around! Change!

But now the crowds were gone. John was in jail.

There in jail, silenced, his death looming before him, John had time to think. He thought, "If the forerunner of the Messiah can be so easily silenced, then what of the Messiah?" John's thinking led him to ask a rather devastating question of Jesus: "Are you the Messiah, or should we be looking for some-body else?"

It is a shocking question. It was the question asked by Jesus's worst critics. It is one thing for his enemies to ask such a question, but now the question has been asked by Jesus's best friend, his cousin, John the Baptist. Are you the Messiah?

I dare say none of us are shocked that John the Baptist was in jail, arrested by Herod. After all, you know enough about church history to know that this is the way tyrants handle troublesome preachers. There are lots of preachers right now in jail in China. Totalitarian governments like Herod's can't tolerate meddlesome preachers. That doesn't surprise me.

But what is shocking is what this preacher said, what he asked of Jesus. He . asked, are you really the Messiah, or should we look for someone else?

Maybe, at the beginning, as Jesus began, it was easier for John to look at him and see the Messiah. His ministry began with great power and prominence. Sure, there was resistance, but Jesus seemed to overcome it. John had said that there would be one who would come preaching with fire, with mighty deeds, and he had been right.

Some of John's disciples came and John said, "Take this message to Jesus. Bring his answer back to me. Here is the message: 'Are you the Messiah, are you the one whom we are looking to for salvation, or should we look for somebody else?'"

John's whole ministry had been pointing to Jesus, saying that he was the one. Now John asks Jesus, "Are you the one?" Has John somehow forgotten his own sermons?

When Jesus had come to John for baptism, John had refused, saying, "If anybody ought to baptize anybody, you ought to be baptizing me!" It is an amazing statement for one with such "ego strength" as John the Baptist. He was no shrinking violet. And there at the baptism, the Holy Spirit appeared. Had John forgotten all of that?

What did John mean by, "Are you the one?"

In even the most stunning religious experience, no matter how dramatic, there is always some let-down afterward. You can't stay on a spiritual mountaintop forever. We learn to be patient with the new believer, so confident, so convinced, and enthusiastic. Give the new believer some time, and then what was once a life-changing experience becomes just another Sunday. Fire seems to run out of fuel.

John preached, "The Messiah is coming! He is going to fix everything, set things right."

But now the Messiah has come. Anticipation of the Messiah has now met the reality of the Messiah. And perhaps that's John's problem. Jesus just does not deliver what John expected in a messiah, leading John to ask, "Are you the one?"

Nothing is more eager and energetic than the eyes of a child in first grade. But go back and look at those same eyes in the eleventh grade. Dullness has set in.

Oh, those first days of expectation and exhilaration in ministry, the joy of realizing that God has called me for this work. I am going to get to work for God! I am going to get to change the world with Jesus!

And then the reality: fights over the carpet, pettiness. This was not why we were called. Between the expectation and the reality, there is the difficulty.

Maybe John worked better with the anticipation. Maybe John found it hard, more difficult to be a preacher of the present, the reality.

Perhaps Jesus did not meet John's expectations. He had spoken of the Messiah as this powerful, mighty one, who would come with fire, with power of judgment and force.

And yet, when they looked at Jesus and his ministry, they thought of what Isaiah had said, about the suffering servant, about the one who would come and be so gentle and tender, he would not quench a barely burning wick, or bruise a fragile reed. Maybe John was just disappointed.

Here came Jesus, the one who was mighty, and he is telling people to turn the other cheek, to "Do good to those who hate you." We expected so much of Jesus. And he delivered so little. When they put him on a cross, we expected him to act like God's Son, to be able to throw himself down from the cross, to say, "Now it is payback time." Instead, he looked down from his cross, hanging there in utter misery, and said simply, "Father, forgive."

I love it when someone says, "We came here one Sunday, and we said this is what we are looking for in a church. And we came back, and we've been here ever since."

But I hate it when they say, "Yes, we did come to your church a Sunday or maybe two, but we just didn't feel like we were being fed. It wasn't what we were looking for, not what we expected."

The great challenge, I think, is not to "scale down our expectations," as we sometimes say. I've got a friend who said, "In all things you ought to aim for the sun. Chances are, you'll probably only hit the moon, but still, the moon isn't so bad." Scale down your expectations. Get realistic.

Maybe a better way is to have more proper expectation. Fire can take many forms. Some of them are destructive, terrible in their effects. Others are warm, gentle, life-giving. Maybe the way for John to find light is not to ask less of Jesus but to ask different things of him.

An Advent question: Will you receive the Messiah, Jesus, as he is rather than as we would have him to be? Will you let God come into your life as God wills, not as you desire? Will we allow our expectations for God to be schooled, formed, reformed by the reality of God in Christ?

Relating the text

Burnout is the disease of our age. *Time* magazine had an editorial way back in the 1980s about "the burnout of just about everybody." I concluded that the metaphor of burnout was not quite right, particularly when applied to those of us in the church. *Burnout* is a term that is borrowed from rocketry, when a rocket rising from the earth runs out of fuel, "burns out," and falls to the earth. Burnout implies that our problem is a lack of energy. I have concluded that many people who think they are "burning out" do so, not from the lack of energy, but from a lack of meaning.

We are tired and despondent. The French call it *ennui*; the Bible speaks of the "noonday demon," depression.

Advent is an appropriate season to ask, "Wherein will renewal and restoration be found for tired people like us?"

The prophet Isaiah may be of some help here. "Those who wait for the LORD shall renew their strength" (Isa 40:31 NRSV).

I wonder about the Hebrew. Is the Hebrew here best translated as, "Those who wait on God (that is, those who serve God) will renew their strength"? It is a Christian claim that service to God is renewing, that in taking up the burdens of Christ, he gives us what we need to carry them.

Or is it those who wait for God (that is, those who expect the advent of God) are promised that they will receive God?

Or could it be those who wait with God (to stand with God expecting the advent of God's mercy and love) will not finally be disappointed?

It makes a difference.

Waiting is difficult because it implies some linkage to something else. When we wait on someone we are engaged in service to another, which is not easy in our society. Or either we are waiting for someone else to come make our day. Waiting for someone implies that we are not self-sufficient unto ourselves, that we need someone to come and save us. Or sometimes we wait with someone in the late-night vigil, in a hospital room as someone waivers between life and death.

None of this is easy.

And yet such waiting requires that we live through resources not of our own creation, that we reach out to God to enable us to do that which does not come easily or naturally.

The promise of the text is that those who wait on, and those who wait for, and those who wait with will run, will soar, yes, they will mount up with wings as eagles.

But not without a wait.

I was with a group of preachers the other day. The youngest among us was a kid out of seminary, not more than a year. He was telling us all the wonderful things that were happening in his church. They had experienced a dramatic increase in attendance. A dying Sunday school program for children had been revived. It was just like a miracle, he said.

When the young man left the room, one of the older, wiser, and more experienced preachers turned to another and said, "He'll learn. I was naive like that when I was just out of seminary." There was widespread agreement in the group.

"There is nothing better than the first couple of days of class," the students say to me.

"And nothing worse than the last days of class."

As a preacher, I often feel this way when I am presiding at weddings. Such an outlay of money: the flowers, the beauty, things so well-planned, everything so perfect and beautiful. Come back to that same couple, living in a little apartment out on the edge of town. They spent $15,000 for their reception. And now they cannot find $11 for this week's groceries.

Fourth Sunday of Advent

Isaiah 7:10-16
Psalm 80:1-7, 17-19
Romans 1:1-7
Matthew 1:18-25

Unto Us a Child

Selected reading

Matthew 1:18-25

Theme

Christ is the incarnation of God. In Jesus, we are encountered by a God who loved us so much as to take upon himself our flesh, our humanity, our world in order to bring us to himself.

Introduction to the readings

Isaiah 7:10-16
Isaiah foretells of the coming of God's peace in the form of a baby born to a young woman.

Romans 1:1-7
Paul opens his letter to the Romans with an acclamation of the grace of God in Christ.

Matthew 1:18-25
Matthew tells of the birth of Jesus.

Prayer

Lord, you came among us, not in a way we expected, but as a baby. We had great difficulty seeing you in so small a form, so vulnerable an incarnation.

Lord, you came to us where we least expected. You were born among a poor family, to an oppressed and victimized people, in an out-of-the-way part of the world.

Lord, you came to us when we least expected. We thought that all hope for humanity was lost, or that it was up to humanity to save ourselves or we would not be saved, or that some god or other would swoop down from the heavens and deliver us. Then you came to us in the dark of night, born to Mary and Joseph; you came to us as a baby.

Lord, forgive us when we don't see you because we look in the wrong places, or because you give us hope for your advent, or because we expect you to come in power, majesty, and glory rather than in humility, poverty, and meekness.

Lord, help us to experience your birth among us. God with us. God with us not on our terms, but on your terms, as a baby, Jesus, a human one who took upon himself our humanity that we might be brought back to God. Amen.

Encountering the text

Our Gospel this day is the nativity as reported by Matthew. The predominate tone of Matthew's account is one of embarrassment. Poor Joseph! Poor Mary! This child was an unexpected intrusion into their lives.

The child is to be called Emmanuel, meaning "God with us." Evidently, when God is with us, God is not with us in placid, nondisruptive ways. God's intrusions among us cause consternation and difficulty. The angel urged Joseph not to fear (Matt 2:21), but how could Joseph not fear when his whole world was being rocked by a birth so unexpected?

Children are intrusions, not only the baby Jesus, but any child, for that matter. We adults like to get our world fixed, secure, safe from disruption. But some adults find their worlds considerably turned upside down by children. Today's text is about a couple named Mary and Joseph who could tell us a thing or two about the disruptions caused by pregnancy and birth.

Sometimes we Christians overlook what a strange, peculiar thing it is for us to point to a God who comes among us in the form of an infant. Unto us has come a God who intrudes among us, not as a warrior, not as an all-powerful messiah, but as a baby—a small, fragile, vulnerable, disruptive, unexpected, threatening baby.

The meaning of this miracle is our challenge in today's sermon.

Proclaiming the text

"A child is born to us, a son is given to us" (Isa 9:6).

It had been a long, frustrating wait: the tests, the treatments, the discouragement, the unknowing. We wanted a child. But we were learning that a child is one blessing that is a gift—unearned, unachieved, undemanded.

"We know more about how to help couples not have children than how to help them have children," the doctor had said.

But at last the hoped-for, prayed-for dream became reality. The gynecologist, who in today's upside-down world had spent his day helping people avoid pregnancy, gave my wife the news.

Through the fall, she grew bigger—"great with child," as Matthew would have said. As the December days grew short and cold, we watched this mystery of mysteries unfold.

Patsy said that she knew the Christmas cantata was not written for our child, but as our little church choir struggled through John Peterson's maudlin *Love*

Transcending, sometimes she caught herself singing for our baby growing in her womb, rather than for Mary's baby. On the night of the cantata, when she processed with the choir, she knew that she was on her way to Bethlehem.

When the lector spoke of Mary's being "blessed among women," Patsy said Gabriel was speaking to her. We rejoiced, like Elizabeth and Mary before us, when they had talked about the advent of their babies.

That December, we found that there is no better time to be waiting for a child than Advent, when the whole world waits for a baby.

A few years ago, a sermon by a fellow preacher chided us for our seasonal, sentimental infatuation with the baby Jesus. He urged us to think less about the sweet baby Jesus and more about the grownup Christ. "Away with the manger!" he said. Today I know more than I did then. Now I find myself standing before the season of the babe at Bethlehem, prodded by a second reading of Raymond Brown's *Birth of the Messiah*, thinking again about the advent of our baby—and Mary's.

I know the dangers of our annual attempt to reduce the majesty of the incarnation at Bethlehem in Judea to cute, infantile proportions here in our living room creche in North Carolina. I know the sentimental mush of "Away in a Manger" and its theologically questionable cooing over the "little Lord Jesus." But now I know also, from firsthand experience, how threatening babies are.

Herod knew. King Herod—the old fox, sitting in Jerusalem with all the military clout of the empire to back him up—knew how dangerous babies can be. Herod knew that he had better take matters into his own hands while he still had time, before the child could mock the impotence of the old man. It was not time to wait for the unknown, growing child to come to fulfillment. With babies, Herod knew, it is the unknown that both attracts and repels.

We fear childish impudence and disrespect in the face of our adult pompousness. The Central African Empire's Emperor Bokassa knew this when he enacted the massacre of the innocents after some impudent schoolchildren refused to wear state-imposed uniforms. I have found it is difficult to retain my delusions of adult authority and omnipotence when the wee one across the breakfast table sends her bowl flying in my direction and then laughs at how funny I look with oatmeal on my suit. Every baby challenges Herod's, Bokassa's, and my claims of power and immortality. The future is that child's, not mine, not yours. With each passing day we decrease as they increase. Is that why our society wavers between the extremes of romantic glorification of childhood on the one hand and toleration of child abuse and child neglect on the other?

I know that a baby is supposed to bring out the best in us. But never forget that a baby mirrors the worst also. Why did we so desperately want a baby? To make secure our claims of immortality in this mortal world? To reap security for our old age in this insecure time? To achieve vicarious fulfillment by living out what we regret in our past through our plans for her future? Like all human creations, even the creation of a child is tinged with our subtle, deceptive human pride.

And why did Judea want a baby—this child Messiah? To bring us the gift of immortality through his entrance into our mortal flesh? To offer us self-fulfillment by championing our causes and choosing us, and us alone, for the benefits of his love? To promise us eternal security and peace that free us from earthly insecurity? The advent of the Christ child, like all of God's incarnations, was impossible without his advent into the realm of our subtle, deceptive human pride—into the realm of all our ambivalent expectations.

There, in the baby, "the hopes and fears of all the years" are met by a God who meets us where we live—with our pride masquerading as faith, with our false hopes and selfish fears—and claims us at the infantile point where we all began our meandering life journey. Starting at the beginning, at the source, he confronts our very deepest and darkest fears, re-creating our humanity from the womb onward.

But even this does not adequately describe the mystery we sense at seeing God in the manger. The most disturbing quality of the baby Jesus, the mystery of his advent that scandalizes even as it inexorably beckons, is the vulnerability of his incarnation.

Nothing is so helpless, so dependent, so fragile, so frail as a baby. I know of no other religion so bold as to admit to the possibility of its God appearing in so vulnerable a form. How scandalously condescending is the love of this God who deems to meet us first as a baby. How threatening is this God to my human desire for an aloof, platonic deity who lives in the realms of the abstract, self-contained ideal rather than in the stable out back, who is wrapped in swaddling clothes and lying in a manger. For most of the year we preach about humanity's need for God. But on Christmas, can we be so bold as to speak of God's need for humanity—a God who comes, reaching out to us, as a baby, needing the love, warmth, and nurture of an utterly human family?

I have noted that within some of the rituals and festivals of churches in impoverished nations, great prominence is given to the infant Christ. An old man in a poor Italian village first explained this to me as we stood one December in his little church before an altar creche and the Santo Bambino.

"The bambino," he said, whispering to me in toothless solemnity, "is poor, little, and outside like us." Then he smiled.

Not too far up the road from this old man's town, Francis of Assisi had done much reflection upon the holy child, seeing the babe as a paradigm for God's suffering servanthood among the poor of God's earth. Perhaps we more powerful ones can do no better than to sentimentalize and trivialize this fragile babe. Perhaps it must be left to the poor, the outsiders, and the "little ones" of the world to see the powerful, revolutionary, messianic, divine-human solidarity that the presence of the babe declares.

With the vulnerability of the babe comes his claim upon us. A baby, because of its vulnerability, dependence, and potential, evokes a response from us, demands a commitment unknown in the majority of human encounters. This claim arises not only because babies need us but also because somewhere within our deepest selves, we know that we need babies. Some deep, human instinct tells us that babies are a sign of our human creativity at its best, that they are a reminder of our dark, biological, primordial origins in the waters of creation and a hopeful hint of our still open future. Call it life. One finds it difficult to be neutral in the face of such smiling mystery.

A parishioner of mine once explained it to me this way: He had interpreted and kept his marriage vows rather loosely, had thought little about his past, and had not the slightest interest in the future. He had spent the first years of his marriage mainly on the road making money.

"But one night," he said, "I got turned around. That was the night I walked into the hospital room and held my little baby in my arms for the first time and realized that she was part of me even if she was better than I deserved. I said to myself, 'You're going to have to stop your foolishness and start living like somebody, because she's somebody.'"

The birth of that baby summoned forth the best in the man's humanity and laid hold of his life in a manner that could only be called rebirth.

Did Joseph and Mary feel such a claim upon their lives as they stood by the manger, or did the shepherds and the magi? What is that wonder we feel reflected back upon us when we encounter the babe? Is it a glimpse of ourselves at our best, in our primal innocence? Or is it a vision of one who is part of us yet is better than we deserve? Who are those fortunate somebodies who stand around the manger, blessed by so close a love? Who could expect the magi to return home the same way after such a meeting?

This December, if a messenger in white—whether a gynecologist or the angel Gabriel—should tell you that you were blessed and that you were going to have a baby, I hope you would sing as Mary sang. You could spend your Advent wait in less productive, less creative ways, I can assure you. Waiting, you might discover firsthand the truth of God's incarnation among us.

As for me, I know I'm supposed to keep my categories clean and carefully define the limits between the divine and the human. But, God help me, I know that while I may be singing about the baby Jesus this season, I'll always be seeing baby Harriet—that little one who, now in the third advent of her life, stands before me demanding that I lay aside my pen and tell her a bedtime story, as she and I wait in the December darkness for the God who came first as a child.

And so I begin: "Once there was a woman named Mary, and she was told that she was going to have a baby..."

Relating the text

"What is the glory of God? The majesty that had nowhere to lay its head; the grandeur that was meek and lowly; the beauty that had neither form nor comeliness that anyone should desire him; the splendor of a lonely Wanderer, weary and footsore, with nails through his hands and feet.... I have found in and through him all the God I want. Nothing less than that. All that I know of God, I do not say that I have learned it from him; I say that I have seen it in him. And when I celebrate the day of his birth, I celebrate the day when God made himself so manifest that men have not been able to get away from him."

—Paul Scherer, *Love Is a Spendthrift* (New York: Harper, 1961), 16–17

"Jesus gave us a new and paradoxical definition of God, a definition of the humility of God. Many people were offended. They wanted a God of glory, not entering the world at the bottom, not from a despised place like Nazareth in Galilee, but he must come in from the top. He must be properly introduced, by the right people, and with the appropriate protocol. But instead the people got the man from Nazareth, and he was only prepared to give them a message of the humility of God, of the identification of God with the people and things that don't count for very much in this world. He carried his message of God to the extreme, driving the humility of God all the way to the cross."

—Carl E. Braaten, *Stewards of the Mysteries* (Minneapolis: Augsburg, 1998), 27–28

Baby Talk

Selected reading

Hebrews 1:1-4, (5-12)

Theme

After trying all these years to get through to us, the God of Israel attempts a remarkable experiment in communication. God comes to us as the Son, a baby in a manger. Here, in the flesh is "the Word made flesh," dwelling among us, a sign, a visible embodiment of God's great love for us.

Introduction to the readings

Isaiah 52:7-10

Isaiah joyfully proclaims the announcement of good news to the suffering people of Israel.

Hebrews 1:1-4, (5-12)

After attempting to speak to us in so many and diverse ways, God now speaks to us through the Son.

John 1:1-14

John speaks of the great mystery of the incarnation, the light into the darkness, the word into the silence.

Prayer

Lord Jesus, you have caused this holy day to shine with the brightness of your great light. You have come to us, the world's true light.

Grant that we might see your light, that we might be drawn to your love, that we might show forth your light into all the world, that many might see your light reflected in our lives.

Babe of Bethlehem, Mary and Joseph's son, the one for whom there was no room at the inn, speak to us this glorious Christmas Day, be born again in our hearts, take form in our lives, redeem our humanity, making us your own.

Lord, we thank you that, having tried to speak to us in so many ways down through the ages, you at last speak to us through your only Son, Jesus the Christ, who reigns this day and for ever and ever. Amen.

Encountering the text

The letter to the Hebrews is an amazing pastoral document. Here is an early Christian communicator who, in an attempt to minister to a struggling congregation, reaches for a whole range of metaphors, images, and devices in order to be heard. Placing image upon image, symbol upon symbol, reaching back into the recesses of Israel's history with God, Hebrews proclaims the good news of Christ.

Our text today, Christmas, is the stunning opening refrain of Hebrews. God's way with us is depicted as a pageant of communication. "In many times and many ways" (Heb 1:1), God has spoken to our forebears in faith. Now, "in these final days" (1:2), God speaks through a son, a child, heir of all that is God's.

This is language of incarnation, fitting accompaniment to the Christmas Gospel, John 1:1-14. There, it is said that the Word became flesh. Here, the Word is acknowledged as Son. This text says both that God is incarnate in Jesus and that because Jesus is the Son, he rules. The incarnation speaks both of the accessibility and the availability of God in Christ and also of the exalted power of the Christ who is God. These themes of availability and exalted power, linked in Jesus, will be recurring themes in the letter to the Hebrews.

This Sunday's sermon may fit the theme of incarnation as availability and exalted power, linked in Jesus, will be recurring themes in the letter to the Hebrews.

This Sunday's sermon may fit the theme of incarnation as availability, accessibility, or "the condescension of God," as theologian Karl Barth spoke of Christmas.

Perhaps our chief homiletical challenge at Christmas is overcoming the suffocating sentimentality of what we've done as a culture to Christmas. Now, on this day, to insert all this talk of babies into the mind of the congregation is to risk falling into the grossest of maudlin sentimentality. You know how we love to speak about babies.

Which—if you've ever actually been with a baby for some length of time—is strange. Babies are excruciatingly fleshly carnal. Babies have diapers that need changing, emit foul odors, demand to be attended in the middle of the night, and cry. All of this carnality makes rather amazing our sentimentalization of infancy.

In the incarnation we are witnesses to the dramatic loving incursions of a living God. This God condescends to us. There's nothing sweet or sentimental about that. The great God enters our pain, our fleshly existence, and comes to us where we live.

That God might love us, not just on Christmas, but forever.

Proclaiming the text

"In the past, God spoke through the prophets to our ancestors in many times and many ways. In these final days, though, he spoke to us through a Son" (Heb 1:1-2).

Luther said it: when God speaks to humanity, God always speaks in baby talk. God does this, says Luther, because God is love. Therefore, God never forgets that no matter how old or how big we become, we are still helpless, dependent, unknowing babes so far as our faith is concerned.

So God bends to our infirmities. When God speaks, he tells us only as much as we need to know, only what we can take. God knows we cannot stand the full weight of the full truth. The creator knows the needs and limits of us creatures. So God talks baby talk to us.

God does not bother Adam and Eve with lessons in animal husbandry or botany. God simply says, "You're in charge. But stay off that tree over there." Like any busy parent, God never gets around to telling them why; he simply tells them the way it is. But you know Adam and Eve. From the beginning, we want to know too much for our own good.

God speaks to Moses out of a burning bush, knowing that children are fascinated by fire and things like that. But when he speaks, it is with ludicrous simplicity: "Go tell people that I AM sent you."

And the law, in basic kindergarten morality, is (as literally translated): You no kill. You no lie. You no steal.

And for the prophets: Broken jars and scrolls and other object lessons for children talk of lions, lambs, and stories that only little ones understand. Baby talk.

Have you ever watched people talk to babies? *Goo goo. Ga ga.* I sat one day in a sunlit park with my own baby and watched perfectly intelligent, sensible adults stop before the stroller and, one after another, be reduced to nonsensical babblers. *Goo goo. Ga ga.* You should have seen the old banker, in the park for a lunchtime stroll, bending over, dangling his gold chain over the head of the little one, puffing up his fat, rosy cheeks, and pursing his lips as he buzzed and wheezed, clicked and sputtered. Watching the man, I thought: if only your bank tellers and depositors could see you now!

And yet, child developmentalists say that such baby talk is essential for language development, coordination, perception, and a host of other human characteristics. Our local hospital even employs a woman to walk around the neonatal care unit and talk to the smallest babies. There are research reports indicating that infants who are not talked to frequently during the first months of life suffer stunted development and sometimes even die.

Erik Erikson believes that trust is developed in a child during the very first weeks of its life, in all the little rituals of greeting that the infant and its parents go through when it wakes in the morning. All the cooing and tickling, grinning and silly chatter that occur between parents and their young, Erikson says, is this building of trust that is essential for one's whole life. The absence of baby talk leads to serious deficiencies.

All subsequent chatter of learned theologians, says Luther, is but a series of footnotes on the primal baby talk. This later, abstracted, generalized reflection must not deafen us to the first, simple childlike ways in which God speaks to us. When it does, we begin complicating the faith, talking big, claiming to know more than we have experienced, forgetting our essential condition, smothering the elemental power of it all. Babies do not have to be told what Mommy means by "cootchie cootchie coo." Love needs no explanation.

And so, stooping once more to our level, bending over into this violent playpen we call home, God again speaks—this time not simply speaking to babies but coming as a baby, as one of us.

To the outside observer just passing through, all this excited talk over the bassinet—the toothless shepherds grinning and peering over the edge of the crib, the wise old men from back east reduced to babbling fools—seems strange. But here in the nativity is truth, not as complex theory or lofty ideal, but truth wrapped in swaddling clothes, lying in a manger. "In the past, God spoke through the prophets to our ancestors in many times and many ways. In these final days, though, he spoke to us through a Son" (1:1-2).

When the child becomes a man, he still speaks in stories, parables, simple declarations of the way things are now that God has come in the flesh. With a crisp "Follow me," he invites all to a kingdom where only the little ones are citizens—the very young, the very old, the very oppressed, the very sick, the very poor—a kingdom where to receive a child is to receive him. Here is a Walt Disney World–like place where everything is turned upside down, the lowly ones are great, the great are brought low, and there are surprises for everyone. In this kingdom, grownups who use words that are too large and pray prayers that are too long and get too big for their britches have trouble getting through the door. Baby talk.

Later, when, in a sort of frivolous, childish gesture, he enters the capital city clownishly bouncing on the back of a fuzzy donkey, his beard does not hide the child beneath the man.

On that day, a long way from the manger at Bethlehem, he is welcomed into Jerusalem, not by the mayor with the key to the city, but by children with palm branches.

These babies look at him and see one of their own.

Relating the text

"In what then does the greatness of humanity consist, according to the doctrine of the Church? Not in its likeness to the created world, but in its being the image of the nature of the Creator."

—Gregory of Nyssa, *On the Making of Man* (London: Aeterna Press, 2016), XVI.2, 44.180A

"This is the season of the year when so many things stand out in stark outline against the background of our days. We think of little children all over the world; children in refugee camps who have known aught else throughout the length of their days; children in orphanages in our own land, in other lands; rootless children; children in families where there is so little love that they are unaware that their own lives are touched by its gentleness and strength; sick children, those who have walked and will never walk again; those who have looked out on the beauty of the world and will never see it again. Our hearts are touched and melt in the quietness as we remember the children of the world."

—Howard Thurman, *The Mood of Christmas* (Richmond, IN: Friends United Press, 1985), 107

The great philosopher Kierkegaard told a parable about a great king who fell in love with a lovely servant girl. He wanted to tell her of his love, but he wanted to approach her in a way in which she might freely, willingly love him.

As a high and mighty king, he would overwhelm her. She would perhaps fear him, or respect him, but could she love one so high and so remote from her and her world?

So the king devised a plan. He took off his royal robes and dressed as a poor peasant. He slipped away from the palace, descended into the village below, and took up the life of a poor peasant. There he wooed the young woman. Making her acquaintance, he gradually got to know her and she gradually got to know him. Eventually, she grew to love him. They moved toward marriage. At last he revealed himself to her as king. They live happily ever after in the palace, as recipients of true love.

Take this as a parable. In many ways God attempted to reveal himself to us. Now, God has been revealed to us as a Son, Word in the flesh, God with us.

I understand something of Hebrews 1:1-4. After all, I'm a preacher. I know what it's like to struggle to communicate. Almost on a weekly basis, I must stand up and talk about matters that are woefully beyond my ability to communicate.

I struggle to find appropriate analogies. I grope for usable metaphors. I collect stories, quotes, and sayings, all in the interest of speaking the gospel. As a young preacher I was told that this was the central task of Christian communication—to make contact with where people live, to put the good news of Jesus Christ on their idiom.

Hebrews 1:1-4 suggests that God is also involved in such communicative struggle. In many ways God attempted to speak to us, groped for ways to get through to us, to reveal his love and plans for us. Now, at last, God speaks to us through a Son.

"I'll admit it, I've got this problem with control. I need to be in control of things around me. I put a high premium on order, predictability, control. Sometimes my need for control gets me into trouble."

"Don't worry too much," I said. "God is getting ready to cure you completely of your need to be in control. In a few months, you'll have no need of control, order, and predictability."

In two months his wife is to give birth to twins. Twin boys.

"Children are gifts of God," she said.

"Yes," he agreed, "and sometimes the gift that God means to give with children is humility."

In children God gives us not always the gift we thought we wanted but the gifts, in God's wisdom, God knows we need.

"No contact between the finite and the infinite is possible without some vulgarization of God. No potter, whatever his skill, can form even the most exquisitely delicate vessel without getting clay on his hands. If God were to touch only the fingertips of our highest and best, 'E'en then would be some stooping' (Browning). And if our God, like Browning's duke, chose 'never to stoop,' we would be without hope. God loves us where we are or not at all.

"Men [and women] in our time are troubled by the religion of the Bible. By the way in which it shuttles back and forth between cosmos and province, by its mixture of theology and geology. And they always will be for it speaks of the most profound of all mysteries, the way in which the Eternal moves among and touches the lives of men. It is the biography of that classical Christian affirmation, 'In the beginning was the Word...and the Word became flesh and dwelt among us.'"

—William Muehl, *All the Damned Angels* (Philadelphia: Pilgrim Press, 1972), 56–57

"Christians have drawn out the ethical significance of a religion of the Incarnation. The material creation is not alien to God if the Word has become flesh. Christian spirituality takes the body seriously as the vehicle, not the enemy, of spiritual life. Christian involvement in the thoroughly earthly problems and needs of their fellow human beings is patterned on the divine 'kenosis' (self-emptying) of the Incarnation. This is bound to take on social and political dimensions. A religion of the Incarnation cannot hold aloof from the political problems of injustice and oppression. Incarnational theology is at once a sacramental theology, finding spiritual significance in the things of the earth, and a political theology, drawing on those spiritual resources for a renewal and transformation of the condition of life on earth."

—Brian Hebblethwaite, "Incarnation," in *A New Handbook of Christian Theology*, ed. Donald W. Musser and Joseph L Price (Nashville: Abingdon Press, 1992), 254

Christmas Day

Isaiah 52:7-10

Psalm 98

Hebrews 1:1-4, (5-12)

John 1:1-14

The Word with Us

Selected reading

John 1:1-14

Theme

Paul says that the Christian faith is an auditory phenomenon: "Faith comes from listening" (Rom 10:17). The proclaimed word, uttered through the voice of a preacher, received within the context of the gathered congregation, is the wellspring of our faith. The advent of the Christ, the incarnation, is announced through a preacher named John. Jesus comes into the world preaching. The proclaimed word is at the heart of the Christian experience, a primary means whereby God's people are guided and sustained. Jesus is born among us as the Word.

Introduction to the readings

Isaiah 52:7-10

Isaiah speaks of the beauty of those who speak the message of the redemption of God.

Hebrews 1:1-4, (5-12)

The letter to the Hebrews notes all the ways that God has communicated with God's creation down through the ages. But now, on this day, "[God] has spoken to us by a Son" (v. 2 NRSV).

John 1:1-14

John begins the story of Jesus with, "In the beginning was the Word." Jesus is God's great act of self-communication and revelation to the world.

Prayer

Dear Lord Jesus Christ, in your incarnation you united all things—things in heaven and things on earth, things above and things below. In your person and work you united God and humanity.

Help us to receive you when you come to us. Help us to welcome your embrace, to awaken to your intrusion into our lives, and then to courageously follow you throughout our lives, not only on Christmas, but every day, now and forever. Amen.

Encountering the text

Our Gospel is the prologue to John's Gospel, a most fitting Gospel for the nativity. John's Gospel employs a host of metaphors for Jesus—he is the door, the good shepherd, the vine, bread, water, and life. But this great, vividly metaphoric Gospel begins with Jesus as the Word: "In the beginning was the Word and the Word was with God and the Word was God. The Word was with God in the beginning" (John 1:1-2).

John's Gospel shuttles, almost immediately, from high-flown talk of "the Word" toward a man sent from God, whose name was John (1:6). So quickly we move from God to humanity. So swiftly the Word—the eternally begotten Word—becomes flesh, our flesh as we are made to look at a man whose name was John. We are told little about this man whose name was John—nothing of his parentage or his hometown—only that he was "sent from God." In a way that man is a parable for any of us who are attempting to be disciples. We are here because we have been summoned, called by God. So every one of us has no credentials and no certification other than that we are all "sent from God."

The Fourth Gospel does not call him John the Baptist. It just calls him John. John's main activity is speaking, and the location for his preaching is the "wilderness" (1:23), so the parable extends itself. This wild man addresses those who are in a wild, trackless, threatening waste of the wilderness. John was a forerunner of those who, like John Wesley, stood out on street corners or in open fields to preach. The Word goes out to those who need it most, out to the wilderness. John's location, his pulpit in the wilderness, reminds us that there are some words that are too true, too lively to be fully contained in a temple, synagogue, or church. God's word is to be heard at these confined, established, sacred sites, to be sure. But the Word, the living incarnate Word, cannot be contained. It reaches out, pushes out, even into the wilderness. The Word is greater even than the beautiful religious platforms that are built to present it.

This one sent from God has only one function: to "witness." A witness is someone who testifies, who simply tells what he or she has seen and heard. The witness is not to embellish or exaggerate. The witness has little significance in and of himself. His significance is in what the witness has to say about what the witness has seen and heard. We want an honest account of what the witness knows to be true. Except for two brief references to this "witness" (5:33-36; 10:40-42), these few verses are all that we hear of John. He speaks, and then he disappears.

Let us simply, directly proclaim the Word this Sunday of the nativity: God's creative, saving Word has come to us, is born among us. Hallelujah.

Proclaiming the text

Christmas is the beginning of the story of Jesus. The story of Jesus begins, in the Gospels, not with Jesus, but with ordinary people. Mary and Joseph get the story going in Luke and Matthew. An ordinary peasant couple are enlisted to bear the Christ into the world.

John's Gospel, as we have heard this morning, begins with John the Baptist, a "voice" crying in the wilderness. When asked, "Who are you?" John replies that he is a "voice." He has no body, no substance or enduring significance other than the sound of a voice, a voice crying in the wilderness "so that through him everyone would believe" (1:7).

Theologian Karl Barth says that John the Baptist is the model for every preacher of every age. John is only interesting as a voice, a witness, someone who points toward the coming Christ. He is transparent like a pane of glass to the One who comes after him who is greater than he. As a witness, John is simply to testify to what he has seen and heard, no more. He must decrease as the One toward whom he points increases. His significance is not in himself but rather in the truth that he tells to those in the wilderness.

It is right that John's Gospel should begin the story of Jesus not with a birth in a manger, but with the words of a preacher. The Fourth Gospel says that Jesus is the Word (in the Greek, *logos*) who came down from heaven and dwelt among us. Although this is the only place in John's Gospel where Jesus is called the Word, it is a powerful image of the Christ, a wonderful introduction to the incarnation. As the Word, Christ is God's self-communication, the major means of the establishment of divine-human communion. God didn't just say to the world, "I love you." God's great message of love became a human being who speaks.

John says that the eternal Word came to "tent" among us (that's what the verb *dwelt* literally means in the Greek, "pitched his tent among us"), and his primary way of dwelling among us is as the Word (1:14). And that's why we joyously sing praises to God this day.

Jesus is more than words can say but never less than words. In Jesus, the words about God became God-in-the-flesh and dwelt among us as the Word. Jesus is God's Word to the world, God's sermon to us, God's Word to which all our words in all our sermons point. As Paul put it, "We don't preach about ourselves. Instead, we preach about Jesus Christ as Lord" (2 Cor 4:5).

Did you hear, in John 1, an echo of the creation story found in Genesis 1? God begins the creation with a word, "Let there be light" (Gen 1:3). True, as John's Gospel said, people "loved the darkness more than the light" (John 3:19). But how does God overcome our love of the dark? Through words.

The creative purposes of God for the world are not forever stumped. The creative work of God continues, John seems to say. When Jesus comes into the world, John 1 says that it's almost like Genesis 1 all over again. Creation continues. God will get what God wants. The light shines in the darkness and nothing that we have ever done, even the worst of it, has been able to overcome the light. To those who receive the Word has been given the gift to "become God's children" (John 1:12).

The incarnation, the Word made flesh, is the supreme example of God's determination, from the beginning of the world, to be with us, no matter what it takes. Jesus the Christ is fully human and fully divine, without any subordination or mixing of either the human or the divine. Jesus was not just "the greatest person who ever lived," not just "a great moral example," not just a wonderfully insightful peripatetic wisdom teacher. He was more. He was God in the flesh.

Jesus is God's supreme act of self-communication. God didn't just say, "I love you." God became flesh and moved in with us as Jesus. Or as it is said in Hebrews: "In many and various ways God spoke of old to our fathers by the prophets; but in these last days he has spoken to us by a Son" (Heb 1:1-2 RSV).

So here I stand on this Sunday of Sundays to announce to you good news: God is with us. God speaks to us, not as words, but as the Word. And the Word this day is good. Merry Christmas. The light shines in the darkness. The Word has become flesh and dwelt among us. Hallelujah!

Relating the text

"Blessed are those who have not seen yet believe," says the risen Christ toward the end of John's Gospel. Johannine irony is at work here all the way to the end of this Gospel; we have not seen Christ as his first followers saw him and yet here we are, believing on the basis of nothing more than John's words about the Word.

"These things are written," says the Fourth Gospel, "so that you will believe" (John 20:31). And despite all the setbacks and perfectly good reasons for not believing the testimony of a wild man with a voice like John's, we do believe, we gather here in church and celebrate the Word made flesh, dwelling with us.

"For the sake of the proclaimed word the world exists with all of its words" (Dietrich Bonhoeffer, quoted in *Worldly Preaching*, ed. Clyde E. Fant [New York: Thomas Nelson, 1975], 129). In other words, God has given us Creation, not merely as the result of the creative Word but rather as that sphere that has been created to hear the Word, to be evoked continually by the Word. The purpose of the world and all its rich array of creatures, including us, is so that the Word might have an appropriate, grateful audience. The world is the stage on which the great drama of redemption is being played. "In the sermon the foundation for a new world is laid," says Bonhoeffer.

When Jesus walks through his congregation in the words of the sermon as the Word, the congregation experiences Jesus as God in the Flesh. Jesus Christ is the self-attestation, the self-proclamation, the self-revelation of God.

Christmas is the feast of the incarnation. Christians are those who claim that when we hear of the birth, life, death, and teaching of this Jew from Nazareth who lived briefly, died violently, and rose unexpectedly, we have heard as much of God as we ever hope to hear. God was so fully present in Jesus the Christ, in the flesh, incarnate, reconciling the world to himself, that early Christian writings like John's Gospel just quite naturally called him "the Word."

It was not that the disciples encountered Jesus as a wonderful person then, after his death, got all worked up in their grief and began thinking, "He is almost like a God." It was rather that, when they encountered Jesus, particularly as they encountered him after his resurrection, everything fell into place, their eyes were opened, and they were able to say with one voice, "You are the Messiah, God's Son!"

At the same time he was not some divine automaton, dropping down out of heaven, moving like a hard-wired robot to his predetermined death, an angelic being for whom his human form was only apparent. He was the enfleshment of God. His human life was not some fleshly husk that he could discard once his divinity took over his humanity. He never got over being fully human while he was fully divine. The incarnation is the great mystery of God being veiled and unveiled, near yet distant, human yet divine, understandable yet mysterious, divine yet human, God Almighty tenting among us as the Word. Sometimes we had difficulty hearing him because of his humanity—God so near to us, as a suffering servant, that it was hard to imagine. Sometimes we had difficulty hearing him because of his divinity—God whose ways and thoughts were more strange and distant from us than we had imagined. Sometimes we heard him precisely because of his humanity—God so near as to be unavoidable. And sometimes we heard him precisely because of his divinity—God revealing to us that which we could not hear except as a gift of God. Everyone who speaks of this incarnate one will find that his or her speaking participates in this same veiling and unveiling that characterized the Word made flesh.

The incarnation is the great mystery that makes preaching possible. As we stressed earlier, preaching is a divinely wrought, miraculous act. Preaching is God's speech. Preaching is God's chosen means of self-revelation. If a sermon "works," it does so as a gracious gift of God, a miracle no less than the virginal conception of Jesus by the Holy Spirit. (One reason why Christians tend to believe in the likelihood of miracles like the virgin birth of Jesus or the resurrection of Christ is that we have experienced miracles of a similar order, if not similar magnitude, in our own lives as we have listened to a sermon. Something has come to us from afar, something has been born in us that we ourselves did not conceive. A word has been heard that is not self-derived. It's a mysterious, undeserved gift. It's a miracle.) Thus preaching is theological not only in its substance but also in its means. Preaching is not only talk about God but also miraculous talk by God.

At the same time, preaching is an utterly human, mundane, carnal, and fleshly thing. Bonhoeffer says, "The proclaimed word is the Christ bearing human nature. This word is... the Incarnate One who bears the sins of the world... The word of the sermon intends to accept mankind, nothing else. It wants to bear the whole human nature" (Clyde E. Fant, *Bonhoeffer: Worldly Preaching* [New York: Thomas Nelson, 1975], 128). Even for Almighty God to speak to us, and to speak in ways that we comprehend, is an incarnational exercise. Aristotle defined a human being as a "word-using animal." For God to speak words to us animals, to become embodied in the words of Scripture or a sermon or the words of the risen Christ, is for God to condescend to us, to stoop, to take up our nature, to risk enfleshment. A less secure, less sovereign, and free godlet might have kept silent rather than risk intercourse with us on our level. To talk with us is to take up the sins of the world, to risk entanglement in our sinful evasion of the truth. If Christ has not preached to us, presumably we would have little reason to crucify him. His sermons, in a sense, brought out the worst in us. He told us the truth about God, and we hated him for it.

First Sunday after Christmas
Nativity of Our Lord

Isaiah 63:7-9

Psalm 148

Hebrews 2:10-18

Matthew 2:13-23

Let's Keep Herod in Christmas

Selected reading

Matthew 2:13-23

Theme

We tend to sentimentalize Christmas, the incarnation. Yet the Gospel writers bend over backward to convince us that Christmas is about a true God entering into the reality of human life, even the bleakest aspects of that reality.

Introduction to the readings

Isaiah 63:7-9

Isaiah sings joyfully of the gracious deliverance of God.

Hebrews 2:10-18

Christ came not "to help angels" (v. 16) but to the children of Abraham, says the letter to the Hebrews in this treatise on the incarnation of Christ.

Matthew 2:13-23

Warned in a dream, the holy family flees to Egypt, and Herod the king launches a slaughter of boy babies in Israel.

Prayer

Holy God, we marvel at the mystery of your incarnation among us, the message of the angels, the song of Mary, the birth of the babe at Bethlehem; give us grace to see all the ways you stand beside us, share our pain and sorrow, and celebrate our joy.

Because you came among us, dispersed the gloom of night, and dawned in our darkness, we know that you care. Therefore, for all of those who this joyous season are sad, we pray for mourners, for the sick, for those whose families are divided, for misunderstood youth, and for little children who are in fear.

Lord, you deemed it good to be born among a people in an occupied land, amid war and strife, where kings raged and soldiers ravaged with the sword. Therefore, we pray for all of those who suffer from war and civil unrest.

Because you have come to us, we come to you, bringing all those problems of our lives that seem so insoluble, offering up to you all of the fears that seem so great, all those matters that perplex us so deeply that we know not what to ask or pray; yet you know. Grant us that peace that only you can give, give us what we need, despite what we think we want. Amen.

Encountering the text

Today we continue the celebration of the incarnation, a celebration begun on Christmas. Yet our sermon will underscore the power of the incarnation, not by an exclusive focus upon Christ, but rather by reflection on the sort of world into which Christ was born. The birth of Jesus is described by Matthew, not in Christmas card sentimentality, but in political realism. Jesus's birth caused a great bloodbath—the massacre of the innocents. What does that tell us about the way in which God comes among us in Jesus?

Bishop Spong (*Born of a Woman: A Bishop Rethinks the Birth of Jesus* [San Francisco: Harper San Francisco, 1992]) says flatly that Herod's massacre of the newborn infants couldn't have happened. (It is amazing when one considers all that these would-be skeptics are so certain about!)

To this, a much more faithful and scholarly bishop (N. T. Wright) replies:

> It is, frankly, incredible to me that someone living in the century of Hitler, Stalin and Pol Pot should find it difficult to believe that rulers can slaughter children for their own political ends. Furthermore, everything we know about Herod the Great (mostly from the Jewish historian Josephus, who had access to Herod's court records) suggests that he was exactly the sort of man who would have had all the babies in a particular village executed if he had had the slightest suspicion that anyone was talking about a future king being born there. After all, Josephus tells us that this same Herod, around the same time, had several of his own family murdered because of his paranoia about plots against his life.... It is no strain on the imagination to think that this same Herod would do what Matthew says he did. (*Who Was Jesus?* [San Francisco: Harper San Francisco, 1992], 87)

What is the significance for our understanding of Christmas that, when Jesus was born, Herod ordered the murder of innocent Jewish children? After the warm glow of Christmas Eve and Day, now the church ponders the political, realistic significance of the incarnation.

Proclaiming the text

Adapt the material in today's "Relating the text" to your congregation. This Sunday we have a wealth of good, vivid illustrative material with which to work.

A good place to begin would be with Kerry Bond's meditation on the significance of Herod in the story of Jesus.

You might organize your sermon in this way: use contemporary, up-to-the-minute illustrations from this week's newspaper, which show that the world in which God becomes incarnate in Christ is a world torn by various sorts of strife.

Then move to a reflection on the way Matthew tells the story of the birth of Jesus. There, in Matthew, are the wailing mothers, the crying babies slaughtered, the holy family fleeing for their lives as refugees into Egypt.

Note how this way of telling the story of Christmas is somewhat at variance with the Christmas story, which we all know and love, as told by Luke. Ponder the significance of telling the story of the birth of Jesus the way that Matthew tells it. Herod is there as a cold, realistic reminder of what sort of world this is for many of God's people. Herod ensures that the nativity is a realistic story and a political story.

Ask what good could the incarnation do us if God had not become incarnate in this world, among us? Why is it that we sentimentalize Christmas, making it sound so calm and sweet? Is this just another means of keeping Jesus irrelevant? Detached from the "real world"?

Matthew's nativity, with Herod and all, reminds each of us this Sunday after Christmas: into the world—the real world where we live and work and struggle—has come a savior who is Christ the Lord. He does not remain above the human fray. Rather, he enters into the fray that he might bring us to God.

Let's keep Herod in Christmas.

Relating the text

"What happens when we banish Herod from Christmas? We market an insipid version of Christmas completely detached from the reality of the evil world we live in.

"But if we leave Herod in the Christmas narrative, our sermons can address the shadow of evil hovering over Christmas to this day. Herod still stalks the earth. He may be disguised in the military fatigues of a dictator. He murders street children in Brazil by sending death squads when darkness falls. Herod sells Thai children as prostitutes to wealthy westerners. He detonates a car bomb that kills innocent people."

—Kerry Bond, *The Living Pulpit* (October–December 1995): 15

Dr. Karen Westerfield Tucker tells of a children's Christmas pageant at her church. At first, the pageant went the way of all such childhood theatricals. The magi appeared in long robes, carrying large, expensive-looking boxes wrapped in gold and silver foil. There were shepherds in bathrobes. They all gathered around the manger. Yet the highlight occurred when Mary unwrapped the babe in the swaddling clothes and revealed, not a cuddly baby doll, but rather a cross. In silence, Mary held the cross high over the manger for all to gaze upon.

What a symbol of Christmas as Matthew presents it! As the favorite hymn puts it, "Love came down at Christmas." Love came down, down to us, down to where we live, amid our "wars and rumors of wars," amid our violence and strife. The babe at Bethlehem's meaning is understood best in light of the cross. Love came down at Christmas.

It was a hot, dusty day when we visited Bethlehem. We had very little time in the Shrine of the Nativity, which is the only thing worth seeing in Bethlehem. Almost before we got off the bus, the guide was herding us back on. We traveled about a mile, just outside the city limits of dusty, dreary Bethlehem, when we were then deposited by our guide at the gaudiest of gift shops for an hour of harrassment by the clerks to buy souvenirs.

Miserably, as we finally settled back on the bus for our trip back to Jerusalem and the hotel, someone muttered, "What a place for God to pick to be born in."

And then it hit us. What a place! The dust, the misery, the ugliness. Bethlehem.

This is the glorious truth behind the incarnation. God comes to us where we are, in Bethlehem, or Boston, or Bangkok. God with us. God with us.

Second Sunday after Christmas

Jeremiah 31:7-14

Psalm 147:12-20

Ephesians 1:3-14

John 1:(1-9), 10-18

Amid the Darkness

Selected reading

John 1:(1-9), 10-18

Theme

Jesus Christ is the light of the world. Unfortunately, we are often dazzled by the lights in this world. The fourth Gospel begins with a warning not to confuse the momentary thrill of following the flamboyant lights with the lasting life and grace that come to those who believe in the Word made flesh.

Introduction to the readings

Jeremiah 31:7-14

This is an oracle describing the joy of the scattered Israelites when they are gathered together under God's protection.

Ephesians 1:3-14

Paul pours forth thanks to God for abundant spiritual blessings upon believers and for their participation in God's eternal plan for all of creation.

John 1:(1-9), 10-18

This is John's beautiful prologue to his Gospel, which testifies to the Word who became flesh, to whom John the Baptist testified.

Prayer

Lord, we vow to follow you, but our hearts have wandered away. We desire to be faithful, but we allow other desires to crowd out our good intentions. We are dazzled by the world's charms. We are like spoiled children who become bored, even when surrounded with a thousand good gifts from you.

Teach us to see through the false promises that surround us. Enable us to remain focused on the true light of the world, Jesus Christ our Lord. Amen.

Encountering the text

The beauty of John's writing is astounding. He begins his Gospel with words that exude power and meaning. However, while we can appreciate the rich language and theology of this prologue, we must not overlook the Gospel writer's desire to immediately establish a comparison between Jesus Christ and John the Baptist.

In the opening verses, we are introduced to the Word/God/light/life-giver. This divine description is put on hold just long enough for us to hear a humbler description: "A man named John was sent from God" (John 1:6). John "wasn't the light" but is the witness who testifies, crying out for all to look at the true light (1:8). We are then plunged back into the salvific description of the Word. John's posture will not change throughout the Gospel. In 5:35, Jesus explicitly describes John as "a burning and shining lamp" but not the true light. It is easy for us to forget the charismatic appeal of John the Baptist in first-century Palestine. Reread Matthew 3:5-10, 14:5, and Mark 1:5 and contemplate the popularity of a man who makes a king tremble. This flamboyant desert preacher made a lasting impression on the community.

All the Gospel writers waste no time in pointing out his testimony to Jesus. They certainly intend John's witness to lift up Christ, but equally important is the need to refocus those who might still want to follow the "witness" rather than the light.

Today's text gives us the opportunity for reflection with the congregation on the many ways in which we still allow our focus to move off the word and onto the glittering vessels that are meant to lift up the word.

Proclaiming the text

One of my favorite services of the Christian year is the Christmas Eve candle-light service. The sanctuary is decorated with familiar trappings from the past, and in the dark of the evening, everything appears softer, more holy than usual. I love that moment when we have sung enough favorite carols to feel "Christmasy," and someone turns out the lights, leaving only the lighted Christ candle. The silence in that near darkness seems so peaceful, so sweet.

One year, in that moment of silently gazing upon the Christ candle, a small voice cried out in the darkness, "Somebody turn on the lights!"

That little voice understood the truth of the gospel, the purpose of Christ's entry into the world better than those of us caught up in the soft, romantic glow of candlelight. He understood that darkness is frightening, and we need someone to bring light into our lives! He experienced the reality of darkness and called out for salvation from it.

In worship, and in life, we can try so hard to create a certain mood, to manufacture an inspiring moment or an emotional rush that we often forget about worshipping the true light that has entered the world.

There is no doubt the Gospel writer wants us to hear the message that Jesus Christ is the light of the world, the true light that enlightens everyone. However, there is another message intertwined in these opening verses, a message of warning. Be careful, the writer says, be very careful to see the difference between worshipping the true, underived light that is Jesus and being dazzled by a bright lamp such as John the Baptist who is sent to illumine our path to Christ.

The people of Palestine were enthralled by John. So many poured out of the Judean countryside into the desert to hear him preach that powerful religious leaders feared his wrath and endured his insults. King Herod wanted to kill him but feared the masses would retaliate. This flamboyant prophet was the religious celebrity of his day. And the Gospel writer feared the people would not see the true light for gazing upon the "man sent from God," the lamp named John.

Five different times in this Gospel, we will hear John witness to the truth of Christ. Five times we will watch John point his followers to Jesus. John was not only trying to witness to the Word made flesh, he was trying to convince his own people there was another who was greater than he.

My extended family gathers at my grandparents' home for our annual Christmas Day free-for-all. As we watched my three-year-old niece Katie open her gifts, we were amazed to see the drama that played out. As each gift was handed to her, she would throw her hands in the air and shout. Tearing off the paper, she would see the unopened box but have no idea what was in it. At once, her hands would return to the air, she would yell with great sincerity, "Thank you, it's just what I wanted!" and then reach for the next present. It took four adults to convince her the gift was inside the boxes.

Sometimes the wrapping can seem so pretty, we forget about the gift that has been given. We have a difficult time getting beyond the glamour to the substance. We get so caught up in the moment, the flamboyant, the shiny packaging, the charismatic, that we forget to look deeper to what is really important.

I remember as a student attending a worship service where a very famous preacher was to proclaim the word. Afterward, one of my classmates asked, "How was worship?" "It didn't grab me," I replied. I remember hearing those words come out of my mouth and feeling ashamed I had such an attitude toward the worship of God.

I had not come to seek the light, to praise God, to receive the gift of grace found in the Word made flesh. I had come to be grabbed, to be enticed, to be seduced by the beautiful setting, the elegance of the ritual, the pretty lights, the words spoken by someone famous. The church worships because God deserves worship. We do not come to feel moved. We do not come with spiritual aloofness saying, "Thrill me, and then I will have worshipped."

We come because we recognize the truth of the Gospel message. Jesus Christ is the light of the world. Jesus Christ is the true light that we need because the world is dark and frightening. If the flowers are drooping, and the hymns are unfamiliar, and the choir stinks, and the sermon is boring. If the glittering lamps that are meant to lift up Christ do not dazzle us, well, praise be to God. Jesus Christ is still the light of the world. The light shines in our darkness, and the darkness will not overcome it.

Relating the text

Stonehenge is the most famous example of many prehistoric sites that were designed around the idea of tracking the sun's movements. Almost all of these temple observatories took special care to mark the winter solstice, that day when the sun rises the least in the sky. The next day the sun begins to rise a little higher each noon. This is an important day for a primitive agrarian community. Not only does it give hope that winter is ebbing, but it also alleviates the fear the sun will continue to sink, plunging the world into permanent night. After discussing this early preoccupation with light, Father Matthew, a monk at Gethsemani Abbey in Kentucky, commented: "Even back then, before they knew about Christ, the people were looking for light in the midst of their darkness. Pretty good, huh?"

There is still a small sect in the Holy Land called the Mandeans who trace their history back as followers of John the Baptist. They never got beyond the messenger to hear the message. They never got beyond John's words to hear the Word.

"Light is not only the revelation of the logos; it reveals the nature of all who come in contact with it, and the judgment upon each person is determined by his or her response to it. Light shines in darkness. It reveals. It also exposes."

—R. Alan Culpepper, *Anatomy of the Fourth Gospel*
(Philadelphia: Fortress, 1983), 191

When a minister asked how many people were going to take down their Christmas tree on Epiphany (the end of the twelve days of Christmas), one woman reported that she had removed all her decorations by 2 p.m. on Christmas Day. When asked why, she replied, "After we opened all the presents, I got depressed. I was so tired of Christmas stuff; I just couldn't stand it. Christmas is never as good as the advertisements lead you to believe."

"Grant to us, O Lord, not to mind earthly things, but rather to love heavenly things, that whilst all things around us pass away, we even now may hold fast those things which abide forever."

—Saint Leo the Great, quoted in *Earliest Christian Prayers* by F. Forrester
Church and Terrence J. Mulry (New York: Macmillan, 1988), 110

In her book *Reaching Out without Dumbing Down*, Marva J. Dawn draws on Neil Postman to make critical comments about culture creeping into our worship:

"He asserts, 'I believe I am not mistaken in saying that Christianity is a demanding and serious religion. When it is delivered as easy and amusing, it is another kind of religion altogether' [Neil Postman, *Amusing Ourselves to Death: Public Discourse in the Age of Show Business* (New York: Penguin, 2006), 121]. We must always ask if what we do and see in worship reveals the truth about discipleship. Perhaps our crosses are too beautiful—we forget that they are meant to die on."

—Marva J. Dawn, *Reaching Out without Dumbing Down* (Grand Rapids: Eerdmans, 1995), 270

"If, then, the tribulation of the Church be its guilt; if the guilt of the Church be its steady refusal to acknowledge the tribulation imposed upon it by its own peculiar task and its own peculiar Theme; and if the refusal of the Church to acknowledge its theme be nothing less than the Church's avoidance of God—then the very fact of the possibility of this refusal and avoidance points to another opposite possibility. The Church, on its own showing, cannot fall back on the excuse that it is being driven simply by blind fate and necessity. The Church is itself responsible precisely because it fails to lay hold of this opposite possibility. Therefore in the darkness the light shines.

"This is of great importance, not merely in order that we may not doubt that the tribulation of the Church lies in its burning guilt, but in order that we may perceive the hope of the Church to be manifest precisely where its guilt is proven. In the midst of the possibility of the Church lies the impossible possibility of God. The Church is therefore enlightened by the light of eternity, by light from light uncreated. The question is whether the Church is able to recognize this light."

—Karl Barth, *The Epistle to the Romans* (London: Oxford University Press, 1933), 374

The Epiphany of Our Lord

Isaiah 60:1-6
Psalm 72:1-7, 10-14
Ephesians 3:1-12
Matthew 2:1-12

Arise! Shine!

Selected reading

Isaiah 60:1-6

Theme

As Christians, we have seen something. A light has shone into our darkness. That light is Christ, the light of the world. Having seen the light, we are now commanded to share the light, to share the good news of Jesus with the whole world. Epiphany is the season of mission, that season when we are reminded that the light of Christ is meant to shine into the whole world.

Introduction to the readings

Isaiah 60:1-6

"Arise! Shine! Your light has come," the prophet Isaiah proclaims to exilic Israel (v. 1).

Ephesians 3:1-12

Paul speaks of the coming of Jesus as the Messiah as a mystery that was kept secret through the ages but has now been graciously revealed in our time.

Matthew 2:1-12
Matthew tells the story of the journey of the magi to Bethlehem.

Prayer

Almighty God, your Son, our Savior Jesus Christ, came into the world, that we might have light in our darkness, life rather than death. Grant that your people, enlivened by the reading and preaching of your word, and refreshed by your sacraments, might rise, might shine forth into all the world the radiance of the glory of Christ.

May Christ be seen in us, worshipped by the world, obeyed by all, to the distant ends of the earth, now and always. Amen.

Encountering the text

Today is Epiphany, the beginning of that season when we celebrate the revelation, the manifestation of God in Christ. Just as the magi came to Bethlehem because they had seen the light of the star (today's Gospel), so we have gathered here in church to celebrate God's epiphany among us as Christ.

And yet gathering is not enough. Having gathered, we are to go forth to share the light that we have seen. Epiphany is traditionally the season when the church celebrates mission. The magi came "from the East." They were not Jews, had no part of the sacred promises of God to Israel. And yet they were the first to bend the knee and worship the baby Jesus. The magi therefore remind us that God intends for this good news to be spread to all people everywhere.

When someone receives some good news, the natural tendency is to want to share that news with others. That's us today. We have received the gospel of Christ. This Sunday, in the sermon, let us encourage the congregation to "Arise! Shine!" The prophet speaks of a dawning for Israel. It is not enough to receive the light. We are urged as Christians to share that light.

Proclaiming the text

There is a great deal of useful illustrative material in the "Relating the text" section for this Sunday. Here is a possible approach to your sermon:

Begin by noting how Isaiah calls upon Israel to shine forth before all the nations as a testimony of the graciousness and goodness of God. This is the season of Epiphany in which we celebrate not only the manifestation of Christ to the church but also the church as God's means for sharing the light of Christ with the whole world.

Use the St. Martin-in-the-Fields statement of mission as an example of a church that is attempting to see the light of Christ and then to share that light with others. Paraphrase the account of the minister who visits a church, or give your own account from your pastoral experience of the way some people feel when they visit your congregation. How well does our congregation let its light shine into the world?

End the sermon by challenging members of the congregation to share their light, wherever they are, with others. Arise! Shine! Our light has come.

Relating the text

"The day of the professional minister is over, the day of the missionary pastor has come. . . . The day of the church culture is over, the day of the mission field has come. . . . The day of the local church is over, the day of the mission outpost has come."

—Kennon L. Callahan, *Effective Church Leadership: Building on the Twelve Keys* (New York: Harper and Row, 1990), 4

On a recent trip to England, I discovered a congregation that seemed to be doing this well. The congregation is St. Martin-in-the-Fields, an Anglican parish in the heart of London. It has devised a three-year mission action plan. Its mission statement is clear: "St. Martin-in-the-Fields exists to honour God, and to enable questioning, open-minded people to discover for themselves the significance of Jesus Christ."

Along with their mission statement, they have publicly declared and distributed a charter synthesizing their outlook. I include it here, for I believe it can serve as a model for other churches seeking to articulate their theological perspectives.

St. Martin-in-the Fields' ten-point charter:

1. We believe in and proclaim both the mystery that is God, whom we partly know and partly do not know, and the human need to worship.

2. We believe in and proclaim the person of Jesus Christ who distinctively reveals the nature of God and the meaning and purpose of life, and who calls us to follow him through the death of the cross to the place of Resurrection.

3. We trust in the Holy Spirit who prompts liberty, beauty, truth, love and joy against the waywardness of human nature.

4. We are committed to using the Bible in a way that takes account of all truth and relates it to the real experiences, both good and bad, that people have of life.

5. We are committed to a church that conveys the Christian revelation in signs and symbols, particularly in the sacraments of Baptism and Holy Communion.

6. We are committed to exploring the meaning of the Kingdom of God and to making connections between what we profess and the way in which we live and work.

7. We draw inspiration from our patron saint St. Martin who, by cutting his cloak in two, demands that we look both at the resource we create and possess, and the way that it is shared.

8. We are committed to taking all people seriously wherever they might be at their particular point of understanding, while at the same time sharing with them whatever insights may have been gained by our relationship with God.

9. We acknowledge the destructive power of human sinfulness, and we welcome gratefully the forgiveness that God offers to those who are prepared to turn to the truth.

10. We are committed to identifying and affirming what is good and identifying and opposing what is evil, and living as best we can in the mess in the middle.

"Every congregation looking for revitalization must declare its mission succinctly, and then outline the essential tenets that encompass its theological outlook and emphases. The congregation then should declare periodically its commitments through its liturgy. To strangers in our midst, this practice will clarify the basic character and beliefs that motivate the congregation to make a difference in the immediate neighborhood and surrounding society."

—Carnegie Samuel Calian, *Survival or Revival* (Louisville, KY: Westminster John Knox, 1998), 60

In an article titled "Cross-Multicultures in the Crossfire: The Humanities and Political Interests," Martin E. Marty suggests that multicultures within the larger society are "products of response to [the following] four needs in the late modern world":

Identity: the need to answer, "who am I?" . . .

- 73 -

Loyalty: the need to spell out, "to whom do I belong?" Whom shall I trust? . . .

Values: the need to answer, "by what shall I live?" What do I pass on to my children? What would I like to see prevail in respect to the true, the beautiful, and the good? . . .

Power: the need to answer, "how can I protect myself?" or "how can I make my way over against others?" How do I throw off the oppressor and how can I be free?

—Martin E. Marty, "Cross-Multicultures in the Crossfire: The Humanities and Political Interests," in *Christianity and Culture in the Crossfire*, ed. David A. Hoekema and Bobby Fong (Grand Rapids: Eerdmans, 1997), 17

It is important for the church today to realize that it just doesn't exist to "speak to the culture." The church is a culture, a counterculture. One way we let our light shine in a darkened world is by providing people an alternative to the ways of the world. In what ways does your congregation act to respond to Marty's four criteria?

First Sunday after the Epiphany
The Baptism of Our Lord

Isaiah 42:1-9

Psalm 29

Acts 10:34-43

Matthew 3:13-17

Miraculous Baptism

Selected reading

Matthew 3:13-17

Theme

Jesus's baptism was "from heaven"—that is, it was a miraculous moment of divine intervention. Most of the really good things that come into our lives come "from heaven." In the Christian faith, revelation, insight, truth, comfort, and the Christian life itself all come "from heaven," as a miraculous act of a God who cares enough about us to come to us.

Introduction to the readings

Isaiah 42:1-9

The prophet tells of the coming of one who will be "my servant...my chosen," the one who will bring forth "new things" (vv. 1, 9).

Acts 10:34-43
Peter proclaims that the great, expansive love of God "doesn't show partiality" (v. 34).

Matthew 3:13-17
When Jesus is baptized by John the Baptist in the Jordan River, the Holy Spirit proclaims from on high that he is the Messiah, the Christ.

Prayer

Lord Jesus, rip open the heavens and come to us, reach down, reach in, disrupt, touch, embrace, speak to us. Do not leave us, O Lord, to our own devices. Abandon us not to our own voices. Speak to us, miraculously appear to us, and then give us the grace to listen. Amen.

Encountering the text

The story of the baptism of Jesus is a story about Jesus, a story about revelation of Jesus's identity for the rest of the world. Yet, by implication, it can also be a story about us. That is, we have no way of knowing who Jesus is, without the gift of revelation. We can't find out who Jesus is by doing historical research on him. (Sorry, you "search for the historical Jesus" devotees!) Though human reasoning and evidence gathering and empirical research are usual means of making sense of the world, we cannot make sense of Jesus in these ways.

To know who Jesus is and what he means has got to come to us through revelation, as a gift, as grace. It has got to come to us, in the words of today's Gospel, "from above."

All of the Synoptic Gospels begin the story of Jesus with the story of his baptism by John the Baptist. Each of them asserts that Jesus is superior to John—possibly in response to some of the claims of John's disciples. Luke does this not only by having John say that he is inferior, as do the other Gospels, but also by placing the account of the arrest and imprisonment of John right after Jesus's baptism (Luke 3:18-20). The Gospel of John does not give an account of John's baptism of Jesus, although it also opens with a presentation of John as a witness to Jesus.

Perhaps more importantly, all the Gospels connect Jesus's baptism with the work of the Holy Spirit. The baptism of Jesus is presented, unlike any of John's other baptisms, as a baptism in which the Holy Spirit takes over, taking it out of the hands of John and placing it in the hands of God. John's baptism is a prophetic, preparatory washing and cleansing for the coming of the Messiah. But the baptism of Jesus is a baptism in which the heavens are open, there is a voice, and the Holy Spirit makes Jesus's unique identity manifest.

Proclaiming the text

It may surprise you to hear me say this, but say this I will. I don't know how to preach. I've only been trying to preach for the last forty years and, after forty years, I know less about how to preach a sermon than when I began.

I've learned this: when it comes to sermons, people don't listen; more accurately, people don't hear. There are too many obstacles to successful communication: the skeptical modern world, science, attention deficit disorder, hormones, and sin.

I work on a sermon, do my homework. Then I stand up here and thrash about for twenty minutes. Tell some sappy stories. Gesture from the torso. But you don't hear! Even though the lights are in my eyes up here, I can see that you don't hear!

I don't know how to preach. I tried every technique, different forms, and different arrangements. It's particularly hard to hear the things of God. How can you talk to someone about God? How do you speak in such a way that people don't just hear about God but are brought to God? I have learned that it is just about impossible to get people to get a sermon.

But sometimes they do. People undeniably hear. Most of you keep coming back because, having had the lightning strike once, it could well strike again, and you want to be here for it. Having once shuffled in here—distracted, unfocused, unsure—you have, despite all, irrefutably heard.

You know what annoys me about you? It's when I preach a sermon that was meant to be good but wasn't good. It could have been a good sermon if I had another month to work on it. After a sermon like that—poorly illustrated, badly supported, turgid, and opaque—here you come, with tears in your eyes, gripping my hand and saying, "Thank you. That was wonderful. That was life-changing! Got it!"

Got what? I have the manuscript for that sermon. I'm an expert on preaching, and I know a bad sermon when I hear one. Nothing there!

Now why, despite my worst efforts, did you hear? Who pulled back the veil between us and God? Not me.

A clergy friend of mine, for his sabbatical, didn't read books and write thoughts. He chose to travel about the country, visiting churches, listening to sermons. I asked him what he learned in his thirty-sermon tour, and he said, "I think it's a miracle that anybody ever hears anything."

And yet, you do. Why? I think it's a miracle.

Pascal is one of the greatest minds ever, always incisive, probing, struggling with the big questions, looking for answers, and frustrated. In the middle of the night, Pascal wrote, "Not the God of the philosophers, but the God of Abraham, Isaac, and Jacob, Fire! Fire! Fire!" Even so great a mind as Pascal couldn't climb his way up to God; so the living God inflamed him.

In today's Gospel, it was another day at the river. John was baptizing, washing people up, getting ready for the Messiah. It was a ritual that Jews sometimes went through, a kind of purification rite sometimes associated with preparation for the coming of the Messiah.

"Messiah's coming," John preached. "Someday, sometime, someplace, Messiah's coming." People were filled with expectation. John didn't say, "Messiah's here!" No, John preached, "Messiah's coming."

Just going through the motions, expecting the Messiah. People interrupted his sermon with, "Are you the Messiah?"

"No," John answered them. "I couldn't tie the shoelaces of the one who is coming after me, the one you are expecting. I baptize with water; the one who is coming after me, more powerful than I, will baptize with wind and fire!"

John said, "I just wash you up; he will burn you up! Purify you!"

There's a heap of difference between expecting God's word and hearing it. A great distance between anticipating the possibility of the presence of God and getting God.

Well, John is baptizing. "Next." Wade in the water, stoop to the water, up out of the water. "Next." Wade, stoop, up. "Next."

And then, with this one from Nazareth—dove, Spirit, voice—the heavens were ripped open, the veil was torn asunder, and there was fire.

This dove, Spirit, and voice is the Bible's way of saying that God was present. The Spirit hovering over the muddy Jordan waters reminds us of that primal Spirit that hovered over the waters at creation, bringing life, light.

You know enough about the Bible to know that, through much of the Gospels, Jesus can be enigmatic. Jesus tells these cryptic, incomprehensible, often pointless parables. Who can understand him? But here, in this moment, at the first of the year, the veil is pulled back, there is a voice all the way from heaven, and we hear, "You are my Son, you're Beloved." It is a voice directed not at us but at Jesus, a conversation within the heart of the Trinity, but we get a miraculous overhearing. And it is enough.

- 79 -

The voice is "from heaven." It is not of the earth. It is not a voice, like most of what you hear, that arises out of your infantile background, from the damage that your mother inflicted upon you during your latent stage, or something you are dealing with from adolescence, an upsurge of the human spirit. It is a word not psychologically, sociologically, or anthropologically derived. It is "from heaven"—that is, it is from God. It's a miracle.

I don't know how many heard the voice that day. I'm glad that somebody heard it, saw the dove, felt the fire, and had the guts to tell us. Because maybe then we, though sorely limited by our modern epistemological restraints, might be open to such a voice and such a vision.

We baptize babies. Why? A baby can't believe the Apostles' Creed, can't think theologically, and can't obey the Ten Commandments, which makes a baby utterly dependent upon the grace of God to do for the baby what the baby can't do for herself. If this baby is going to get back to God, it will take a miracle.

Get my drift? We baptize in promise, expectation. God will work in this child's life. We baptize anybody, any age, into the same promise. Everybody here requires a voice, a dove, a heavenly aperture, not of our own devising or you won't get home.

One of you has been attending this church for years. And yet you told somebody that you understood only one sermon in a hundred in all those months of Sundays and you keep coming to church, Sunday after Sunday. You understand only one sermon in a hundred! Why? I don't mean, "Why don't you understand," because, as we have noted, there are dozens of reasons why people don't hear God's word. I mean, "Why do you keep coming?"

Because four years ago, during a sermon, by a guest preacher, there was fire! The heavens opened, a dove descended, and you heard God so close you could feel the breath.

I can't preach God's word to you. Forgive me when I try to explain Jesus, attempt to talk you into the faith. I can't. And it's not because I'm not so hot as a preacher; it's because revelation, recognition—when it's about God—is always a gift. A miracle. It's got to come "from heaven." I can't preach, and you can't hear, except as miracle.

I'm not saying that the baptism of Jesus happened just that way with a literal dove descending upon an unembellished baptism, with an actual, audible voice. I'm not saying that this "fire" was not somewhat figurative. I'm not saying that visions like this happen every day. I am saying that it will happen to you!

One day you're being baptized, taking a bath, taking a break, or listening to a sermon. You're staring off into space, doing nothing. And then, just when you thought your world was safe and silent, the once hushed heavens will open, there will be a voice, inexplicable but undeniable, and there will be wind. And you, despite reservations, dare wade into the water. You draw near the fire.

Relating the text

"You can order a Visa card from the Internet with a picture of Jesus on it. A Jesus Visa. The website pitches this credit card with the line, Show the world your love for the Most High. The idea is, apparently, that the more you use your credit card, the more you can show the world your love for Jesus.

"You can load a Jesus screen saver onto your computer. You can buy Jesus playing cards, Jesus bumper stickers, Jesus bookmarks, key chains, lapel pins, and earrings. The idea is that these trinkets enhance your relationship with Jesus. Some Christians claim to find comfort and encouragement in them. Others find them an outrageous commercial gimmick.

"Jesus is not only used to support the cause of healthy profits and entrepreneurial strategies. Ever since Jesus walked and talked with his followers two thousand years ago, people have enlisted him to support a hopelessly long, often contradictory, and sometimes spectacularly foolish list of causes and convictions. Popes, bishops, and soldiers in the Middle Ages understood Jesus as summoning Europe to the cause of the Crusades. Both sides of brutal religious wars have shouted his name. Some have assumed that Jesus approved the colonial conquests of Africa, Asia, South America, and North America in the age of empires. Others have claimed that he allowed, even required, the institution of American slavery."

—Leanne Van Dyke, *Believing in Jesus Christ* (Louisville, KY: Geneva Press 2002), 1

The way I read church history, most of our really big theological mistakes have occurred in the interest of evangelism. In reaching out to speak to the world, to reach the world for Christ, sometimes we fall in. We offer the world nothing of much difference than what the world already has.

A recent study of evangelist preaching in the last few decades contends that there are two primary ways of presenting the gospel. The gospel is advocated either as something that can be historically verified (thus historical criticism) or as a means for getting something that you want like a sense of joy, well-being, or whatever it is you happen to want in life. In other words, the gospel is presented as a technique for getting something else that you want, even more than you want the gospel! In my experience, it is this utilitarian approach that is most popular in the churches of my experience.

The gospel is thereby rendered into something useful and is commended to the world on the basis of its alleged utility. Do you want more joy in your life? Come to Jesus. Would you like to have a happier family life? Come to Jesus.

Sometimes, in this manner of presentation, the gospel is subservient to something else that is considered more valuable than the gospel—joy, peace, a sense of meaning, and so forth.

But what if the gospel is more than a technique, more than a means of getting to something else? What if, in the light of this Sunday's scriptural interpretation, the gospel is about the presence of Christ coming into your world, into your life?

What if the gospel is not so much a technique for getting something else but rather an encounter with someone else? What if the Christian faith is mainly a matter of being met by the risen Christ?

In my experience, that encounter may bring joy or peace, but it could as easily bring a profound sense of disease, dislocation, and pain. What if the Christian faith is not a means of our getting what we want from God but rather what happens in us when God gets what God wants from us?

Second Sunday after the Epiphany
RC/Pres: Second Sunday
in Ordinary Time

Isaiah 49:1-7

Psalm 40:1-11

1 Corinthians 1:1-9

John 1:29-42

Untidy Lives

Selected reading

John 1:29-42

Theme

Jesus is the Lamb of God. John makes it clear in his Gospel that Jesus has become the true Passover Lamb for the world—his death bringing salvation for the children of God. However, it is questionable whether we can, in our overly sanitized culture, fully appreciate the meaning of this sacrificial image. Perhaps this loss of connection with the messy side of life also explains our struggle with ministries to the painful and broken side of people.

Introduction to the readings

Isaiah 49:1-7

The Lord declares it is not enough for Israel to be called, gathered, and honored as the chosen people. They will also be a light to all the nations.

1 Corinthians 1:1-9
Paul reminds this young church that God has given them every spiritual gift they need and will strengthen them in the use of those gifts until Christ's return.

John 1:29-42
John the Baptist proclaims that Jesus is the Lamb of God who takes away the sin of the world.

Prayer
Lord God, you and you alone deserve our worship. Enable us to offer ourselves in praise and thanksgiving as a holy and living sacrifice in union with Christ's offering for us. May our worship form us as your people. May we be taught to live in the harmony of the songs we sing. May our hearts be united in the prayer that forms on our lips. May God's word dwell in our lives as it is read and proclaimed in our gatherings. May we learn to share the gifts you have given us as we share our bread that is your Son, our Savior Jesus Christ. Amen.

Encountering the text
For both John the Baptist and John the writer, the Passover image of the Lamb of God is central to their understanding of Jesus Christ. The repetition of this concept in the baptizer's witness and the Gospel's theological structure reinforces our need to examine this critical title of Christ.

John's passion narrative is written so that we understand Jesus is condemned to death by Pilate on the preparation day for Passover at noon (John 18:28; 19:14), the hour when priests begin to slaughter Passover lambs in the temple. It is this Gospel alone that records that the soldiers do not break any of Jesus's bones "to fulfill the scripture" (19:36). This reference corresponds to Exodus (12:46) and Numbers (9:12) where none of the Passover lamb's bones were to be broken. Then, the soldier pierces Jesus's side and out flow blood and water (John 19:34), traditionally interpreted as signs of the life-giving sacraments of holy Eucharist and baptism.

John the Baptist would not have had to explain these images for the Jews of his day. He proclaims that Christ is the Lamb of God and his disciples follow. They understood the power of such a connection.

Unfortunately, it is questionable whether we or our congregations can grasp the theological significance in connecting Jesus with the Passover lamb. We have had similar dilemmas before. We have difficulty understanding the complex historical/theological setting of concepts such as the Messiah or the second Adam. However, in this case, it may go beyond merely comprehending the background for a term. We might intellectually grasp the idea of Christ as willing sacrificial victim whose blood is literally poured out on the cross, but that does not change our discomfort with the idea.

The text ends with John's disciples following this Lamb of God. But in time, even the disciples will struggle to understand what death, blood, and a cross have to do with hope and salvation. Perhaps this is a good time for us to struggle with the same issue.

Proclaiming the text

On a recent shopping excursion, I was trying to weave my way from one side of a superstore to the other, from the automotive center to the peanut butter section. I had gone about a half mile when I passed through "kill-an-animal-at-any-cost" territory. A mother had obviously hesitated far too long, and her child, who appeared to be around six years old, had stopped, fascinated with a video on deer hunting. She rushed her innocent child away with the words, "Come on. We don't want to watch this." They walked briskly down the aisle and into the hamburger franchise serving the rear of the store.

I have no doubt that woman understood the irony of the situation as much as I did. Reverse the roles, and I would have done the same thing. Yes, we know where meat in the supermarket comes from; we just don't want to think about it more than we have to.

We are comfortable with our sterile environment, our overly sanitized culture. We like it this way. Death no longer happens at home. At one time, slaughtering animals for food or gathering around a relative's deathbed were considered commonplace in most families. No more.

As those intimate, life-and-death moments have moved out of our ordinary lives, we have grown increasingly uneasy dealing with death, illness, and other such disturbing subjects. We are much more comfortable in orderly, neat places with orderly, neat people abiding by orderly, neat schedules—like our worship services.

Everyone knows that worship should be tidy. Sanctuaries are supposed to be clean. People are to be courteous and quiet. Even sermons should be tidy, wrapping up the nagging questions of life.

Death and illness are the last things we want to bring into our weekly worship experience. Sure, we have funerals, but those are special occasions during which we break out special language and rituals. At one time, church families took care of preparing bodies, digging graves, and "sitting up" with the deceased all night before the funeral. Now we hire professionals to manage these details. Death and illness are messy, and we don't deal well with messy. Let the hymn be in the wrong place in the bulletin and we feel uncomfortable!

In seminary, professors of worship and liturgy give out tips on making ritual come alive. "During holy baptism, splash the water around, get everything good and soaked," they say. "Let the congregation experience the 'wetness' of the moment." One student pastor informed me that putting this advice into practice in his church had resulted in the first anonymous note of his career. "Spill water on our carpet again and there will be real trouble."

How different from where we began. When God gave specifics on how to worship to the children of Israel, it became clear the Lord is not such a neat freak. "Build a temple," God said, "a great temple where my name will dwell.

And take animals into the temple—very small animals like doves and great big animals like bulls—and slaughter them there. Take their blood and pour it over all the sides of the altar. This is what I require of you."

Or go even further back than that to the Passover, the great salvation event of the Old Testament! "To save yourselves from death, you must take a lamb," God said. "Slaughter it and paint your doorposts and lintels with its blood." Worship in our family has always relied on blood to be spilt. Our sin is so great, our salvation so costly, something or someone has to die to pay for it.

That did not change with epiphany of Christ; we still rely on blood. We may no longer have to slaughter animals every week, but only because Christ became the final sacrifice of that blood. John called out, "Here is the Lamb of God who takes away the sin of the world!" Jesus is the Passover Lamb for us. His blood will be spilt, and we won't just talk about splashing it on the doorposts or on the carpet. We get plunged into it headfirst, singing, "What can wash away my sin? Nothing but the blood of Jesus!"

The disciples of John understood the power of that image. Hearing the prophet proclaim Jesus is "the Lamb of God," they turn and follow a new teacher. The early church, having celebrated Passover, having watched sacrifices in the temple, would have equally understood the connection. Can we?

Don't get me wrong. I am thankful that sacrifice was final. I can't imagine going to seminary to learn how best to bleed an animal. I hate to think what that temple smelled like after a long day. But surely we can realize we have lost something in this transition if we do not remember that the blood of Christ was just as real as the blood of those sacrificial animals. Simply because it isn't thrown against our altar every week does not mean we can overlook its meaning. After the host is broken at Eucharist, the priest proclaims, "Christ, our paschal Lamb, has been sacrificed for you."

The life and death of Christ were not neat and clean. Life is messy; sacrifice is always messy. To remember and glorify that sacrifice made for us means we cannot become obsessed with keeping worship neat and tidy. If we celebrate a

God who is with us in every aspect of our messy lives, we sometimes have to get messy too. Neat and tidy worship might be comfortable, but we cannot allow our worship to become sterile.

Church researchers have pointed out that one reason many hard-living people give for not coming to worship is they don't feel they have the right clothing. That is sterile worship.

Ask congregations why they don't make efforts to reach out to the homeless or those with mental and physical challenges in their community, and they will talk about smells or how uncomfortable it makes them. That is sterile worship.

Go to congregations around the nation and try to find children. We may talk about being church family, but we don't allow crying or squirming in this family. That is sterile worship.

Ask church members why they didn't come to worship last week and they might tell you, "My back was hurting, and I didn't think you would want me to get up and walk around in the middle of the service." God forbid! That is sterile worship.

Sterile. It means not only clean but also lifeless, unable to sustain life. Is it surprising we live in an age when the church struggles with attendance? Worship doesn't seem to be relevant, to relate to people's real life!

Life is messy. Birth, illness, death, and all parts in between are messy. And God is involved in every one of them.

In fact, Jesus identified himself with those whose lives were, at best, untidy. We are taught to see him in the outcast, the broken in society. If that is true, we should be careful about inviting Jesus Christ to our worship service; it could get messy.

Relating the text

I arrived at Gethsemane Abbey, a Trappist monastery in Kentucky, for a retreat the day after a monk had died. While preparations were made for the service and guests were arriving, his body was covered with a pall and laid in the sanctuary near the altar. Just as they had been next to him during his illness, the monks now all took turns, two at a time, sitting at this brother's side, singing the Psalms. My lasting impression of that experience was that for these people, death was not a lonely, isolated experience. Death was something that came to them while they were surrounded by the community of faith.

When I came home and told a Bible study group about the experience, silence filled the room and hung there uncomfortably. Finally, someone asked, "You don't expect us to do that, do you?"

How different from a few years back when there was no funeral home. At that time, the church prepared and buried its own. Dying and death have never been easy, but at one time, they were understood as burdens we all took up together. It was an opportunity, like other painful situations, to show loved ones our love.

As a young candidate for deacon's orders, I attended a Board of Ordained Ministry retreat to be examined and evaluated. We were asked to respond to several real-life scenarios we might possibly encounter. One of those scenes went something like this: "A young woman comes to you, interested in the faith and holy baptism, but she is upset by the words to the hymn 'There Is a Fountain Filled with Blood.' She doesn't like the idea of being plunged beneath the blood drawn from Emmanuel's veins. What do you say to her?" Indeed. What do we say?

"I believe that one of the most important discoveries of trinitarian theology in our time is the discovery of the suffering love of the suffering triune God. All cheap and easy talk about a God of sovereign power who is in control of a world in which there is so much poverty, suffering, and injustice is obscene. All self-confident talk about a powerful church that has the mandate and the ability to transform society with this or that conservative or liberal social-political agenda or with this or that evangelistic program is increasingly absurd in a disintegrating church that cannot solve its own problems, much less the problems of the world. The only gospel that makes sense and can help in what Moltmann calls our 'godless and godforsaken' world is the good news of a God who loves enough to suffer with and for a suffering humanity. And the only believable church is one that is willing to bear witness to such a God by its willingness to do the same thing."

—Shirley C. Guthrie, "Human Suffering, Human Liberation, and the Sovereignty of God," *Theology Today,* April 1996: 32

"Man lives because of the sacrifice of the wheat and the vine, and he, in his own turn, is a sacrifice to the birds and the worms, or to the bacilli which effect his death. This is the inescapably grim fact of being alive, and which most civilized peoples do their best to conceal.

"From the relative standpoint of time and space this mutual slaughter is hardly a sacrifice in the accepted sense; for every true sacrifice is voluntary, whereas the wheat which was ground for our bread, and the lamb which was slain for our roast could not exactly be called the willing victims of their fate. On the other hand, the Mass represents a true sacrifice, in that Christ submitted deliberately and willingly to his crucifixion, which took place at the very moment when the Jews were sacrificing the Passover Lamb at the Temple. The reason why the new Christ/Sacrifice redeems and the old Passover/Sacrifice does not is that the Victim of the former is willing, the performer of a self-sacrifice, at once Priest and Offering."

—Alan Watts, *Myth and Ritual in Christianity*
(Boston: Beacon, 1968), 147

My first year in seminary brought with it an opportunity to work for several small churches in rural North Carolina. As my supervising pastor was driving me around a small town, I noticed what I thought was a small covered picnic table sitting in front of the Episcopal church. This was not too unusual because many churches in this area had outdoor pavilions for "dinner on the grounds." However, unlike most picnic tables, there were no boards for seats and the table itself was raised to chest level. "That's the smallest pavilion I've ever seen," I said.

The pastor replied, "That is where the church members used to prepare the bodies of their deceased members. Around here, it used to be an honor to be asked by the family to help do that sort of thing."

Third Sunday after the Epiphany
RC/Pres: Third Sunday
in Ordinary Time

Isaiah 9:1-4

Psalm 27:1, 4-9

1 Corinthians 1:10-18

Matthew 4:12-23

The Long Search

Selected reading

Matthew 4:12-23

Theme

One reason why we come to church and listen to sermons is that many of us are engaged in a search—a search for God. We spend much of our lives looking for the meaning of life, the point of it all, the identity of the one who made us and the world. In many and diverse ways, God has reached out to us, reaching out most dramatically in the Christ.

Introduction to the readings

Isaiah 9:1-4

Isaiah speaks of light shining into the darkness for suffering Israel in exile.

1 Corinthians 1:10-18
Paul writes to the Corinthians urging them to lay aside their divisions and be unified in Christ.

Matthew 4:12-23
Jesus begins his ministry by reaching out and calling a group of people to work with him as his disciples.

Prayer

Lord Jesus, we have come here this day searching for you, because we believe that you are searching for us. In countless ways you have reached out to us, tugged at our hearts, courted us, spoken to us. We confess that sometimes we have searched for you in all the wrong places.

We admit that sometimes we have thought that we found you when we only found cheap substitutes for your love. Find us this day, Lord Jesus. Discover us anew so that we might find you and, in finding, love you, and in loving you, serve you in all that we do. Amen.

Encountering the text

We are in the season of the Epiphany, meaning "manifestation" or "revelation" of Christ. The Christ is not something that we discovered but rather is God's unique means of discovering us. We could not find God in our groping, so God, in great grace, found us.

This great truth is revealed in the Gospel lessons of Epiphany and in no more beloved a lesson than this Sunday's lesson, Matthew 4:12-23, the calling of Jesus's disciples. Jesus does not sit back and wait for people to stumble upon him; he reaches out, goes forth, calls to them to "come, follow me."

Conventional rabbis did not "call" disciples, I am told. It was considered bad form for a rabbi to go out, beat the bushes, and ask people to become his disciples. The greatness of one's teaching was supposed to naturally attract students.

Jesus called disciples, reached out, saying, "Come, follow me."

He still reaches, still goes forth, still calls. That reaching, that loving search, will be our sermon on this day as we ponder the significance of the God who came to us in Christ. Our God is an actively seeking, relentlessly searching God, not a possessive, inactive, aloof God. Even as the shepherd searches for the one lost sheep, the father waits constantly for the return of the prodigal son, or the woman tears apart her house looking for the one lost coin (beloved stories that Luke tells elsewhere), so the Christ searches, waits, looks for us.

Proclaiming the text

He had made a rather sudden lurch to the right. He became interested in evangelical Christianity. Rumor had it that he was at a fundamentalist Christian church on the edge of town. He bragged to someone that he was in a Bible study every night.

Then came the 1990s. He made a trip out to the West Coast. He spent two weeks at a retreat with the theme of self-discovery. When he returned, all of his talk was about "astral projection," "out-of-body experiences," and other ideas that someone attributed to his "New Age thinking."

As the century changed into a new millennium, I saw him at a meeting of the Democratic Party. People said that he was planning to run for public office. Other people said that, whether or not he planned to run, politics had become his "new religion." He was totally wrapped up in political matters, out every night, going from here to there to work for various causes.

Now he is what I would call a searcher. His interests last about a decade, and then he moves on to something else. Some years ago, I read a book about us North Americans entitled *A Nation of Seekers*. That's who we are, or at least we enjoy thinking that is who we are. We are a nation on the move. All of us are looking for something. Some of us, like my friend whose spiritual changes I have just chronicled for you, are intense seekers. Others of us are on a more restrained journey.

A number of years ago, on public television, the distinguished scholar Houston Smith did a survey of the world's great religions and called his program "The Long Search."

When I began the Christian ministry, back in the 1970s, my denomination participated with many others in a nation-wide program of evangelism. As I recall, the program was called "I Found It." As part of the program, we were to hand out bumper stickers at our church. We were to affix these bumper stickers to our cars. The bumper sticker said in large letters (what else?), "I FOUND IT." The implication was that we had been looking for something, and now we had at last found it. The "it" that we had found was Jesus. In a nation of searchers, anyone who is able to stand up and to proclaim at last, "I found it," ought to be able to draw a crowd. We are a nation of seekers.

I certainly find this sense of being on a journey to be a major characteristic of the college years. On our campus, the years of college are expected to be years of searching. From what I can tell, the students have the notion that the important thing is to be on a journey; it is not important ever to arrive at a destination. In fact, anyone who stands up and proclaims, "I found it," is regarded as someone who detoured from the path too soon. The search is better than the destination.

During the course of one week in the spring, we had a local businessman give a lecture entitled "My Five Years with a Zen Master." Two hundred students sat in rapt attention for two hours, taking notes, nodding in agreement as he talked about the joys of studying Zen Buddhism.

Two nights later, I attended a talk by a graduate student entitled "My Semester in a Benedictine Monastery." Again, about two hundred students were in attendance, in rapt attention for over an hour. And they were the same students!

We are a nation of searchers.

And though intellectual curiosity is good, and though the Christian Gospels all depict Jesus as inviting people to be on a journey, this image of our long search, our groping for God, is not at all how the Bible tells it. I'll summarize it simply: the Bible is not so much a long record of our search for God; rather, it is the amazing account of the extraordinary lengths to which God will go to search for us.

You will notice this in the accounts of Christmas. Hardly anyone in all the stories of Christmas was looking for God. They weren't searching for something more meaningful in their lives. They were not looking for some way to find deeper significance. True, old Elizabeth and Zechariah are portrayed as awaiting the fulfillment of the promise of God to Israel. But what were Mary, Joseph, and the shepherds looking for? I suspect most of them were simply trying to get by in life, probably because they were poor. They were searching for their daily bread, nothing more. The magi, the wise men, were on a search, following the star, looking for the king. But they are portrayed as not knowing where to look. In their search, they naively go and ask King Herod where this new "king" can be found.

Thus, John begins the stirring first chapter of his Gospel by talking about the "people who have sat in darkness have seen a great light." That's probably a good way to characterize our search. We search, but our search is little more than a groping about in the darkness.

So the first Christmas is not a story about how we found God, groping in our darkness, but rather it is an amazing account of how God found us! And the story continues. Here is Jesus. And hardly ever does anyone look at Jesus and say, "This is what I have been looking for! Here is the teaching that I have been wanting to hear!"

In fact, people seem to do almost anything to avoid Jesus. But Jesus is intrusive, resourceful, relentless in reaching out to people. That's the way the Bible tells it. I recall the time that he met a little man named Zacchaeus. Zacchaeus climbed up the sycamore tree in order to get a glimpse of the celebrity walking by. But then the celebrity stopped and said, "Zacchaeus, I'm going to come to your house for dinner."

Zacchaeus climbed down from the tree, and Jesus climbed into Zacchaeus's life. Jesus intruded, giving Zacchaeus some of the most important revelation. At the end of the Jesus story, in the twenty-fourth chapter of Luke's Gospel, two disciples are walking away from Jerusalem. They are walking away, probably trying to get away from the horrible events of the past week when Jesus was crucified. Then a stranger suddenly appears and walks with them, talks with them, teaches them. Later, they find out that the stranger is Jesus.

Jesus told stories about a shepherd who goes and beats the bushes, goes to great lengths, just to find one lost sheep. For he said God's kingdom was like a woman who rips her house apart, searching from top to bottom until she finds her one lost coin. There is in Jesus this reaching, this constant seeking and searching. In regard to Jesus, there is a search going on, a long, relentless search. But it is not our search. It is God's search for us! The main requirement to get found by God, according to Jesus, is to be lost. And here is the Messiah, a savior, who just loves to seek and to save the lost.

I expect this may go against the grain of why you think you are here. Perhaps you think you are here because you are searching for something. Your life is rich and rewarding in many ways. But in other ways, there is flatness about things, sometimes an emptiness. So you come to church, hoping that something will be said or sung that will help you in your search.

No, that is not the way the Bible tells it. According to scripture, you are here because you have been sought, called, summoned. You are here because God has reached in, grabbed you, put you here, enticed, wooed, allured you here.

And when you hear stories about the long search—that is, God's long search for you—it should condition you to pay attention. Notice those little coincidences in your life, those strange happenings, and those thoughts that you find you have difficulty putting into the context of other thoughts. Perhaps all of this is part of God's continuing attempts at enticement.

Because we tend to bed down with darkness, we have a propensity to look in all the wrong places, to want all the wrong things, this God could not leave us to our own devices. This God came among us, "tented among us," as the Gospel of John puts it. So Christianity is not so much a religion of discovery. It is a religion of revelation. It is the self-giving of God, the self-disclosure of God that makes our relationship with God possible.

So keep looking over your shoulder as you go through life. Keep being attentive to the strange little things, the odd, glorious things that happen to you.

The long search is over. You have been found. This is the good news.

Relating the text

"He who thinks that he is finished is finished. How true. Those who think that they have arrived, have lost their way. Those who think they have reached their goal, have missed it. Those who think they are saints, are demons."

—Henri Nouwen, *The Genesee Diary* (New York: Doubleday, 1980)

"One of my favorite *Peanuts* cartoons starts with Lucy at her five-cent psychology booth, where Charlie Brown has stopped for advice about life:

"'Life is like a deck chair, Charlie,' she says. 'On the cruise ship of life, some people place their deck chair at the rear of the ship so they can see where they've been. Others place their deck chair at the front of the ship so they can see where they're going.'

"The good 'doctor' looks at her puzzled client and asks, 'Which way is your deck chair facing?' Without hesitating, Charlie replies glumly, 'I can't even get my deck chair unfolded.'

"Charlie and I are soulmates."

—Mike Yaconelli, *Messy Spirituality* (Grand Rapids: Zondervan, 2009)

Looking for love in all the wrong places—isn't that how a once popular song put it?

We are hungry for love, for tenderness and caring, for a sense of belonging and embrace. Yet we seek love through sexual promiscuity, pornography, and series of illicit affairs. We will do almost anything to get people to like us. We will sell our souls, compromise ourselves, make fools out of ourselves, all in a vain attempt to get people to love us.

The incarnation is a vivid statement that, while we were frantically searching for love in all the wrong places, "Love came down at Christmas," as our beloved hymn puts it. Love came to us as the Christ. Our search was over.

———

"Your search is over!" proclaimed the billboard along the highway. What search? What glorious discovery have we happened upon at last?

Underneath the large letters, we could read the words "Perfect yogurt at reasonable prices."

Our search really has been scaled down considerably, hasn't it?

———

He came to me at the end of last semester, telling me that he was in trouble with his parents. His direction in life had reversed. No longer headed for grad school, he was now headed for Soweto to work with the poor. While the young man was there last summer, God had gotten hold of him, he said, had convicted him, grabbed him, made him miserable all semester, demanded that he put his life there.

I asked him, "How do you get along with your parents? What did you have to eat for dinner last night? Do you have a girlfriend?"

After an hour or so of conversation, I could come up with no satisfactory precedent, no rationale for his remarkable move, no psychological cause that would explain why he was at this point, so I was forced to conclude, "Well, I guess Jesus really has risen from the dead and is loose, up to his old tricks."

To be a Christian is not to believe a half-dozen impossible things before breakfast. It is to be intellectually open to the possibility that something's afoot, that the life you live may not be your own, that God really does mean to have God's way with the world through you. It is to believe that God really is determined to have you, come what may, that God has plans for you. We are here because God, in Jesus Christ, journeyed out and got us and put us here.

The great theologian Karl Barth had a strange interpretation of Jesus's parable of the prodigal son. He said that it was not so much a parable about us, about our tendency to run away from the father's house, to get lost in the "far country," and to live like a pig.

Barth said that it was a story about Jesus, about the way in which God loved us so much that he allowed his only begotten Son to journey out into the far country of sin and death, to share our lot, to suffer, to be lost in death and then, by the grace of God, to come home.

Jesus is the one who went out to the far country and recklessly sacrificed in order to love us.

Jesus is the one who went on a long, perilous journey of suffering, rejection, death, and resurrection in order to find us.

Fourth Sunday after the Epiphany
RC/Pres: Fourth Sunday in Ordinary Time

Micah 6:1-8

Psalm 15

1 Corinthians 1:18-31

Matthew 5:1-12

Message of the Cross

Selected reading

1 Corinthians 1:18-31

Theme

The message of the cross is strange knowledge about God that only God can give. The message that God is crucified, that the powerlessness of God is God's great victory, is a message that is foolishness to the world. But to those of us who are being saved it is the power of God.

Introduction to the readings

Micah 6:1-8

The prophet Micah says that God has a controversy with God's people. The people have strayed from God's ways. What does the Lord require? "To do justice, and to love kindness, and to walk humbly with your God" (v. 8 NRSV).

1 Corinthians 1:18-31
Paul speaks about the peculiar "message about the cross" that is "foolishness to those who are perishing" (v. 18 NRSV).

Matthew 5:1-12
Jesus opens his Sermon on the Mount with a series of blessings.

Prayer

Lord Jesus, you have revealed yourself to us as God other than what we expected God to be. We said that we wanted God to come to us to reveal God-self to us, but when God came to us on a cross, well, we were shocked. In this time of worship, enable us to see your cross as the unique, unsurpassable revelation of who you really are and what God is really doing for us and for our salvation. Amen.

Encountering the text

Today's epistle sets the tone for Paul's theology of the cross in which he contrasts the truthful message of the cross with the foolishness of human "wisdom." Set alongside Jesus's beatitudes in the Sermon on the Mount, it gives the church an opportunity to reflect upon the wisdom of that which the world considers foolish, namely, the cross of Christ.

In today's selection from 1 Corinthians, Paul begins by noting how the "message of the cross" can be compromised by fancy rhetorical displays in preaching. (Let us preachers beware!) Presumably, some in Corinth had preached that they were in the possession of some special, arcane "wisdom" that gave people the key to what Jesus really meant. But they also must have taught that they had discovered the core ideas whereby we could storm heaven and climb up to God.

I think that Paul is here particularly troubled by our propensity to tailor the Christian message to the limits of human reasoning. This is what Luther called "ladder theology," in which, by our human reasoning, we attempt to climb up to God through the ladder of our human reason and humanly derived concepts. A crucified messiah is an affront to human reason, an unresolvable paradox that cannot be handled the way we humans are accustomed to thinking about things. For Paul, it is arrogant to think we can put God in the dock and cross-examine God through the use of our reason.

Paul says that the cross tends to polarize us into two groups: "those on the way to destruction" and "those on the way of salvation" (2 Cor 2:16 MSG).

To "understand" the cross we must experience the cross as our saving event. Somehow we must subjectively engage this strange truth of the cross, or more properly, be engaged by it. The cross, so experienced, transforms the way we construe reality.

The cross is an affront to human presumption, including our presumption that we have at last discovered the human knowledge (knowledge = *gnosis*) that gives us a handle on God, a ladder to ascend to God. (Many think that Paul was attacking, in his theology of the cross, ancient Gnosticism.) God's wisdom makes a mockery of human wisdom, a truth that is well-attested in scripture, as Paul reminds his congregation. The cross becomes only a "stumbling block" when we attempt to conceive of it. The powerlessness of God in Christ is an affront to our definitions of God as well as to our own desire to be powerful.

The cross is therefore God's self-definition that devastates all of our human attempts to define who God is and how God ought to work, including contemporary gnostic-like attempts. Note Paul's stress upon the cross as the supreme sign of God's initiative, "God chose... God chose... God chose" (1 Cor 1:27-28). Our only boast is in what God has done, not what we do.

Guided by Paul's theology of the cross, let us proclaim this great, fundamental mystery as we continue to explore God's epiphanies among us, contrasting Paul's theology of the cross with the thoughts of those whom Tom Long has called the "new Gnostics."

Proclaiming the text

In this Sunday's epistle, Paul tells the church at Corinth that the "message of the cross" is a challenge to worldly wisdom. The cross of Christ, says Paul, looks foolish to the world's idea of smart. As someone who is charged, on a weekly basis, with delivering a message to you, I sit up and take notice. I want to present the gospel to you, to speak about Christ in such a way that you will assent to the truth of my message and be persuaded that what I am saying is a message that you really want to receive.

And yet Paul says, in his words to the Corinthians, that's where the difficulty begins. We attempt to make the gospel meaningful to people, to make Christ comprehensible, but we do so in the ways that the world makes sense, whereas, the gospel requires a kind of thinking that the world may consider to be downright foolish. How does one speak about God Almighty coming to us as the crucified Christ? A God on a cross? It's, well, foolish.

There is a group of Christian communicators that includes well-meaning people like Karen Armstrong, Elaine Pagels, John Shelby Spong, Marcus Borg, and Bart Ehrman (some of them members of the infamous "Jesus Seminar" of some years ago) who have been getting a favorable reception from many of us mainline Protestant Christians. These scholars say that they want to help preachers like me communicate the gospel to thoughtful, contemporary people like you. They contrast themselves with the Religious Right, saying that they are "progressive" alternatives to various fundamentalisms (many are former fundamentalists themselves). They say that they want to introduce people to recent scholarship, charging that we preachers have sometimes attempted to protect you people in the pews from the grand discoveries of modern biblical scholarship.

What's wrong with wanting to communicate newfound Christian knowledge in a contemporary way? Not much that I can think of; except that Paul notes that sometimes we slip into pushing worldly wisdom as a substitute for the gospel foolishness of the cross and we end up offering the world something that, while more palatable to the world's tastes, is not really the Christian faith, the "message of the cross."

Tom Long, in his book *Preaching from Memory to Hope* [Louisville: Westminster John Knox Press, 2009], examines the work of these "progressive" interpreters of the faith. While Long credits these writers and scholars with "yearning for what all Christians should desire: an informed, intelligent faith," nevertheless he accuses them of a return to the ancient heresy of Gnosticism, or at least, of "a gnostic impulse." The Gnostics, among other things, believed that they had discovered a special, secret knowledge that gave them a unique handle on understanding Christ.

Long points to four core themes of this group that together constitute "a gnostic impulse": (1) humanity "saved" by gnosis, by knowledge, by thinking the right thoughts in the right way; (2) an antipathy toward incarnation and embodiment and a preference for keeping the faith something vague and "spiritual"; (3) a focus on the spiritual inner self, the "divine spark," within as the main thing in spiritual life; and (4) an emphasis on present spiritual reality rather than a future eschatological hope.

In this sermon I mainly want to focus on just a couple of these new gnostic-like claims. I want to contrast, just as Paul did to the Corinthians, the worldly wisdom that Christianity is something "spiritual," some inner "divine spark," and say, as Paul, that Christianity is about a crucified God. I'd like to challenge those mainline Christians who blithely dismiss cruciform claims with their vague, "I'm spiritual but not religious."

Long says that Borg and others breathlessly proclaim that they have uncovered a new take on Christianity, that they have discovered a new way of thinking about the faith that removes so many of the objections to belief. The old Gnostics believed that we are "saved" by knowledge. We Protestants have long believed in the value of education, but this takes things a step further. Here's Long: "Perhaps the most characteristic marker of the gnostic impulse is the belief that human beings, given the proper knowledge, given illumination, can learn their way to wholeness."

This is what Paul would call "the wisdom of this world." Through this special knowledge we can ascend to God in our thinking. In making such a grand claim for the human quest for God, God's own quest is neglected. All of these new Gnostics assume that human beings are engaged in a noble quest to find God, to read the right book or think the right ideas that will enable us to discover God, to uncover the truth of things. That may be a flattering way to think of ourselves, but it's not the gospel way. The truth that Paul lived was not that he was an earnest searcher for God but that God had searched for and found him!

In my experience, many who brag about their earnest "spirituality" stress our search, our quest, our spirituality, and various spiritual practices we might learn and perform in order to find or access peace or enlightenment or God. This not only tends to create a spiritual elite of those really in the know or who are "more spiritual," but also overlooks the God who has come in the cross of Jesus Christ. It overstresses salvation as mostly something we are to do, to think, or to experience. The Gnostics imagine an all-loving but inactive God who is the object of our religious search rather than the God who has, in Jesus Christ, searched for us. Thus we are urged to "deepen our spiritual awareness," or to think in a more progressive and enlightened way, but we are not told the strange news that because we couldn't come to God, God came to us in a form we didn't expect—on a cross!

Among the things that the cross tells us is that we are sinners. God came to us in Jesus Christ and we responded not with, "Here is what I've been searching for!" but rather, you know, "Crucify him!"

So many of our religious ideas and spiritual practices—the cross also suggests—are just clever ways of putting ourselves in place of God, imagining God on our terms rather than as God came to us—as the crucified savior.

Long concludes, "Given the cultural realities of our time, the story of a highly spiritualized faith that one acquires through knowledge and that puts one in direct and unmediated communion with God is quite appealing to many intelligent people…but the gnostic impulse is a spectrum shift away from the gospel."

As we move closer toward Lent, the season of the cross, let Paul call each of us back toward a bold embrace of the theology of the cross—the strangest, most healing, and life-giving truth about God that we have been given to tell a dying world.

Relating the text

If you so choose, you could preach the beatitudes in the same way we have utilized Paul. Here is topsy-turvy thinking quite different from that of the world in Eugene H. Peterson's *The Message: The New Testament in Contemporary English*:

Arriving at a quiet place, [Jesus] sat down and taught his climbing companions. This is what he said:

"You're blessed when you're at the end of your rope. With less of you there is more of God and his rule.

"You're blessed when you feel you've lost what is most dear to you. Only then can you be embraced by the One most dear to you.

"You're blessed when you're content with just who you are—no more, no less. That's the moment you find yourselves proud owners of everything that can't be bought.

"You're blessed when you've worked up a good appetite for God. He's food and drink in the best meal you'll ever eat. . . .

"You're blessed when your commitment to God provokes persecution. The persecution drives you even deeper into God's kingdom" (Matt 5:2-6, 10).

Nicholas Wolterstorff, one of our finest Christian philosophers, in grieving the death of his son, reached a profound understanding of Paul's theology of the cross as well as Jesus's "blessed are those who mourn." In *Lament for a Son*, Wolterstorff grieves his loss and he also ponders the meaning of the beatitudes:

"God is not only the God of the sufferers but the God who suffers. The pain and fallenness of humanity have entered into his heart. Through the prism of my tears I have seen a suffering God...

"God is love. That is why he suffers. To love our suffering sinful world is to suffer. God so suffered for the world that he gave up his only Son to suffering. The one who does not see God's suffering does not see his love. God is suffering love...

"To believe in Christ's rising from the grave is to accept it as a sign of our own rising from our graves.... So I shall struggle to live the reality of Christ's rising and death's dying. In my living, my son's dying will not be the last word."

—Nicholas Wolterstorff, *Lament for a Son* (Grand Rapids: Eerdmans, 1987), 81

"She was really one of the finest students I have ever taught," I said to my friend as we drove down the highway. I had mentioned to him that one of my favorite students was now serving a little church near where we were driving. "I can still remember the wonderful paper that she wrote on a theology of the Trinity. And I remember her not only as very bright but also having a pleasing personality. She was launched on a great career in banking, and then God called her into the pastoral ministry. She walked off that job and came to seminary, where she had a great run."

My friend said, "Well if her church is near here, why don't we drop by and see if she might be there."

I took the very next exit off the highway, and we drove three or four miles into the countryside. Sure enough, just as I remembered, there was a little brick church at the end of a narrow road. We pulled in to the little gravel parking lot and sat there looking at the church. The church had obviously seen better days. The sign out front was peeling and in need of repair. There on the sign was printed "The Rev. Julie Jones, pastor." The church looked forlorn, remote, and small.

After a moment of silence, my friend said to me, "Damn, what a waste."

To know why Julie's ministry was not a waste, one would have to know a story about a savior who died for sinners, "wasting" his life on the cross.

Fifth Sunday after the Epiphany
RC/Pres: Fifth Sunday in Ordinary Time

Isaiah 58:1-9a, (9b-12)

Psalm 112:1-9, (10)

1 Corinthians 2:1-12, (13-16)

Matthew 5:13-20

Teaching (and Doing) What Jesus Commands

Selected reading

Matthew 5:13-20

Theme

Jesus loves us enough to teach us how we need to live in order to be lights to the world. Jesus expects of his followers not only that we love him but also that we obey him. In obeying all that Jesus commands us, we give the world an example of what the power of God can do in the world. The church has a responsibility not to hold back, not to trim down Jesus's demands to what is permissible and possible, but rather to share Jesus's peculiar vision with the whole world, teaching the world all that Jesus taught.

Introduction to the readings

Isaiah 58:1-9a, (9b-12)

Isaiah becomes an instrument of God's truth-telling as he announces to rebellious Israel the depth of their sin in this stirring call for national repentance. The call to repentance ends with the announcement of divine mercy for the penitent.

1 Corinthians 2:1-12, (13-16)

Paul talks about the way in which he tried to tailor his style of proclamation to the peculiar quality of the gospel, saying that among the Corinthians, he only preached Christ as crucified.

Matthew 5:13-20

Jesus continues his sermon on the mount by urging his followers to be salt and light for the world by obeying all of his commandments.

Prayer

Lord Jesus Christ, you come among us as the incarnate one. Your advent into our world is an ever-present reminder that we are not left to fend for ourselves in this world. You came not only to redeem us, to forgive us, and to bless us, but also to teach us, to reveal to us the ways of God, and to guide us in that way.

Give us docile, teachable spirits. Instill in us a fervent desire to know you, to love you, and to obey you. Preserve us from thinking that we don't have the courage or the talent to follow you faithfully. Push us to discover new dimensions of faithfulness to you. Be patient with us when we disappoint you. Keep teaching us, continue to reveal God's will to us, and give us all we need to be faithful disciples. Amen.

Encountering the text

What challenging words in today's Gospel! Is Jesus serious? Does he really expect the crowds before him not to remarry after divorce, to turn the other cheek, to go the second mile, to forgive their enemies, and thereby to let their lights shine before the whole world?

In Matthew's Gospel, Jesus is the teacher. In this "sermon on the mount" Jesus gets quite specific about the demands of the reign of God. He goes into detail about how his followers are to live their lives, how we are to respond when we are unjustly attacked, when we are wronged. He teaches a "higher righteousness," repeatedly saying, "You have heard that it was said...but I say to you..." He says that he has not come to relax the demands of the law of Israel—already demanding enough as they are—but rather he comes to intensify those demands, raising the bar on the righteousness of God.

Does he really expect the mass or ordinary people to live their lives in this way? Is his "higher righteousness" taught for everyone?

In our interpretation of today's Gospel we will focus upon Matthew's presentation of Jesus as the teacher of this "higher righteousness." But we will also link today's Gospel from Matthew with the very end of Matthew's Gospel, Matthew 28, in which the risen Christ continues to teach his disciples by telling them to go into all the world and make disciples by "baptizing them" and "teaching them to obey everything that I've commanded you" (28:19-20).

Jesus not only teaches us but also commands us to teach the whole world as well. We are to hold nothing back. We are to teach others as we have been taught.

In today's Gospel Jesus teaches. He loves the multitudes enough to share with them the fullness of God's reign and its demands. He gives specific, though demanding guidance on just how they are to handle dilemmas that come up in their daily lives. He tells them what they need to do to be "lights of the world."

And he commands us to do the same.

So today's proclamation will be a teaching sermon about the importance of teaching in the life of faith and in the life of the church.

Proclaiming the text

Last Sunday we began Jesus's so-called sermon on the mount. This is not so much a sermon, as we use the word, but more of a lecture. Jesus is teaching. And when Jesus is doing the teaching, there are always fireworks. The sermon, or the lecture, whichever you want to call it, begins well enough. Jesus blesses the poor, the hungry, and the persecuted in his beatitudes. Today the sermon continues with Jesus saying, "You are the light of the world," and "You are the salt of the earth" (Matt 5:13-14). Followers are to "let your light shine before people, so they can see the good things you do and praise your Father who is in heaven" (5:16). True, in speaking the beautiful words to us, Jesus incases them in warnings—the salt that does not savor is worthless; the light that is hidden is nothing but more darkness.

Jesus has begun by saying that he is offering us new teaching: we always heard it said, but now Jesus says to us. He comes overturning much of what we considered to be immovable tradition.

But now Jesus qualifies what he is saying. He says that he has not come to abolish the law and the prophets. He has not come to wipe away revered, time-honored wisdom. That is, he has not come to wipe away ancient wisdom, but rather he has come to "fulfill" ancient wisdom. He is not doing away with the time-honored laws; rather he is pumping them up, raising the bar, pushing the ancient law even further in its demand upon us.

When one considers how much difficulty we have had in keeping the ancient laws—in fulfilling the demands of the Ten Commandments or in aspiring to embody the words of the prophets—it is rather amazing that Jesus wants to make the law even more demanding and the words of the prophets even more stringent. And yet that is what he does.

In fact, he says that anybody who breaks these commandments, or teaches anybody else to relax or slack off on the commandments, "will be called the lowest in the kingdom of heaven" (5:19). He tells us that our righteousness must exceed even that of the Scribes and Pharisees. Who were the Scribes and Pharisees? They were people who knew scripture backward and forward, people who were basically full-time students of and full-time observers of the law.

One of the most frequent designations of Jesus is "Teacher." People call him "Rabbi," which means simply "teacher." But when Jesus does the teaching, rarely is the teaching that simple. Not only does he teach complicated notions with deceptively simple presentation (such as in his many parables), but also his teaching is meant to be understood and obeyed, embodied, and performed to the fullest extent. Jesus the teacher does not want simple intellectual agreement; he wants wholehearted and engaged embodiment of his teaching.

And Jesus taught many demanding things. Wouldn't it have been much easier if he had presented his teaching as a set of noble ideals to be admired rather than as a set of practices to be followed? Consider what Jesus teaches: "If people slap you on your right cheek, you must turn the left cheek to them as well" (5:39). Do not retaliate, do not return evil for evil, but go the second mile.

Those dear folk who sometimes say, "I don't know if I believe Jesus is divine, God's Son, but I will grant you that he was a noble, moral teacher"—I wonder if they have ever actually read any of the moral teaching of Jesus!

Jesus says not only are we to obey these demands but also we must teach others to do the same (5:19).

We are now early in Matthew's Gospel. But when Matthew's Gospel ends, Jesus is still teaching a demanding righteousness. Matthew ends his Gospel with the resurrected Christ gathering his disciples and preparing to leave them in order that he might ascend to his father in heaven (Matt 28). And what is the last thing he tells his disciples? He tells them not only to go into the world and baptize people from every nation in the world but also to "make disciples."

And how do you do that? By baptizing? No, more than just baptizing, Jesus commands his disciples to teach "everything that I've commanded you." How is baptism fully accomplished? How are disciples faithfully made? Jesus answers that in his last words from his earthly ministry. The last thing he says to us in this Gospel of Matthew is: teach everything that I have commanded you. Everything?

Sometimes as I drive past churches I enjoy reading the signs that the church puts out front. The signs, meant to attract visitors I suppose, are succinct statements of what that church most wants to say to the world. "Celebrate Recovery!" read some of the signs. "Cappuccino and Christ—Decaf and Regular." (Okay, I didn't actually see that sign out in front of a church, but one day I expect to!)

Imagine a church that puts on its sign these words: "We will teach you everything Christ commanded." Would you give that church a try?

Some years ago many of our churches—attempting to be more faithful in evangelism and in obedience to Jesus's command to make disciples—adapted a "user-friendly" approach to church. This usually meant adapting their worship services so that they would be easily understood and completely comprehended by first-time visitors. They took out the music that was difficult to sing. They removed most of the scripture reading. Everything was shortened, reduced, and simplified.

I agree with them that it is important to obey Jesus's command, "Go make disciples," to reach people and to baptize. But please note that in Matthew 28 Jesus tells us much more than simply to "go." Jesus tells us to "[teach] them to obey everything I have commanded you."

So in today's Gospel Jesus teaches us that not only is he the light of the world but also our light is to shine before all the world. We are to witness, to be witnesses. People are to see our good works and perceive the reign of God in action through our good works. And it is our job to teach everything that Jesus commanded.

When Jesus commands us to teach "them to obey everything that I've commanded you," Jesus is also giving people a great gift. Life can be confusing.

This world can be an insoluble intellectual quandary. But the church loves people enough not to hold back, intellectually speaking. We teach everything that Jesus commanded out of love for people and their questions and intellectual dilemmas. This is a great gift that Christ gives us to give to the world.

Let's recommit ourselves to continued growth in the faith and to share the riches of our faith with a new generation of Christians in obedience to our Lord's command to teach them "everything that I've commanded you."

Relating the text

It is one thing to reach people for Jesus Christ. It is an equally great challenge to teach people for Jesus Christ. John Wesley, founder of the Methodist movement, was a big evangelist. He believed in reaching people for Christ. Many people think of Wesley as one of the forerunners of modern evangelicalism. But did you know that Wesley produced a multivolume history of Christian thought? He published, in inexpensive form, nearly thirty books that contained the greatest of Christian wisdom, most of it writings from the early church fathers. For whom did Wesley publish these works? For the laity! Wesley believed that it was much too difficult to be a Christian in eighteenth-century England without help from the wisest of friends. Therefore, he made the very best, deepest, and thickest Christian thought available for everybody.

I wonder if we preachers are making a big mistake to try to put the gospel on the bottom shelf. We have been taught that we are to do anything possible to ensure communication with everyone. We therefore are tempted to simplify the gospel to the point of silliness, to remove all intellectual impediments in the interest of "reaching people."

Today's Gospel reminds us that one of the reasons people suffer and are in difficulty is because they are confused. They can be helped through sound, compassionate teaching. People come to church with big questions, and the good news is that Jesus Christ loves people enough, along with their questions, to give them big answers. We are therefore enjoined by Jesus not only to reach people but also to teach people.

Perhaps we preachers ought to be reminded that we get paid by the church (not paid all that well, but still on most weeks paid!) to reflect, to pray, to meditate, and to read. For the mass of people whom we preach to on Sunday morning, the only intellectual stimulation they will have during the week is the sermon. Therefore let us take the intellectual needs of our people as seriously as we regard their other needs. Let us teach, in the name of Christ.

In my experience younger members of my congregation seem to crave more teaching about the Christian faith than some of my older members. Not long ago, when I visited a congregation with a high percentage of young adult members, and when I listened to the sermon that the pastor preached, I was impressed that the sermon was rather long (by my standards) and full of substantial intellectual content. It was definitely a teaching sermon in which the pastor patiently, in some detail, sought to explain an aspect of the faith.

When I commented on this teaching sermon the pastor replied, "You know, my sermons have gotten longer and more content-oriented as the average age of my congregation has declined."

"Do you think that younger Christians like teaching sermons because they are less well-formed in the faith?" I asked.

"That's part of it," he responded. "Another reason may be that young people are attempting to follow Jesus into an often-confusing world where there are few props and crutches for Christians. They are also at a time in their lives when there are so many important decisions to be made. I think for all those reasons they are grateful for a church that takes the time to show them the way."

Tertullian famously said, "Christians are made, not born." Christian discipleship does not come naturally. We are not innately Christian. Christians must be "made" through teaching, long-term moral formation, and discipline.

In today's Gospel, Jesus teaches. He tells people things that they would never have known had he not taught them.

There is a model here for the church of any age: we must make disciples. How? Through baptism (God's gift of the Holy Spirit, washing from sin, and moral regeneration) and through teaching (instructing them in the odd way of faith).

Perhaps there was a time when the church did not need to engage in so much teaching. In the North American culture of fifty years ago, home, school, and church all colluded in an alliance that felt like a vaguely Christian culture. Christianity felt normal, natural, as if it were innate. The Christian faith was the only game in town.

If the church were ever justified in thinking that way, that time is no more. There is a new sense that Christianity is odd, countercultural, against the stream. If we are going to keep our children in this faith, if we are going to raise up a new generation of Christians, then we will have to make them that way.

In short, our time is a time of a renewed call to Christian teaching.

Sixth Sunday after the Epiphany
RC/Pres: Sixth Sunday
in Ordinary Time

Deuteronomy 30:15-20 or Sirach 15:15-20

Psalm 119:1-8

1 Corinthians 3:1-9

Matthew 5:21-37

You Have Heard It Said... But

Selected reading
Matthew 5:21-37

Theme
The righteousness commended by Jesus is more than just conventional common sense. Common wisdom is insufficient to comprehend the higher, more demanding way of Jesus. Jesus's teaching overturns our commonly held notions of what's right and what's wrong, calling us to a more demanding way, a way closer to the will of God.

Introduction to the readings

Deuteronomy 30:15-20

The Lord God speaks to the Israelites in the wilderness, saying to them that in giving them the commandments, he has set before them the way of life and the way of death.

1 Corinthians 3:1-9
Paul speaks of his fellow workers who have labored in the church at Corinth.

Matthew 5:21-37
In his Sermon on the Mount, Jesus commends a higher righteousness, saying, "You have heard that it was said...but I say to you..." (vv. 21-22).

Prayer

Lord Jesus, we come to church this Sunday not only to praise you and to worship you but also to be taught by you. Teach us, Lord, even when your teaching challenges our cherished assumptions. Even when your message disrupts our lives, teach us. And when you teach us, give us the grace to hear you and, even more, to practice in our lives what you preach to us in your Sermon on the Mount. Amen.

Encountering the text

It might be possible to say that Jesus makes common sense, that the way of Jesus is basically the way of reasonable, conventional propriety and common wisdom—until we are encountered by a text like this Sunday's assigned Gospel.

Matthew presents Jesus as a kind of new Moses. Just as Moses had to go up a mountain to receive the commands of God, so Jesus ascends a mountain to give new commandments of God. And the thing that impresses us in listening to Jesus's words here in chapter 5 is that they are new.

Though Jesus is connected to what has gone before (he's presented like Moses the law-giver), Jesus is clear that his teaching is also in tension with, even in conflict with, the inherited morality of Torah. Jesus's repeated antitheses— "You have heard that it was said...but I say to you..." (Matt 5:21-22)—underscore that Jesus is teaching a new kind of righteousness.

The righteousness that Jesus teaches may not be so "new." It is the Mosaic righteousness intensified and underscored, in which Jesus again and again repeats some stricture from the Mosaic law, already tough enough to fulfill as it is, and intensifies it, making it even more demanding.

Our first lesson from Deuteronomy sets the tone. Jesus speaks in the tradition of Israel, a people who know that the law of God, the instruction of God, Torah, is not a burdensome demand or an unfair stricture. The law is a gift of God, grace, in which God graciously shows us the way to life.

And yet Jesus clearly shows that he intensifies the faith and the ethics of Israel. In him the way of God, Torah, is not abrogated but rather intensified. "You have heard that it was said...but I say to you..."

Proclaiming the text

You have heard it said, "Christianity makes sense. Your life will go better if you sign on with Jesus." But I say to you that if you listen to Jesus, if you try to take his demands seriously, then you may find that he complexifies and complicates your life. Take today's Gospel for instance.

You have heard it said, "It's important to try to be compassionate and caring toward those in need, but sometimes you have to be realistic and simply go along to get along." But I say to you that Jesus, judged from his comments in this sermon, appears to have little interest in "realism" and none in "just getting along." Not returning evil for evil, as Jesus clearly teaches, is not very "realistic."

You have heard it said, "Violence is wrong unless it is used in self-defense." But I say to you that Jesus appears to advocate some higher value even than self-defense, judged by his comments in this sermon.

You have heard it said, "Religion is fine, as long as you don't take it to the extreme, as long as you are not a fanatic." But I say to you that the way of life Jesus appears straightforwardly to advocate in this sermon seems, well, down-right "extreme." How many ordinary folk have you known who are willing to obey Jesus in all that he demands here in this sermon?

You have heard it said that people respond best to positive messages and sermons that are affirming and supportive of them. But I say to you that in this sermon Jesus appears to attack some of our most widely affirmed practices. His intent seems to be to make us downright uncomfortable, if not angry!

You have heard it said that the main thing you ought to ask in coming to church is, "What are my deepest needs that I need met?" But I say to you in this sermon that Jesus appears not to give a rip about our needs. In fact, I daresay that if you really took seriously what Jesus demands in this part of his sermon, you would leave church with more needs than when you arrived!

You have heard it said, "The purpose of a sermon is to help make religion rational to thinking people, to present Jesus in such a way that people will see that he is the answer to their questions and the solution to their problems." But I say to you that this Sunday Jesus seems to want to provoke even more questions and instigate even more problems.

I expect that many of you didn't have a problem with Jesus until you came to church this morning and heard Jesus preach, "You have heard that it was said...but I say to you..."

Relating the text

"Who teaches you? Whose disciple are you? Honestly. One thing is sure: you are somebody's disciple. There are not exceptions to this rule, for human beings are just the kind of creatures that have to learn and keep learning from others how to live. Aristotle remarked that we owe more to our teachers than to our parents, for though our parents gave us life, our teachers taught us the good life."

—Dallas Willard, *The Divine Conspiracy: Rediscovering Our Hidden Life in God* (New York: HarperCollins, 1998), 271

Presumably, many of the people who heard Jesus's sermon that day thought they were righteous and good—until they heard Jesus speak about righteousness and goodness! So much of our lives is based upon the illusion that we are in control of our lives, that we have things well in hand—until some mystery intrudes into our lives and we are forced to see the true insecurity of our lives.

"I hope as much from the justice of God as from his mercy. It is because he is just that he is compassionate and full of tenderness...for he knows our weakness. He remembers that we are dust. As a father has tenderness for his children, so the Lord has compassion for us. I do not understand souls who have fear of so tender a Friend.... What joy to think that God is just, that he takes account of our weaknesses, that he knows perfectly the fragility of our nature."

—Therese of Lisieux, quoted by Brennan Manning, *The Wisdom of Tenderness: What Happens When God's Fierce Mercy Transforms Our Lives* (Grand Rapids: Zondervan, 2010), 22

"Nobody is too good for the meanest service. One who worries about the loss of time that such petty, outward acts of helpfulness entail is usually taking the importance of his own career too solemnly. We must be ready to allow ourselves to be interrupted by God.... It is a strange fact that Christians and even ministers frequently consider their work so important and urgent that they will allow nothing to disturb them. They think they are doing God a service in this, but actually they are disdaining God's 'crooked but straight path' (Gottfried Arnold). It is part of the discipline of humility that we must not spare our hand where it can perform a service and that we do not assume that our schedule is our own to manage, but allow it to be arranged by God."

—Dietrich Bonhoeffer, *Life Together* (New York: Harper Collins, 1954), 99

During World War II, an American Marine, badly wounded on the island of Saipan, lay bleeding to death. A Navy corpsman rushed to his aid. At the risk of his own life, the corpsman played the good Samaritan, pouring oil and wine on the wounds of his bleeding brother.

It would be an understatement to report that the Marine was neither grateful nor gracious. He demanded to know what had taken the corpsman so damn long to get to him. When the battle subsided, the regimental commander, who had watched the scene from the safety of a bunker, approached the corpsman and said, "Kid, I wouldn't have done that for a million dollars!"

"It is important to cherish a pure thought of God, consciously imprinting it upon our memory as if it were an indelible seal. In this way we grow in love for God: it stirs us to fulfill God's commandments and in so doing, the love of God in us is nurtured in perpetuity."

—Saint Basil the Great, *The Longer Rules*, 5

"We are not asked to love the neighbor as neighbor, but as ourselves."

—Geevarghese Mar Osthathios, Metropolitan of the Orthodox
Syrian Church in Kerala, India

"The good news calls our whole way of existence into question. If we are indeed 'in God's image,' then the central task of our life is covenant-making and covenant-keeping. It is a promise both rich and heavy for us to say that finally we shall be like God. . . . Our Central human vocation is to be with brothers and sisters and for brothers and sisters. That is who God is . . . that is who we are called to be, expected to be, promised to be."

—Walter Brueggemann, *The Bible Makes Sense* (Winona, MN:
St Mary's College Press, 1977)

"Our passionate concern for the masses must find incarnate experience in helping our neighbors, and we need not have to ask who they are."

—Robert F. Morneau, *Ashes to Easter* (New York: Crossroad, 1996), 19

"The world is overcome not through destruction, but through reconciliation. Not ideals, nor programs, nor conscience, nor duty, nor responsibility, nor virtue, but only God's perfect love can encounter reality and overcome it. Nor is it some universal idea of love, but rather the love of God in Jesus Christ, a love genuinely lived, that does this."

—Dietrich Bonhoeffer, *Meditations on the Cross* (Louisville: Westminster John Knox, 1998), 47

"Our Lord asks but two things of us: Love for God and for our neighbor.... We cannot know whether we love God...but there can be no doubt about whether we love our neighbor or no."

—Teresa of Ávila, *Interior Castle* (Nashville: TAN Books, 2011), ch. 3

"Jesus' approach is always fresh, surprising, new, and unexpected. Consequently, it always provoked a direct reaction.... He shattered firmly formed convictions and beliefs. He often used nonreligious language, avoiding the religious language of his contemporaries, a language that had been used so long, and so often by so many people, that it had lost its meaning almost completely. He continually used examples from everyday life to express himself."

—Joseph G. Donders, *Praying and Preaching the Sunday Gospel* (Maryknoll, NY: Orbis, 1988)

"You cannot love others and harbor resentments toward them at the same time. The love we are speaking of is not romantic love, but a spiritual love that views another through the eyes of compassion. Love produces a quality of life that is more enjoyable and healthy than a life filled with resentment and anger."

—Sage Bennet, *Wisdom Walk: Nine Practices for Creating Peace and Balance from the World's Spiritual Traditions* (Novato, CA: New World Library, 2007), 81

"The spirit in which Scripture should be read is to seek there first of all to know God and the mysteries of our religion, and ourselves; and to learn therein the ways to advance toward God and make good use of creatures. In a word it is to seek only truth and justice in such reading by practicing charity and the other virtues.

"The specific conditions are purity of heart, humility, simplicity, and suppression of curiosity and impetuousness."

—Jean Mabillon, *Treatise on Monastic Studies: 1691* (Lanham, MD: University Press of America, 2004), 109

Seventh Sunday after the Epiphany
RC/Pres: Seventh Sunday in Ordinary Time

Leviticus 19:1-2, 9-18

Psalm 119:33-40

1 Corinthians 3:10-11, 16-23

Matthew 5:38-48

Christic the Foundation

Selected reading

1 Corinthians 3:10-11, 16-23

Theme

The church is established by God and sustained by Christ, who is the very foundation and basis of the church. The church is a thoroughly human and therefore fallible human institution, but it is also an institution that rests upon the foundation of Christ. The hope for the church, the church's unique glory and peculiar identity, is its foundation in Christ.

Introduction to the readings

Leviticus 19:1-2, 9-18

Leviticus lists the ethical standards that are demanded of God's chosen people. God's people are to live in a way that is different and distinctive, living not simply on the basis of their own standards, but rather living by God's given way of life.

1 Corinthians 3:10-11, 16-23
Paul says that he works like "a wise master builder" to lay the foundation of the church in Corinth (v. 10). The foundation of this new "building" is Christ.

Matthew 5:38-48
"You have heard that it was said," says Jesus, "but I say to you" (vv. 38-39). Jesus intensifies the demands that God makes upon God's people as Jesus continues his sermon on the mount.

Prayer

Lord Jesus Christ, by your grace our sins are forgiven, the reign of God entered among us, we sinners were called to be citizens of your new reign, and the church was born. You are the foundation for our life together. You are the only good reason to be here. Give us the gifts we need in order to be more faithful members of your body, the church. Equip us for good works so that the world might see the outbreak of your reign in us. Imbue us with your spirit of love and charity so that our life together in the church might more closely resemble your life among us. Amen.

Encountering the text

Paul, in his letters to his young churches, loves to develop some metaphor in order to illuminate the mystery of life in Christ. That's what *metaphor* literally means—to shed light. A metaphor casts new light on some otherwise abstract idea.

In chapter three of his letter to the Corinthians, Paul uses a construction metaphor. Paul says that he has worked in a way that is similar to a skilled "master builder." The Greek word here is actually more akin to "architect." Paul casts himself in the role of a designer, a master planner of the building that some-one else will build (1 Cor 3:10). A successful building must be planned "with care." That is what Paul says that he has done in Corinth. He notes that once the foundation is laid, some later builder can't come along and change the foundation, the one part of the building that can't be modified. Paul says that foundation is Jesus Christ (3:11).

Christ is the basis for everything, the foundation of the church. Any other basis for the church is a false foundation. Paul implies that he can allow others to contribute to the church at Corinth, adding this or that, as long as he has faithfully laid the true foundation—Jesus Christ.

As he continues to expand this construction metaphor, Paul asks, "Don't you know that you are God's temple" (3:16), taking the building image in a different direction.

In our sermon today, let us focus on that central image of Jesus Christ as the foundation. The foundation is that part of the building structure upon which everything rests. If the foundation is neglected in any way, the entire building is in peril. Today's sermon will therefore be a reminder to the congregation of first things, of the basis for our existence as a church, that sine qua non that is the bedrock upon which the church rests. Christ is the foundation, the first and last thing that needs to be said about the church.

Proclaiming the text

We were in England, in a green and pleasant valley, where we came across the ruins of a medieval monastery. Even in ruin, there was a beauty about the place. Romantic poets found inspiration in its crumbling pillars and arches. The roof had collapsed. Only a few of its dozen lancet arches still stood. Grass grew in the middle of the church, where once there were beautiful flagstones.

The church had been destroyed by iconoclasts during the Protestant Reformation. People attacked the church and the surrounding monastery and took what they wanted. The stones had been used to build other buildings in the nearby area. Statues had been broken to bits and the windows shattered.

We wandered among the ruins. Archaeologists had traced the foundations of the buildings. Over five hundred people had lived and worked in this church compound in its heyday, but now, it was only a memory. All you could see left were foundations of what had been a grand, glorious, and soaring building. Nothing but the foundations remained.

The most important part of a building is that part that none of us ever see— the foundation. The foundation goes deep into the earth. The higher and more glorious the building that rises above the foundation, the deeper the foundation needs to be. Get that foundation wrong, and the whole building is in peril, no matter how good it looks to the street-side observer. We have an expensive new building in our town that was just built by the city. Scarcely six months after it opened, it is being vacated for a couple of years. Bad foundation, they say. Cracks are developing in the floors. A couple of the walls have begun to separate from each other. The whole thing is in danger of collapsing. Get the foundation wrong, and the whole building is wrong, no matter how good it appears to the eye.

So Paul writes to the church at Corinth that Christ is the foundation. He uses an architectural metaphor. We are diverse elements of a new building. Out of all these diverse elements, a wonderful new building has arisen, a building that is named the church.

There are times when Paul speaks in his letters of the church using the metaphor of the body. "You are the body of Christ," he sometimes writes to the church. But here Paul the preacher gives us a different metaphor. You are all elements of a great new construction project that is built on the foundation of Christ.

Reading between the lines, in Paul's letter to the Corinthians, we are correct in concluding that the building is not in very good shape. There seem to be tensions between people who had been Gentiles, pagans, before they became

Christians and people who had been Jews before they became Christians. There was a deep wall between these two religious, ethnic groups. The Jews had been on the receiving end of Gentile persecution down through the centuries. And now they have been brought together in the church. Well mostly together. There seemed to have been huge problems. Some of the Jews, because they knew scripture, had been living by scripture all of their history. They were really put out with these pagans who were completely ignorant of scripture.

Some of these former pagans, now that they were Christians, had the nerve to look down on the Jews. They felt that keeping of the old Jewish religious laws was silly. They would not eat meat just because it had been sacrificed in pagan ceremonies. Gentile Christians thought one way; Jewish Christians thought another. The new "building" called the church was in danger of falling down!

And let's be honest. We've got tensions in our congregation as well—tensions between folk who have been part of this church since the earliest days and people who just showed up last week. There are tensions between those who know a great deal about the Christian faith, those who are sure and confident in their use of scripture, and those for whom all this Christian faith is a very new experience. Added to that are stresses between rich and poor, educated and less-educated folk. Are we in danger of collapse? The church is a broken-down shack sometimes, with huge cracks in our walls, a leaky roof, and a boarded-up window or two. At times we are exposed to the elements. Things leak.

Paul is honest about all of these tensions and stresses in the building that is the church. And yet Paul is equally honest about the "foundation" on which the church rests—Jesus Christ. The words and work of Jesus Christ give trustworthy support to the building of the church. True, the church is not always the group of people God intends us to be. But we rest, despite our weaknesses, upon a strong foundation—Jesus Christ.

We are, for better or worse, the form that the risen Christ has chosen to take in the world. If people are going to meet Christ, if they are going to be called into discipleship, if they are going to grow in their understanding of the Christian faith, it will have to be here in the church. It's too great a responsibility for ordinary folk like us if it were not for our faith that all of this rests upon Christ. Your discipleship was his idea before it was yours. The church was his idea before it was Paul's or anyone else's. Christ not only founded the church, we believe, but also promises to stick with the church, through thick and thin, to preserve the church until the end of time, to make the church that which we could never be on our own.

Dig down into any church, digging down through all of our tensions and infidelities, and that's who you will find, down deep, at the bottom of it all—Jesus Christ. And that is our ultimate hope, not in ourselves and our rickety, broken-down attempts to be the church, but rather in Jesus Christ, the foundation for the church.

Sometimes, at some of our meetings, I confess that I lose sight of the true meaning of the church. When we are struggling with finances, when there are sharp differences of opinions among us, it is easy to lose sight of the church as Christ's body and to think of us as just another contentious, ordinary group of people.

But then on Sunday, when we are all gathered here, when we join our voices in a hymn, when we come forward to the Lord's Table, when we pray, I am reminded: this is what it's all about. This is not just another club of people who try to get along. This is the holy church whose foundation is Christ.

Or when you give so generously and sacrificially as the offering is received, is your giving simply motivated by your human generosity? Giving at the highest level, in my experience, tends to be a testimony to the presence of some other basis—the foundation is Christ.

Or when you reach out in service to others who are not your relatives, not part of your family, and you take responsibility for their need, from whence does such service arise? I think it has its basis, its foundation, in some mystery greater than your own desire to volunteer. Its foundation is testimony to the presence of Jesus Christ.

We are the Word made flesh, God's Word made flesh first in Christ, then in us. You dig down deep, to what we are resting upon, down to the bedrock, and you find Christ the Lord. Don't be deceived by some of our trivialities, our triteness, and our many problems in the church. Down deep, where it really counts, there is Christ. He holds all of this up. He is the sure foundation.

Though the storms may shake and rattle the building, though we've got our problems, we rest on a sure foundation. In times of difficulty, we can live with hope because, as we sing "A Mighty Fortress Is Our God," that fortress rests upon the sure foundation of Christ.

I know a preacher who has had a remarkable ministry in a very difficult situation—the inner city of one of American's once great, but now decaying cities. His church has had a real struggle. And yet, his church has had a remarkable ministry.

I asked him to sum up, if he could, his theology of ministry. And this was his response: "I always want to be the sort of church that is so bold, courageous, and risky in its ministry, that if God does not want our ministry, it will utterly fail. On the other hand, I want a church that is so faithful that when people see us they will say, 'there really is no reason for that church being there, other than Christ wants it there. There is no sufficient explanation for why that church is still alive today, still there, still witnessing and serving, still enacting the gospel, except that Jesus really means for it to be there.' That's the sort of church I want to serve."

The most important part of any building is the foundation. We are not, thank God, in charge. Christ is not, thank God, dependent on us for the church to survive. We are not, thank God, the key to the church's future. That belongs to our foundation, Jesus Christ the Lord.

Relating the text

I am a member of a church that has been in some danger of falling down lately. Perhaps you have heard. Charges of sexual abuse by the clergy. One was sent to jail for stealing money from the church, money he was supposed to be protecting. There are holes in our roof and some severe structural problems. My church falls, well, just a bit below the ideal. In a way, it's somewhat of a comfort to hear Paul admonishing the folks at First Church Corinth. It's a comfort to know that the poor old church has, from the very beginning, been in danger of collapse. Our problems are nothing new.

I was talking with a Lutheran bishop some time ago. The man looked depressed to me. I asked him how he liked being bishop, and he said *like* is not the right word to use. I said that I knew that a bishop's job was demanding, taking long hours, a lot of work.

He set me straight. He said it wasn't the hard work. It was rather that as a bishop, he had a front-row seat on everything that was wrong with the church. He spent too little time talking to clergy who were productive, faithful, and engaging and too much time talking to clergy who were unfaithful, difficult, and depressed.

Every year at our annual conference, the very first meeting that we have is the clergy "Executive Session." What a way to begin a church meeting! We read out the names of all of those who are preparing for ministry and all of those who have completed their requirements for ordination. Unfortunately, we also discuss, sometimes at great length, all those who have betrayed their ordination vows, who have been less than they are called to be. It is a depressing way to begin a church meeting, by admitting all of our failures—the crumbling pillars, the leaky roof, the broken windows, and all the rest. Such moments make you think that, if the church is Christ's body, it is an ever-crucified body. If, as John opens his Gospel, the Word is made flesh, then sometimes it is hard to see the eternal Word, the decaying flesh!

In such times the church doesn't look much like this grand building, built by the master architect, God, this glorious structure. It looks pretty sad, humbling, in danger of collapse. In such times we need to recover our foundation. This imperiled structure, the church, has no hope of surviving, no chance of thriving, if it were not for the foundation, Christ.

Eighth Sunday after the Epiphany RC/Pres: Eighth Sunday in Ordinary Time

Isaiah 49:8-16a

Psalm 131

1 Corinthians 4:1-5

Matthew 6:24-34

Free for Whom?

Selected reading
Matthew 6:24-34

Theme
Many of us think of ourselves as free. Yet among many, "freedom" has become another form of servitude as we allow our lives to be driven by our desire for material things. Jesus has some strong warnings against our materialism, and he promises us better lives than the lives that are enslaved by money. He warns us about the temptations of wealth and the dangers of making our money our master rather than our servant. Following Christ requires our wholehearted allegiance. We cannot serve God and money, he says.

Introduction to the readings
Isaiah 49:8-16a

Through the prophet Isaiah, God promises never to forsake or to forget his people in their time of trial.

1 Corinthians 4:1-5
Paul says that he and other leaders of the church are "servants of Christ and managers of God's secrets" (v. 1).

Matthew 6:24-34
"No one can serve two masters," says Jesus as he continues his teaching (6:24). In this section Jesus focuses upon the dangers of subservience to wealth.

Prayer

Lord Jesus, during this hour of worship, give us the courage to take a sober, honest look at our lives. Give us the grace to consider our lives in the light of your creative will for our lives. Help us to see our lives not as our achievements but as your gift. In a materialistic, acquisitive culture, where money is made to look more valuable than it really is, enable us to want more out of our lives than merely restless, constant striving and accumulation of possessions. Guide us to see how our possessions have us rather than us having our possessions. Free us from undue love of the world and worldly things. Help us to stand up straight, as free, unburdened people who, knowing our creator, also know who we are created to be and show the freedom to live the lives for which we have been created. Amen.

Encountering the text

Jesus has been teaching the crowds. He has begun his sermon on the mount with an odd series of blessings, blessing those whom the world tends to curse. Then he has launched into a series of commands and guidelines for those who would presume to be part of his new reign.

This section begins with Jesus's proverbial statement, "No one can serve two masters." The conflict between masters here is rather specific: "you cannot serve God and wealth" (Matt 6:24). Jesus tells us not to be anxious. And the anxiety that is condemned is specifically anxiety over material things. The flowers of the field and the birds of the air are cited as instances of modest creations that appear to have no anxiety about material matters but that are beautiful to behold (6:26-30).

Worry about food and clothing is condemned as not better than the lifestyles and values of the Gentiles. If you want to worry and be anxious, Jesus implies, worry about the demands of the kingdom.

Anxiety is here cast as a function of "Whom do you serve?" Who is your master? That which has mastery over us is that over which we are most anxious. We can't serve both God and *mammon* (the Greek word for "wealth").

Jesus's talk about "masters" may sound strange to us. After all, we are citizens of the most freedom-loving, freedom-enjoying nation on the earth, or so we are told. We are not bound to any master!

Most of us pastors find that much of this culture's talk about "freedom" can be deceptive. Every day pastors work with people who show all the signs of the ravages of enslavement. Jesus's linkage of mastery and materialism is bound to hit home in many of our churches where many people lie awake at night, endanger their health, and break up their marriages in breathless pursuit of "something more." We may be among the first to know that our "freedom" to do what we want, when we want, and how we choose could be just another form of servitude.

It's enough to provoke us to ask, "Whom do you serve?"

Proclaiming the text

If there is one virtue on which all of us can agree, it is on the virtue of freedom. Americans, for example, think of themselves as the freest people on the planet. They fight wars to give others the same freedom they prize. The most severe punishment they can give out as a society is incarceration—taking away someone's freedom. Most of us covet and guard our freedom to choose.

Therefore it sounds strange to us for Jesus to address us with the words, "No one can serve two masters." Perhaps this is one of those biblical moments when the archaic subject being dealt with—whether or not to eat food offered to idols, what to do about polygamy, or how to behave when you are a slave—doesn't apply to us.

There were slaves and there were masters in Jesus's day, but in our day we have (mostly) eradicated the evil of legal slavery. We are free, among the freest people who have ever lived on the face of the earth. How can Jesus accuse us of having some "master"?

As a campus minister I noted that most college students think they are "free" to have alcohol at parties. They are at last free from parental constraint so that they can consume as much booze as they like. But soon they discover that they have become unable to have fun at parties without alcohol. They will say, "I have to start getting drunk on Friday afternoon so I'll be ready for the party that night." This is freedom? They thought that alcohol abuse is a sign of their freedom, whereas in truth alcohol had become their master.

Of course you will note that in today's Gospel Jesus isn't speaking of just any old servitude: Jesus speaks about our servitude to material possessions. This is one of the longest-sustained arguments in Jesus's sermon on the mount, and the subject of this detailed exposition by Jesus is a subject many of us would rather hear nothing about, particularly in church—money!

And Jesus's talk about money seems strange in its linkage of money and subservience because, after all, the accumulation of money is the major way that we hope to achieve freedom. Many of our forebears worked long hours in grueling, backbreaking work with short vacations and constant worry about where the next meal was coming from. We are different. Most of us have accumulated enough stuff—enough insurance, enough of a pension, enough discretionary income, to be free. Our money is our ticket to freedom from worry. Our striving and accumulation is the price that we pay for our freedom. As the army advertisements remind us, "Freedom isn't free."

I'll say. When you examine the way that many of us actually live, *freedom* is not the first word that would come to mind. Why is it that so many of us modern people feel condemned to rush to and fro, choosing this, buying that, accumulating something else, all in a breathless quest to grab and acquire out of the fear that we may risk losing the very thing that would make our lives worth living? Is it because we have mistaken license for freedom? It's like we're on a manic-depressive roller-coaster ride between the dizzying heights of the modern fantasy that our freedom is endlessly expanding, and the despairing realization that we are in truth not free—we are driven, jerked about by our stuff, on a treadmill of ever-rising expectation that brings us more grief than happiness. Our "freedom" has become another form of bondage. Thinking ourselves to be masters of ourselves, in reality we become slaves to our own ever-expanding, omnivorous desire. "Live to shop!" says the T-shirt.

Jesus designates our material things, our money, as mammon. It's a Greek word that can mean either "money" or "the god of money." Isn't it interesting how our material possessions have a way of starting out as a means to adorn our lives, to enrich our lives, and end up taking on a life of their own, become a kind of beast to be fed, a little less than a god. Our helpful servant has become our demanding master.

Jesus presses the point by referring to the flowers of the field and the birds of the air. We consider ourselves superior creatures to them, yet, says Jesus, they don't lie awake at night worrying about how to pay their mortgage for the house they shouldn't have bought. They don't destroy their health and shorten their lives through their constant striving and hoarding.

Unlike the birds of the air, we can plan and envision into the future. That's why we say that we are working so hard; we are trying to provide a good future for our children, trying to make sure that we have a soft retirement. And yet Jesus condemns our "prudence" as sorry servitude to a false god. We think that we are so free when in reality creatures like the birds show a carefree life that makes our driven lives look sad.

In response Jesus refers us to our true creator. The God who created us continues to care for us, to provide a way for us, says Jesus. Jesus has come to reveal to us the true nature of God. In his miraculous feeding of the multitudes that will come later in this Gospel, Jesus shows us what God is really like.

Now I expect that few of us came to church this morning to hear a sermon on money, to have ourselves lambasted for our materialism and our greed, to be called slaves to mammon. We came to church to worship God. But don't you see, that's just what Jesus is trying to help us do? We can't fully worship the true and living God, the God whose full revelation is Jesus, when we are bowing and scraping before false gods. Therefore our false gods must be named and exposed if we are to love more dearly, follow more nearly, and see more clearly the God who created us, who loves us, and in whose life is our true freedom.

I therefore call you to prayerfully consider what you are expending your life for. What do you possess that you just couldn't do without? How has your life slipped into bad habits for all sorts of otherwise "good" reasons? Let us cast off the burdens that our culture attempts to place upon our backs. Let us stand up and be the truly free beings that God created us to be. Let us refocus on the most important things in life. In short, let us worship the Father, Son, and Holy Spirit in all that we do, including our dealings with material things.

Therein is our true freedom to be who God created us to be.

Relating the text

Theologian Reinhard Hutter says in *Bound to Be Free* that there are three levels of freedom. The American tends to think first of political freedom: the freedom that was at stake in the American Revolution—that is, Jefferson's, Franklin's, and Washington's freedom, and by extension the freedom sought by Rosa Parks and Martin Luther King Jr.

But when we think further, we may think about a second kind of freedom, the kind that is the presupposition of political freedom: moral freedom. This is the freedom that enables us to be morally responsible. The philosopher Immanuel Kant made this sort of freedom the basis of his ethics. An act cannot be considered truly "ethical" in which someone does not freely choose to perform this act. Only people who are free to decide between right and wrong and then act on the basis of their decisions can be considered truly moral people. In fact, the freedom to act in a way that you think to be right is the hallmark of what makes a person a real person in the modern world. This sort of autonomous (literally: "self law") freedom is the hallmark of the modern world.

But then, says Hutter, there is a third level of thought about freedom that is peculiarly Christian, thinking about freedom in the company of people like Augustine, Thomas Aquinas, Martin Luther, Jonathan Edwards, Søren Kierkegaard, and Karl Barth. While they differ from one another in various ways, these Christian thinkers all agree that it is this third level of freedom that is most fundamental and decisive: the freedom to live and to love God. The most important freedom is the freedom to be the human beings we are created to be. What makes us essentially human?

It is at this level of freedom that all freedom stands or falls. This third, most fundamental level addresses the question: What constitutes the human as human? What makes us who we essentially are?

In the modern age, this Christian view of freedom was exchanged for the modern view that we are gods unto ourselves. Who is a "god" if not that being that chose to do anything he wants, whenever and however he wants. The modern world thus attempts to fulfill the satanic promise (Gen 3) that "you will be like God"—that is, we can choose to do whatever we want with our lives.

Thus when Jesus tells us, in today's Gospel, that we "can't serve two masters," are there not many whose sad lives are testimonial to the truth of Jesus's claim? We have exchanged the mastery of the creator for enslavement to ourselves. We have nothing to be free for except for ourselves.

And ourselves may be the cruelest masters of all.

In Aldous Huxley's prophetic novel *Brave New World* the dilemma of the contemporary world is chillingly depicted. We have the illusion that we are free, yet we are victims of all sorts of subtle but binding impersonal forces that control our every thought and movement. The modern state, according to Huxley, has attained the perfect dream for a state: its citizens believe that they are free to do what they want but they have been so formed, programmed, and educated to want only what the state wants for them.

Visiting in Japan, I asked my host (who is originally from the United States and is not a Christian) what he thought was the greatest challenge for Japanese society. He answered, "I may be thinking like an American here, but Japanese culture seems to be totally focused on material striving, on working unbelievably long hours, on placing the company before everything else in life, and in getting the latest technological gadget that's available."

"If that's a fair characterization of modern Japanese culture, why do you think that's so?" I asked.

"I think it's what you get when you have a culture that has no real Christian presence in the culture," he said. "As you know, I'm not a Christian myself, but I sort of admire the way that the Christian faith has within it a constant critique of materialism. Jesus was tough on those who hoarded, and his contempt for the rich is notorious. When there's no Christian critique, no Christian 'minority report' against our greed, then there's no check on our materialism. The results can be sad."

I have no way of knowing if my host's characterization of Japanese culture is fair or not, but his comments are an interesting observation about the Christian faith and the warnings about money that are inherent in that faith.

Transfiguration Sunday
RC/Pres: Ninth Sunday
in Ordinary Time

Exodus 24:12-18
Psalm 2 or Psalm 99
2 Peter 1:16-21
Matthew 17:1-9

The Fellowship of Fear

Selected reading
Matthew 17:1-9

Theme
We come to church to be part of that fellowship that dares to be in conversation with and submissive to a living God. Encounters with the true God rarely leave us unscathed. Therefore a typical reaction to particular moments of revelation in the Bible is fear. When God is encountered as the One who is beyond us, not a product of our imagination, a commanding Lord, then we feel fear. The church, seen from this perspective, is the fellowship of fear.

Introduction to the readings
Exodus 24:12-18

"Come up to me on the mountain," says God to Moses (v. 12). So Moses goes up on the mountain with some of his assistants. There on the mountain, in a cloud, Moses is given a privileged vision of God.

2 Peter 1:16-21

The message of the good news of Jesus Christ is like "a lamp shining in a dark place" (v. 19). Scripture is the gift of women and men who were moved by the Holy Spirit to speak God's word.

Matthew 17:1-9

Jesus takes three of his disciples up on a mountain. There he is miraculously transfigured before them, and a voice declares, "This is my Son whom I dearly love. I am very pleased with him. Listen to him!" (v. 5). The disciples, upon seeing the vision and hearing the voice, were overcome by fear.

Prayer

Lord Jesus, teach us, in your loving care for us, not only to love you but also to fear you. Teach us to be afraid of disappointing you by the unfaithfulness of our discipleship. Train us to fear the great gap between what we think is right and what you declare to be your higher righteousness. Show us that your ways are not always our ways and that your thoughts are higher than our thoughts. Preserve us from attempting to whittle you down to our size, to reduce the cosmic, demanding, saving faith in you to something small and manageable and petty. Save us from attempting to use you to get what we want in the world; enable us to live so that we become God's means of getting what God wants in the world. Amen.

Encountering the text

Christians reading about the Transfiguration of Jesus on the mountain before his fearful disciples have always tended to think about Exodus 24 and 34. Just as Moses was transformed and descended the mountain with his face shining in glory (Exod 24:19), so Jesus shines like the sun in glory on the mountain. Jesus, whose true identity has been in doubt and ambiguous to the disciples throughout much of Matthew, now in chapter 17, just before he makes his way to the cross, is made manifest for his disciples to see. There is a cloud, a voice, a vision, and the same voice that proclaimed him God's Son reiterates that claim here on the mountain.

When Moses was transfigured in glory, the special group of onlookers (Exod 24:1) were afraid. So are the disciples of Jesus who are privileged to witness his transformation. In our proclamation of the Transfiguration today, we will focus on this reaction to the revelation of Jesus's true identity—fear. Fear is an all-too-rare emotional reaction in today's church. And yet fear is a frequent biblical emotion. Our sermon will explore this anomaly.

Proclaiming the text

I passed by a church the other day. The name of the church is the Fellowship of Joy. Interesting name for a church. I'm old enough to remember when they named churches for various saints, or even where they were geographically located. I think it's a relatively new development to name a church for an emotion. True, there is plenty of joy in the Christian life. I know one church that had as its motto or slogan "the fellowship of excitement." And excitement is also a Christian emotion, sometimes. I do worry that emotions are notoriously short-lived. But I also worry that "joy" or "excitement" may fall short of the truly Christian emotion. If you had to pick one human emotion that best describes what it means to be with Jesus, which emotion would you choose?

For today, this Transfiguration Sunday, I've got a Christian emotion to suggest. It's not joy. It's fear. Looking through the New Testament, you will find that the predominant New Testament emotion is neither joy nor excitement. The main emotion of the Gospels is fear.

That's right. When people encountered Jesus, their predominant emotion was not joy. They felt fear. Interestingly enough, the people who felt fear when encountered by Jesus were not the anonymous crowds. The people who are reported as being most afraid of Jesus were his own disciples.

When Jesus assists his disciples after a night of fishing failure and they bring in a miraculous catch of fish, they feel fear. When Jesus calms the wind and the waves and saves the disciples in the boat, they feel fear. When the women come out to the tomb, on that first Easter morning, and they find the tomb is empty, what do the Gospels say they felt? They felt fear.

Time and again Jesus has to say to his disciples, "Don't be afraid." You wouldn't have to tell them not to be afraid, if they were not afraid. Something about Jesus tended to make those closest to Jesus scared half out of their wits.

You would think that at last we have come upon an aspect of biblical faith to which we could easily relate. In many ways, we live in a time of great fear. When the great poet Auden attempted to characterize our age, he called us "the age of anxiety" (W. H. Auden, *The Age of Anxiety* [New York: Random, 1947]).

That first Sunday after September 11, 2001, I stood at our church door and watched people scurrying into church, many of whom I had never seen before. And if you had asked me that day what emotion I saw on people's faces, I would have answered fear. I can name for you a dozen people who before that date in September routinely traveled by air to various places. Now they drive. Why? They are afraid.

The doctor comes in after your yearly physical and says, "There's a problem. We need to have some tests. I am concerned about something we saw on your X-ray." What do you feel? Not a sense of relief or joy, excitement or wonder. You feel fear. You are not helped a bit by your doctor attempting to reassure you with, "There, there now. Nothing to be afraid of—yet." It's your doctor's *yet* that causes a huge lump to develop in your throat.

I think the source of fear on these occasions is this: when an alien, unexpected, and unwanted reality invades your life, disrupts your reality, alters the accustomed flow of things, then there is fear. What will tomorrow bring? What will happen in my life? These are among the fearful questions that arise during such moments.

A friend of mine says that he can remember, when he was a very small child and his mother had to teach him to be afraid of the traffic in the street in front of his house. "The street is a dangerous place. You're not even to think about crossing the street without first asking me for permission. You're not to cross the street unless I am holding your hand. The street and the cars in it are very dangerous," his mother had to teach him.

But then he grew older. Eventually he was given permission to venture across the street on his own. He lost that childhood terror of the bad things that might happen to him in crossing to the other side.

The other day my friend, who is now in his fifties, said, "One thing I have found out later in life. My mother was right. Most of the bad things that happen to you in life happen to you while you are crossing over to the other side. A lot of pain could be avoided in this life if we follow the simple rule: 'don't cross the street—unless you are holding on tight to somebody else's hand.'"

Not a bad motto to carry with you through life. It's a fearful world out there.

And yet, that sort of fear is not the sort of fear that Jesus engenders. Fear—that is, New Testament fear—is the fear that comes not as part of the frail and vulnerable human condition, not as an aspect of living in troubled times, but in the presence of Christ. Oh, we say we want a vision of God. We claim that we want God to speak to us. We say that we want some "proof" of the reality and the presence of a living God.

But there, on the mountaintop of the Transfiguration with the strange, mystical cloud, the shining face, the voice from heaven, all these details spell fear. What was the Transfiguration? It was a bright, shining, scary moment when a couple of Jesus's disciples saw Jesus for who he really was. There is Jesus speaking directly with Moses and Elijah, the two greatest figures of the Hebrew faith. And then, there is Jesus alone, greater even than Moses and Elijah. And the predominant emotion of this grand revealing moment? Fear.

Here on the mountain a couple of disciples have a great spiritual experience. Why were they afraid? In order to answer that question, I would have you look at the episode that immediately precedes this visit to the mountaintop:

Jesus predicts his death. He straightforwardly tells his disciples what lies ahead: "I will suffer and be killed."

When Peter protests that it is impossible to conceive of a messiah who is rejected, suffers, and dies, Jesus intensifies the conversation by saying, "And if you want to follow me, then you must take up your own cross and follow me."

If people are supposed to be on a spiritual search, a journey toward the Divine, is this the journey we want?

That is why I would say that the fear that is felt so often among Jesus's followers in the New Testament is not just any old fear. It is fear of Jesus. It is not the fear that is felt when we have some numinous, ethereal, vague, mystical experience. It is the fear when we come face to face with the God whose name is Jesus the Christ, when we sense his particular demands upon us, when we see clearly his narrow way to which he beckons us. And then we are afraid.

Scripture says, "It's scary to fall into the hands of the living God!" (Heb 10:31). False gods offer no fear. If that which we call "God" is only a projection of our own selfish, deceitful aspirations, then what is there to fear in that? But our God, the God who comes to us in Jesus Christ, is a living God. And to see in a moment that loving but demanding face, to sense the perilous journey that lies ahead when we follow him, that is to feel fear.

Encounters with the living God can be not only deeply moving but also threateningly fearful, as well as life-transforming. On the mountaintop Jesus doesn't simply reveal himself to his followers, but he demands that they follow him, that they walk the path that he walks.

No wonder the disciples fall on the ground. And no wonder Jesus says to them, "Get up and do not be afraid!"

Why are more people not here in church this morning? You know the standard reasons. People come and say they can't sing those old hymns. They don't understand that the Christian faith lives by the saints, that we enjoy the spiritual gifts of the past. Or they say that they find our church "unfriendly." They don't understand that the church is much more than a mutual admiration society, a gregarious country club sort of place. We are about larger, godlier things here. Or they say that we use a bunch of strange words, outdated language, and they find the Bible to be impossible to understand. They don't understand that Christian discipleship sometimes takes a long time, a lifetime of discipline of training and formation.

Today I would like to suggest that lots of people avoid church, not because they misunderstand what we are about, but because they understand all too well. Church is about God. Church is about the possibility of a threatening though life-changing encounter with the risen Christ. Church is about seeing God's way and will in our world and then having to say yes or no to walking that way. And knowing that scares a lot of people to death.

Relating the text

Today's proclamation stresses the distance, the awe, and the fearsomeness of a living God. In our own day we have tended to crank God down to our size. God is a personal friend who thinks somewhat like we think. Part of the problem is that we have personalized and individualized God until there is little of God left to stand against us.

One reason why we go to church on Sunday is to risk exposure to the God we could not have thought up on our own, a God who sometimes is against us. When we keep God limited to just what we ourselves think we hear God saying, then it's unlikely that we will have new experiences of God or that we will hear God saying anything to us that really challenges us. The problem is that when any single person prays, refusing to let others who are praying weigh in on what they are hearing or even whether or not what was allegedly heard from God matches what we know about God from Scripture, we risk the absolutizing of one person's religious arrogance. Really now, do you think you would have heard the message that "it is a fearful thing to fall into the hands of a living God" if you had not gotten up and come to church this morning?

A while back a young man met with me and began the conversation by saying, "Look, you're a sort of expert on God, right? Well some things have been happening to me in my life, strange coincidences. And I am going to tell you about them. And I hope that I know what you'll say. I hope that you will tell me that this has nothing to do with God. But then again, I am afraid it might, so here goes."

Then he told me a series of odd coincidences and happenstances, weird revelations and realizations. When he finished, I said to him, "Well in my expert opinion, as a certified religious specialist, this all sounds suspiciously like the voice of God. I think God is intruding into your life, attempting to get you to do something for him."

"Oh, no!" the young man moaned. "I was afraid you were going to say that."

That was what he said—"afraid." He was a smart young man, and while he didn't know everything about the Bible, he knew enough about the Bible to know that encounters with a living God can be demanding. The Bible testifies that few people come close to the true, living God and come away unscathed. In my experience, when most people talk about wanting to get "spiritual," they mean that they want to get warm and cuddly with some amorphous, sweet, and always-smiling sort of godlet.

On the mount of Transfiguration the disciples fall to their knees, overcome by the majesty and the mystery of Christ. In a dazzling moment they see that Jesus is more than a great moral teacher, more even than a miraculous healer of human ills; Jesus is none other than who the baptismal voice proclaimed him to be—none other than God's Son.

In today's church, with our carpeted rooms where we worship, with smiling amiable worship leaders and upbeat praise songs, with preachers joshing with us and everyone so comfortable and so delighted to be together, so well adjusted to Jesus, I wonder, are we in need of a refreshing dose of mystery, of wonder and transcendence? Transfiguration is just the Sunday for that.

The elderly matron had heard that their new preacher was controversial at his previous church. Many in the church were fearful that he might be a divisive, discomforting new pastor for them. So she came to church, on the new pastor's first Sunday in the pulpit, a bit anxious over what she might hear.

After the service she greeted her new pastor at the door with these words: "Mr. Smith, I heard that you were somewhat of a troublemaker, a radical even. But I listened carefully to your sermon, and I am happy to say that I didn't hear you say anything that would make anyone the least bit uncomfortable. You were wonderful! You didn't say a thing!"

First Sunday in Lent

Genesis 2:15-17; 3:1-7

Psalm 32

Romans 5:12-19

Matthew 4:1-11

Lenten Contradiction

Selected reading

Romans 5:12-19 (with reference to Gen 2:15-17; 3:1-7)

Theme

In Lent, we are confronted by a series of contrasts. We were created by God for life in a lush garden. We betrayed that creation with our disobedience. We were intended to be in fellowship with God. We destroyed that relationship in our sin. And yet, God stays with us, reaches out to us, gives us Jesus, "the free gift Christ" (Rom 5:15), in order to heal our contradictions and alienation.

Introduction to the readings

Genesis 2:15-17; 3:1-7

The story of our beginning ends badly in our disobedience by eating the forbidden fruit.

Romans 5:12-19

Paul contrasts the way that "sin came into the world" through Adam's sinful disobedience with Christ's faithful obedience, speaking of Christ as the "new Adam" (v. 12).

Matthew 4:1-11

In the wilderness, Jesus resists the temptation of the devil.

Prayer

Almighty God, whose Son our Lord was led by the Spirit into the wilderness, there to be tempted by Satan, we pray for your grace to resist the temptations that come our way. We pray for the honesty to truthfully confront our sin and falsehood and, having told the truth about ourselves, be embraced by your love. In our weakness, you come to us in your strength. In our waywardness, you move toward us with forgiveness. Be with us during these forty days of Lent and teach us that, having repented and confessed our sin, we might eagerly receive your forgiveness. Amen.

Encountering the text

Lent, in my part of the world, means the first hint of spring. The winter solstice is past, the days grow gradually longer, the light grows brighter, and budding flowers suggest the return of new life. How the natural world around here contrasts with the world inside the Lenten church! There, we have no more "Alleluias." The mood is restrained and sombre. Thus, I call Lent a season of contrast.

The contrasts are greater than the natural world itself. The scripture for this first Sunday of Lent is filled with contrasts. The first lesson from Genesis depicts quite a contrast between the gift of the lush garden and the aftermath of our sin. God gives the woman and the man a garden where all they have to do is to pick the fruit off the tree. Except they must stay away from that tree over there. The moment the creator's back is turned, the creature makes for the tree and the rest is history.

Paul's words to the Romans are a string of contrasts and contradictions: sin came into the world in Adam; grace came in Jesus Christ. Many die in Adam; many live in Christ. Adam brought judgment; Christ brought justification.

Death—abundance. Condemnation—justification. Disobedience—obedience. "Where sin increased, grace multiplied even more" (Rom 5:20). Death came through Adam, "eternal life through Jesus Christ our Lord."

We are in the midst of Pauline rhetoric here, a string of opposites, contrasts, and juxtapositions. The form of this closely reasoned discussion stresses the oddness of the gospel, the way that the coming of Christ set in motion a string of divine countermeasures to contend with our infidelity and sin. In Christ, the history of the world is thrown into reverse, the course of the sinful stream of human events begins to flow in another direction.

Lent—coming as it does into a society of success, fulfillment, human potential, and self-esteem—is a season of contradiction. What the church calls us to do during these forty days of repentance, self-examination, and reflection is a countercultural move, a reverse in our society's predominate way of thinking.

We are swimming against the stream in our seasonal confrontation with sin, finitude, death, and mortality. These are subjects that our culture has elaborate means of avoiding. But not in church. In church, in these brightening first days of spring, we insist that our congregations turn their thoughts toward the shadow, toward the truth about our condition in our sin.

We are able to be so truthful and honest because of the grace that is ours in the work of Jesus Christ on our behalf.

Proclaiming the text

Years ago, when I was serving as a pastor in a coastal South Carolina town, about this time of year we had quite a ruckus. The local Episcopal parish had placed three crosses on the lawn adjacent to their church. They draped them in purple for Lent. After a week or so, the church received a call from the local chamber of commerce. They complained about the three crosses.

"This is a big season for tourists," they said. "We think those crosses could send the wrong signal to visitors at the beach. People don't want to come down here for a vacation and be confronted with unpleasantness."

The church stood its ground. The three crosses stayed. "It's Lent," said the church. "People are supposed to be uncomfortable."

Lent, the season of unpleasant uncomfortability.

I participated in a powerful service on this Sunday, the first Sunday of Lent, a few years ago at an Episcopal church in Florida. I found the service, which included the sombre Great Litany, to be a moving experience. At the end of the service, one of the members of the church said, "I regret that you had to visit us during Lent. This is not a fair representation of our church with these dull hymns and the silent recessional. Normally things are much more beautiful and upbeat at our church."

There is some debate among liturgical experts about just how we are to handle these Sundays of Lent. Sunday is the day of resurrection. Lent is the season leading to crucifixion. There are those who think that we shouldn't give over Sunday, the day of Easter, to the sombreness of Lent. Sundays ought to be a break in our Lenten disciplines, they argue.

But when you think about it, there is something almost invigorating about this time of the Christian year. These forty days from Ash Wednesday to Easter are among the most countercultural and subversive in the church year. Confession of sin, focus upon death, honesty about temptation—these matters do not come naturally to us. We live in a success-worshipping, power-seeking, feel-good culture. Lent moves us in another direction.

In today's Gospel, Jesus is confronted by Satan in the wilderness. The great tempter offers Jesus three possibilities: turn stones into bread, take political power, or perform spectacular spiritual feats. And these are all good, worthy ends sought by most of us. Isn't it a good thing to feed hungry people? Isn't it a worthy vocation to attempt to do good for others through political action?

Wouldn't it be wonderful to witness a miracle so great that struggling believers would be able to believe?

Yet Jesus rejects all of these otherwise good offers. He says no.

In today's first lesson, the familiar story of our creation from Genesis, things begin well enough. Man and woman are created to live in a good and lush garden. We have only one minor restriction, which is to stay away from the Tree of Knowledge, the Tree of Life. And the moment that the creator's back is turned, there we are, eating the forbidden fruit, surrendering to our relentless curiosity. Isn't intellectual curiosity a good thing? Yes. But it is our great intellectual capacity, that wonderful gift of God, that we pervert and use in our rebellion. The contradiction between our high calling in God's creation and the way we despoil that high calling is one of the contradictions of Lent, one of the ironic, deep contradictions of human life.

In today's epistle, Paul writes to the church at Rome, singing to them of the triumph of Christ. He recounts for them the entrance of sin and rebellion into the world. We are those who have gone astray, who have preferred our wills to God's will. The results of this sin are all around us. The history of this past bloody century and the headlines in this morning's newspaper tell the story.

Yet to this story Paul contrasts the story of Christ. Christ brings life to our death-dealing ways. Christ offers forgiveness for our sin. In Christ, it's like God starts all over with creation, from the beginning, and sets us toward a new future.

This first Sunday of Lent, think of church as a place where our contradictions are underscored, examined, and ministered unto. One reason why church can sometimes be so unpleasant is that here we confront so many of those truths about ourselves that we spend much of the rest of our lives avoiding. Here, with God's help, we try to tell the truth about ourselves, and sometimes the truth hurts.

The whole world is busy attempting to climb up the ladder to success; here we kneel down in confession of sin. The world keeps telling itself that we are basically good people who are doing the very best we can. Here, we admit that we are those who wander, who go astray, rebel; in short, we sin.

On a Sunday like this one, perhaps we ought to put a sign over the door of our sanctuary, a warning to the unsuspecting first-time visitor: BEWARE. TRUTH BEING TOLD HERE!

How is it possible for people like us to tell the truth about ourselves? Honesty would be utterly impossible were it not because, in Jesus Christ, we have been loved. As Paul says to the Romans, though our sin was serious, in Christ "grace abounded." Our misdeeds are abundant, as we admit every time we pray a prayer of confession. Yet, as Paul says, in Christ we have received abundant grace. To the unrighteous has been given righteousness. We could not get good enough for God, so God in Christ has made us good through his saving love for us. We could not do right by God, so God in Christ did right for us.

The good God who should have punished us for our failure to be good instead loved us back into relationship with God. This is the great, wonderful contradiction of the cross, the great contradiction of Lent, upon which rests our hope in life and in death. Amen.

Relating the text

Our sin is a complicated matter, a matter of contrasts. How odd that in going out to do "good," we end up doing such "bad." Henry Ford, having ripped small-town America asunder by his creation of the Ford Motor Company, tried to preserve America's past in his wistful construction of Greenfield Village—a museum of how New England looked before the invention of the Model T Ford.

Charles Lindbergh, in midlife, was a pathfinder for American Airlines and a creative architect of global air routes to the far corners of the Pacific. Late in life he devoted his efforts to global conservation movements in order to protect the very Shangri-La that he had helped to endanger through the spread of technology. And critics of these two controversial men can point to their gross racial bigotry and antisemitism and thus to their potential for rigidity, all mixed in with their virtues.

Martin Marty once said of our modern denial of our other side, "sin" has become largely a matter of "improper opinion."

—Martin E. Marty, *The Improper Opinion: Mass Media in the Christian Faith* (Philadelphia: Westminster, 1961)

After discussing Freud's liberation of the modern psyche from any psychological restraints, an existential psychotherapist, Yalom, wonders if modern America (particularly in California?) took Freud too far:

"But what would Freud emphasise were he to examine contemporary American culture, especially in California, which has been the birthplace of so many of the newer therapeutic approaches? Natural instinctual strivings are given considerable free expression; sexual permissiveness, beginning in early adolescence, is, as many surveys have demonstrated, a reality. A generation of young adults have been nursed and spoonfed according to a compulsively permissive regimen. Structure, ritual, boundaries of every type, are being relentlessly dismantled.

"In the religious orders, Catholic sisters defy the Pope, priests refuse to remain celibate, women and gay men divide the Episcopal church on their right to be ordained, and women rabbis lead services in many synagogues. Students address professors by their first names. Where are the forbidden, dirty words, the professional titles, the manuals of manners, the dress codes?

"A friend of mine, an art critic, characterised the new California culture by describing an incident that occurred on his first visit to Southern California. He stopped at a fast-food drive-in and was given, with his hamburger, a small plastic container of ketchup. Elsewhere these containers have a dotted line and the notation to 'tear here'; the California container had no dotted lines, only the simple inscription 'tear anywhere.'"

—Irvin D. Yalom, *Existential Psychotherapy* (New York: Basic, 1980), 223–24

"Robert Penn Warren measured human evil to its depths as a gateway toward new human possibilities. His long-verse poem 'Brother to Dragons' has lost none of its biting power over the years.

"In it, the author recounts a discussion, in some kind of limbo, between himself, Thomas Jefferson and other members of the Jefferson family. The discussion concerns the brutal murder of a slave by one of Jefferson's relatives, Lilburn Lewis, who hacked the slave to pieces with a meat axe because he had broken a pitcher belonging to Lilburn's mother.

"Warren, struck by the fact that none of Jefferson's writings mention this incident, confronts him with the event. Jefferson is unable to square the murder with his deistic, optimistic doctrine of human nature. The cold fact and Jefferson's nice theory simply will not jibe. And Jefferson is forced to recast his view of human nature in the light of what took place on Lilburn's plantation. He has to take seriously the fact of human sin as it exists in Lilburn.

"And not only as it exists in Lilburn. Warren sees more deeply than that. As he talks with all the characters in anyway related to the event, it becomes clear that they all share in the guilt of what has happened. And then Warren reminds his readers that they too were in the hut, participating in that brutal murder: 'We have lifted the meat axe in the elation of love and justice.'"

—Robert McAfee Brown, *Persuade Us to Rejoice* (Louisville: Westminster John Knox, 1992), 39

I was watching a Sunday afternoon program on a national network on "the emerging church." Most of what they showed us was fairly predictable—the usual two-thousand-member megachurch in California where those younger than thirty years old were gathered, where a rock band played throbbing praise music, and where the clergy told sappy stories about "awesome" people who had done "awesome" things.

But one young man who was a pastor of a large congregation with lots of people under the age of thirty was asked by the interviewer, "To what do you attribute the remarkable attraction of your church to young adults?" He answered, "You have a whole generation of young people—beautiful, bright, successful young people—who have never had anyone love them enough to look them in the eye and say, in love, 'Man, you really suck.'"

I might have put the matter differently, but still, it's not a bad message for the first Sunday of Lent.

Second Sunday in Lent

Genesis 12:1-4a

Psalm 121

Romans 4:1-5, 13-17

John 3:1-17

The Spirit Blows Where It Will

Selected reading

John 3:1-17

Theme

God graciously gives us the Holy Spirit, that uncontrolled, untamed force empowering our spirits, enlivening our ordinary moments into occasions for worship.

Introduction to the readings

Genesis 12:1-4a

The Lord promises Abram that he will be the father of a great nation that will bless all the nations of the world.

Romans 4:1-5, 13-17

Paul recalls God's faithfulness to Abraham in contrasting faith and works.

John 3:1-17
Jesus encounters Nicodemus and speaks to him of the workings of the Spirit.

Prayer

Lord, bless us with the gift of your Holy Spirit. Breathe upon us your breath of life. Here, as we march behind your Son, Jesus, during the Lenten journey toward the cross, we flag, we falter, we fall away. Only by the empowerment of your Spirit can we hope to run the race we have begun.

In praying for your breath, your Holy Spirit, we realize that we are praying for a gift that may disrupt and disturb our lives. We come here to be confirmed in what we already know, to tie things down in our lives, to be secure.

Save us from our boring desire for safe harbors and quiet security! Let your holy breath blow upon us, even when it disrupts our ordered lives. Come, Holy Spirit! Amen.

Encountering the text

Today's "Proclaiming the text" walks the congregation through today's Gospel in a rather playful manner, so we will not say too much about the text here. Focusing upon the primary image in the Gospel—wind—today's sermon will be a playful relating of Jesus's encounter with Nicodemus and our own experience of the breath of the Spirit, breathing upon each of our lives, particularly in the context of our life of worship.

Nicodemus comes to Jesus, wanting to get things tied down, secured, figured out, explained. Jesus speaks mysteriously, ambiguously (as he so often does in John's Gospel) of wind, breath, and grace. Nicodemus is there for us, for those of us who come here on Sunday to get things tied down, secured, figured out, explained. Then, just when we get all settled down in the pews, a holy breath comes upon us and we are turned around, disrupted, reborn "from top to bottom."

Proclaiming the text

It's funny. I know less about preaching today than I knew when I started. A few years ago I could tell you what constituted a good sermon, what was needed to do it right. Today, I'm not sure. Why does a sermon work that has no reason for working? Why does a sermon not work when it's got everything going for it? I don't know.

I'm in the middle of a sermon. It's a good sermon, one on which I've worked hard. There I am, preaching, preaching. I look out toward the congregation. Nothing. Dead.

Why did I want to preach this sermon? What did I have in mind? Sometimes sermons backfire, roll over and play dead, limp off into obscurity, miss their mark. And maybe even more frustrating, sometimes they work and I don't know why.

I had a busy week. Monday through Saturday I was with the youth at Walt Disney World. Saturday night I was at the hospital catching up on my visiting. I intended to get on that sermon earlier but... There's nothing to do but stand up and do what I can. So I tell the story about the boy who goes away from home and doesn't know whether or not he ought to come back: tie a yellow ribbon 'round the old oak tree, he ain't heavy he's my brother, Christ has no hands but our hands...I pray that they've never been in church in their lives so maybe they haven't heard any of those. I stagger to the end of my sermon, limp off with a poem by Kahlil Gibran, and pray for the Benediction to rescue me from embarrassment.

Service is over. I'm standing at the door ready to say, "Well, gee, Arnold Palmer had off days too," or "For what you pay me here a dozen good ones a year ought to be enough."

Joe Smith grasps my hand, and there are tears in his eyes. He says, "Preacher, er, uh, well, anyway, thank you...thank you..."

Sarah Jones comes out and says, "Preacher, thank you. I'm going in for surgery tomorrow. After that sermon, I am ready."

What happened? It worked! Why did it work? Wait a minute Joe, Sarah! Come back here. What was it that you heard?

I go back over my notes that I scribbled on the back of that envelope while I was watching *60 Minutes* last night. Nothing there. What happened?

I know less about preaching today than I knew ten years ago, much less than I knew twenty years ago.

And yet . . .

Some time ago, *Engage/Social Action* magazine asked a group of committed Christian activists who were known for their work on behalf of racial justice what factors contributed to their unwavering commitment to put themselves on the line for justice. Nine out of ten listed preaching as number one or two on their list. They were there because of some sermon. I don't know about preaching.

It's tough to invest yourself in an activity that you don't understand. A couple of years ago I did a book on burnout among clergy. I interviewed clergy who had called it quits and those who had thought about calling it quits. To my surprise (why was I surprised?) they listed preaching as one of the most debilitating, frustrating, discouraging pastoral activities.

Why? Well, for one thing, what good does it do? You hurl your voice against the silences, year after year, chiseling your little messages out of the impervious granite of Scripture.

Sometimes I call preaching an art. But if it be an art, preaching is the most fragile, ethereal, and fleeting of all the arts. How I envy musicians. All they've got to do is stand up and follow somebody else's notes. An actor puts a particular twist on Shakespeare, yes. But then the same play can be given tomorrow night. But preaching? It's fleeting, fragile.

"Hey, wasn't that sermon just great? Let's all get together tomorrow and do it one more time!"

No. You had to be there to have heard it.

We can't get these people together again with these cares, these hopes. Words are spoken, they waft out over the congregation, then words die and the silence resumes.

Just words. Just preaching. Just mystery. I don't understand it.

Late one night there was this church official who came to Jesus. His name was Nicodemus. He says, "Teacher, we've seen you do some impressive things, like turning that lime punch into Mogen David last Saturday during the wedding (in violation of church rules about alcohol in the fellowship hall, I must say). Teacher, how do you get into God's kingdom? What do you have to do to get whatever it is that you have?"

Jesus replied, "I have three things that I want to say about that. Point one: You have to be born from above to see the kingdom. Point two: You have got to get the Spirit. Point three: The wind blows where it will."

That was Jesus. Ask him a simple, straightforward question like *What have I got to do to get what you have?* and he answers with parables, talk of birth, spirit, wind.

Nicodemus comes in from the dark, from the night, seeking light. What have I got to do? How is it possible?

And Jesus responds with surprising images: birth and wind.

You want to get into the kingdom? Simple. Just be born from above.

"Well, how can you do that? Can you teach an old dog new tricks? Can you squeeze back into your mother's womb and be born a second time?"

Jesus says, "You can squeeze through your mother's womb about as easily as you can squeeze yourself into the kingdom. You must be born, not again, but from above. [The Greek word is *anothen*, which means 'from above' or 'from top to bottom.' The same word was used on Good Friday when it was said that the veil of the temple was torn anothen, 'from top to bottom.'] You have got to be born from above, from the top down, from top to bottom."

But as so often happens in John's Gospel, somebody hears but doesn't hear. When Jesus first said born from "above" Nick thought he heard him say "again." How can you be born a second time? No, Jesus says, "Turn up your hearing aid. I said born from above." *Anothen.*

Isn't it interesting that when people talk about this passage today, making it the very hallmark of the Christian faith, the one and necessary path to the kingdom, they often speak of the way Nicodemus misunderstood it rather than the way Jesus depicted it. They say, "You must be born again." Like a second time or something. No. Jesus said, "You must be born from above. Flesh is flesh. But Spirit is spirit." What God wants to do with you is a renovation involving an attic-to-basement overhaul. Top to bottom. *Anothen.*

"Well, how?"

"You do it the same way you got born. What did you have to do to get born, Nicodemus?"

"Well, I was just floating along and then I just got pushed out."

"Right! Getting into my kingdom is a lot like that, only more so, top to bottom. *Anothen.*"

"Well, how?"

"Like wind. The wind blows where it will. You don't know from whence it comes. You don't know to where it goes. You can't control it, predict it, harness it. Getting into my kingdom is a lot like that, only more so, *pneuma.*"

"Jesus, did you say *pneuma* in the ordinary sense of 'wind' or *pneuma* in the theological sense of 'spirit'?"

Jesus replied, "Yes."

Do you find it interesting that when Nicodemus asked "how" Jesus responded by citing two of the most mysterious, uncontrollable events in life? Birth. Wind.

How? What did you do to get born? If it were a matter of how—a technique, a method—Jesus wouldn't have called it birth and wouldn't have named it wind.

How? God so loved the world that God gave. Can you say *charis*, gift, Nicodemus?

"Did you say *charis* in the ordinary sense of 'gift' or *charis* in the more theologically sophisticated sense of 'grace'?"

Jesus replied, "Yes."

Charis. Grace. *Pneuma*. Wind. Spirit. *Anothen*. Birth. Gift.

Nicodemus replied, "I don't understand."

And Jesus said, "Now, you're catching on."

"You must be born from above." (By the way, the *you* here is in the plural. Jesus was from Georgia. You all must be born from above.)

And we are. That's what's so confusing about it. For we are such high achievers, do-it-yourselfers, pragmatics. What do we have to do? Is there a technique? Can we read a book about it? Are there illustrated directions?

That's the image I have of us on Sunday morning. We come with our little notepads ready to receive our assignment for the week. "Now this week, church, I want you to work on your sexism, racism, materialism. Come back next Sunday, I'll give you another assignment."

I remember growing up in the South, in summer, before the days of air conditioning. How, when chores were done for the day, in the evening, everyone would gather on the porch and rock and talk in an attempt to escape the heat. And the leaves of the trees would rustle. And the talk would cease. And everyone would fall silent, sit back, and savor the breeze, the gift of the breeze. *Pneuma. Charis.*

You know what it's like to come in here on a Sunday, not really wanting to be here, your mind elsewhere, your heart elsewhere as well. And then, during the service, in the music, or the hymns, or in the sermon even, something gets hold of you, you rise, you soar forth at the end of the service with wings. Now what was that?

I don't know as much about preaching as I once knew. But I know this. Preaching appears so fragile, so unpredictable because preaching is so pneumatic.

As I emerged from the chapel last Sunday morning, an undergraduate asked, "What was that? I didn't get a thing out of it."

And I said, "Look kid, the Spirit blows where it will."

A sermon is a gift. Call it grace. And when you've been there, on those delicious, rare, and delightful Sundays when a cool, refreshing breeze ripples the congregation from the pulpit, it's wonderful. It's grace. I lay down all of my projects, my plans; I cease my eternal posturing. And I just enjoy the breeze. I can breathe again, an infusion of pneuma like the sixth day of creation. It's mysterious, it's amazing, and it's grace.

Relating the text

Every time we read Scripture in our Sunday worship, we pray a "Prayer for Illumination," saying, "Open our hearts and minds, O Lord, by the gift of your

Holy Spirit, so that as the word is read and proclaimed we may hear what you have to say to us today. Amen."

We ought to know enough about us and our defenses to know that, if minds and hearts are ever opened, it will be a miracle, the result of the gift of the Holy Spirit.

The last Sunday of the school year I got a call from the chapel attendant about 8:00 a.m.

"Dr. Willimon. You up?"

"Yes, I'm up."

"Just wanted you to know there's no electricity in the chapel this morning."

"What? Has the choir gotten there yet?"

"Well, I think they may have. I can hear voices down front, but it's too dark to tell if they are choir members or not."

I threw on my clothes and rushed down. It was dark. I mean it was so dark. We took a flashlight. Went downstairs and got every candle we could lay our hands on. By 10:15 we had 232 candles lit. It was about as dark as downtown Durham at 3:00 a.m. We had to redo the entire service because we couldn't use the organ or the sound system. I was a wreck.

But at exactly fifteen minutes till eleven, suddenly, for no reason, all of the lights came back on. So most of the people entered the chapel to be greeted by 232 candles stuck in every window, on every flat surface.

"Well, what do we have in store for us today?" asked a sophomore. "One of your trendy worship innovations? Jack-be-nimble Sunday is it, Dr. Willimon?"

"Shut up and sit down," I said. In love.

From there, everything that could go wrong, went wrong. I was as glad to get that service over with as I was to leave army boot camp. "I've had it," I thought. "There have got to be easier ways to make money."

Then, after nearly everybody had stumbled out, someone said, "Nice try, Dr. Willimon. You'll probably be better by fall."

"Shut up," I said. In love.

After everybody had left, there were these three young women who came up to me. They were smiling. I hadn't noticed them before. One said, "Dr. Willimon, we're all seniors. And this is our last Sunday here. And we were just saying to ourselves that we're really going to miss your sermons. What you've said has really helped us make it through our four years here. Thanks."

And even through thick limestone gothic walls, I felt a breeze.

"In the postmodern era worship celebrates being alive to life, offering people an experience of being alive in Christ. Postmoderns are not going to invest their one and only life in dullness and doubt. If the haunt of our common nature in the modern period was doubt, the postmodern haunt is belief. Whereas good preaching in the modern era struck thoughts and struck attitudes, good preaching in the postmodern era strikes chords and invites poetry.

"Postmodern worship doesn't help people doubt it, but helps them shout it. Worship generates song and poetry. Worship must set vibrating in the soul the full chord of God's awareness.

"Both realists and abstracts expect worship to help them 'experience' life, to unclench spiritually, so as to better hear the wind and see the fire. Worship that is not fresh, preaching that is preplanned will increasingly have the same reception as clothes that are 'prefitted' and products that are 'prefabricated.' Postmoderns can stand hot air—but only in fresh air.

"Worship is not something postmoderns want to 'attend'; worship is something postmoderns want to enact. It is not too far wrong to say 'When a past [forty] adult misses church he will ask, "What did he say?"—meaning "What was the sermon about?" The under-forty adult is more likely to ask, "What happened?"'

"Both groups judge worship primarily on the basis of whether or not they were caught up in something, and most of all, whether joy is felt!"

—Leonard I. Sweet, *Quantum Spirituality: A Postmodern Apologetic* (Dayton, OH: Whaleprints, 1991), 84–91

Third Sunday in Lent

Exodus 17:1-7

Psalm 95

Romans 5:1-11

John 4:5-42

Jesus Is Where He Finds You

Selected reading

John 4:5-42

Theme

Sometimes we think of ourselves as on a search, a search for God. Yet to tell the story of our faith in a more biblical way, we would have to say that Jesus is on a search for us! He comes to us, often at the most surprising and inopportune times, often in the strangest or most ordinary places. He comes to us, speaks to us, and in the encounter initiated by him, we are saved.

Introduction to the readings

Exodus 17:1-7

For a people famished in the desert, by the grace of God there is miraculous water streaming from a rock.

Romans 5:1-11

"The love of God has been poured out in our hearts," Paul tells the Romans (v. 5).

John 4:5-42

In a Samaritan city, Jesus encounters a woman at a well and engages her in conversation.

Prayer

Lord Jesus, give us the vision to see you when you come into our lives. Help us to be patient with your elusive presence. Preserve us from trying to figure you out on our terms; help us to be hospitable and to receive you on your terms. And when at last you speak to us, help us to respond to your voice, to answer when you call our name, then to follow you where you lead. Amen.

Encountering the text

Some have called the third and fourth chapters of John's Gospel the "book of signs." Taking last Sunday's story of Jesus and Nicodemus and contrasting it with this Sunday's Gospel of Jesus and the Samaritan woman can lead to some interesting insights.

Whereas Nicodemus was a "Jewish leader...a teacher of Israel" (John 3:1, 10), a man who comes to Jesus by night in the capital city of Jerusalem, this "woman" is mentioned four times as a "Samaritan" (4:7-10). Jesus comes to her in the middle of the day at noon. In case we miss the point of her Samaritan outcast status, John tells us directly, "Jews and Samaritans didn't associate with each other" (4:9). Her questionable marital status just compounds her sense of distance from the righteous.

Nicodemus is introduced to us as the one who "came to Jesus" (3:2). By the way, that phrase is repeated in his later appearances (7:50; 19:39). When he talks to Jesus, he has very little to say. He has come to Jesus out of curiosity.

What a contrast Jesus's conversation with the Samaritan woman is! When Jesus speaks to her of "living water" (4:10), she immediately engages Jesus in a discussion of "flowing water."

"Sir, give me this water," she exclaims (4:15). She calls Jesus a "prophet," referring to the different locations of worship for Samaritans and Jews.

This woman, who is thoroughly depicted as an outsider, becomes a wonderful image for us of the one who, though marginalized, comes forward in the broad light to follow Jesus. Jesus comes to her, reaches out to her, and engages her in conversation. Nicodemus, by contrast, is the well-informed but misunderstanding traditionalist. Though he is an "insider" and she is so thoroughly an "outsider," Jesus engages her, teaches her, and appears to win her over. The story ends with the woman at least tentatively using that controversial term for Jesus—*Christ*.

Perhaps today's sermon is a good time to contrast the relationship between "insiders" and "outsiders" in Jesus. Whereas the insider sees Jesus, Jesus seeks the outsider. It reminds you of the stories that Jesus told in other Gospels when he was criticized for the company that he kept and where Jesus said that he had come "to seek and to save the lost." Jesus has this thing for the lost. His love is border-breaking, boundary-breaking, and seeking love.

Proclaiming the text

I was born into the church. I can't remember a time when I was not a Christian. When I was a child, my mother read from a large Bible storybook for children every morning. After a few years I knew by heart nearly all of the major Bible stories, Hebrew Scriptures, and New Testament. We went to church almost every Sunday, certainly every Sunday that we were in town.

George, however, was not born into a Christian home. In fact, George noted later that no one in his family—at least no one anyone could remember—had ever been active in a church. George said that as a child, he would see people entering a church on Sunday morning, as his family would be making their way to the lake. He would ask his mother, "What happens at a church?" And all his mother would say in response? "We don't do that."

When I was a teenager, the church was there just when I needed it. We attended a large Methodist church in downtown Greenville. The church had a wonderful program of activities for the youth. During my teenage years, we had a succession of talented and able directors of Christian education. I became active in the church youth group when I entered junior high and continued through high school. I met my best friends there. We went to church camp in the summer and to large youth assemblies across the state. At one of these youth assemblies on missions, I met a professor from our nearby church college, and he talked me into attending that college. So it seemed only natural for me to complete the Christian education that I had received in high school by going to one of my church's colleges.

George, however, had a rather stormy youth. He was in and out of petty trouble. He fell in with the "wrong kind of crowd" as they sometimes say. It was also said that George was the leader of that kind of crowd. He never did anything too serious, though the police did pick him up on one occasion and charged him with vandalism after some windows were broken in the school gym. He was also charged with speeding through a school zone right after he got his license. School was a struggle for him. When it came time to graduate from high school, he had to search far and wide for a college that would admit him. The whole town had a tradition of having a baccalaureate service for our town's high school graduates at First Baptist Church. Just about all of us were there in our caps and gowns the day before our graduation for this service of worship. All of us except George.

I expect that most people here this morning, if you look back over your life, resemble me more than they do George. Most of us have been here, in the church, as long as we can remember. It would be difficult for us to remember all the way back before we were not a Christian. We are here because we were put here.

But there are a few of you who more resemble my friend George. You came to this faith later in life. You arrived here at the church innocent and uninformed. The Bible was confusing to you. The strange language that was used mystified you. It is as if you had entered some strange, new world.

Some of us have been here so long that we feel like "insiders." Others of us are still new, fresh, recently arrived, and we could be labeled "outsiders."

Now today's Gospel is the story about Jesus and an outsider—the Samaritan woman. She is an outsider on at least two counts. She is a Samaritan, which ethnic group faithful Jews regarded as renegades, heretics, and outsiders. For any Jew, the phrase "good Samaritan" is an oxymoron. She is also a woman. She is on the margin of a patriarchal society. She could take no active part in the religious life of Israel. She is the very embodiment of the outsider.

And if you were here last Sunday you remember that Jesus was there in conversation with an insider—Nicodemus. Nicodemus was very much an insider, a "teacher," a "ruler of the Jews." He was an official, an authority. So here, two Sundays in succession, we've got two very different and memorable stories of encounters with Jesus—one an insider and one an outsider.

Nicodemus comes to Jesus, seeks him out, but by night. Jesus initiates the encounter with the woman. He strikes up a conversation with her while she is out drawing water in the middle of the day. She surely had no intention of engaging in a theological discussion when she went out to get water. She wasn't looking for a savior. Jesus came to her. And in coming to her, Jesus engages her in one of the most lively and interesting conversations in the entire Gospel of John. He speaks to her of deep truths, tells her of the availability of "living water," gets personal with her, delving into the innermost secrets of her life.

Jesus's conversation with Nicodemus ends a bit inconclusively, to say the least. Nicodemus has very little to say to Jesus except repeatedly, "How can this be?" He ends the conversation befuddled, staggering forth. We will hear about him later, but having thought about Jesus, we wonder how much he really understood of Jesus.

The woman, however, engages Jesus in lively give-and-take conversation. The encounter ends with her running to tell her friends, "Come see a man who told me everything I ever did! He can't be the Messiah, can he?"

And if you are an "insider," if you have been in church on many Sundays, you probably know, in my contrast of these two stories from the Gospel of John, how things are stacked. Generally, Jesus appears to have better luck with the outsiders than the insiders. Note that the insiders seek out Jesus. They go to Jesus, trying to figure him out on their terms. But Jesus goes to the outsiders. He seeks them out, engages them. Jesus comes to them, before they have a chance to come to Him.

In fact, I don't think it is too much of an overstatement to say that the Gospels are prejudiced toward the outsiders. Jesus got into all manner of trouble for spending so much time with outsiders, the uninformed, the unfaithful, and the uncommitted like this scandalous conversation with the Samaritan woman. "This man received sinners!" was the great charge against Jesus in other Gospels.

"The Son of Man came to seek and to save the lost," was Jesus's reply.

In any church of my acquaintance on any given Sunday that's who still gathers with Jesus. In any church there are mainly two types of folk in conversation with Jesus—insiders and outsiders. The insiders know a great deal about religion, or at least think we do, and we are often depicted in the Gospels as those who are confused by Jesus, who have difficulty figuring him out, who think we know a lot about faith, only to be surprised by Jesus when he uncovers how little we know about him.

The outsiders presume, like the woman at the well, that they don't know that much about religion. And maybe that's the best precondition for knowing. Outsiders are sometimes made to feel inadequate, second-rate, marginalized by us insiders. This is strange since, as we have said, the Gospels bend over backward to show that Jesus seeks out, leans toward, reaches to the outsiders. In fact, I think it fair to say that a church can be judged by how many "outsiders" it gathers on a Sunday morning. If, when we gather here to worship, we have nothing but people like me, "insiders," then we are not the church that Jesus gathers, because Jesus has decided to tilt toward the outsiders.

So this morning, whether you find yourself as an insider or an outsider, know this: Jesus has found you. He seeks us out, engages us, and begins the conversation. He gives us what we need. To the insiders he gives a challenge, prods us, sometimes confuses us, and pushes us off balance so that we are forced to journey with him toward new understandings and experiences of faith. He thereby reminds us that we are on a journey with him and we are not at the destination yet. To the outsiders he gives welcome, conversation, encouragement, and embrace.

Where do you find yourself this Sunday? Would you call yourself an insider or an outsider? Know that today's Gospel, the story of Jesus and the Samaritan woman, is a reminder that wherever you are, Jesus has found you. He calls you. So enjoy the conversation!

Relating the text

A scientist takes a rather cynical view of the notion that God has created a benevolent, purposeful world for us. The world, for this scientist, is empty and forlorn: "If there is a purpose in the universe, it is remarkably elusive. If things were arranged for human habitation and happiness, it's being kept a secret from us, hard though we look."

—William H. Calvin, *The Ascent of Mind* (New York: Bantam, 1990), 200

Jesus appears to get a better response from this outsider, this Samaritan, this woman, than he got from the insider, the man, Nicodemus, last Sunday. If you look out over your congregation, how many "Samaritan women" can you count on a Sunday morning? Or do you mostly look out upon a gathering of Nicodemuses? What does this say about your congregation? Evangelism might be the supreme test for the fidelity of a church. And evangelism might be defined as the enjoyment of Jesus as he engages the outsiders and brings them in. Will we be with Jesus as he reaches out to the world, or will we merely hunker down in our cozy enclave of the elect?

Fourth Sunday in Lent

1 Samuel 16:1-13

Psalm 23

Ephesians 5:8-14

John 9:1-41

All I Know Is . . .

Selected reading

John 9:1-41

Theme

We live in a world in which we have attempted to stablize and fix, to protect and insulate ourselves from intrusions of the divine. Yet, in unexplained, miraculous moments, God intrudes among us, comes to us, and there is healing and vision. Although our modern means of describing our lives and conceptualizing our experience hinder us, we need to testify to what we have seen and heard and to point the world toward a power, a presence, and a love that is beyond our actions and resources.

Introduction to the readings

1 Samuel 16:1-13

David is anointed as king over Israel by the prophet Samuel.

Ephesians 5:8-14
The writer to the Ephesians gives instruction in how Christians should live as "children of light" (v. 8).

John 9:1-41
Jesus heals a man who has been blind from birth. His healing immediately touches off a heated religious controversy.

Prayer

"Awesome Lord, you will forgive us if we prefer you just a bit more familiar. We are sure you do not mean to frighten us, but distance and difference can be unsettling. We love the Grand Canyon but prefer not to get too close to the rim. Come to us, but be less dramatic. We have all the drama we can stand just getting through the day. So we dread how you come to us this and every day—crucified. We stand speechless before the majesty of your cross, frightened yet attracted. How unexpected to learn the awesome distance between you and us by your nearness. Amen."

—Stanley M. Hauerwas, *Prayers Plainly Spoken* (Eugene, OR: Wipf and Stock, 2003), 114

Encountering the text

This wonderfully crafted Johannine story is the story of Jesus and the man born blind. It begins with a man who is unable to see, whose infirmity is debated by those who can see. By the end of the story, only the blind man really sees. He is blind "from birth." This is no temporary or recent malady. It was the way he was born, the way he was created, so the question "Why is he blind?" takes on added seriousness and theological weight.

The belief that illness is the result of sin is well substantiated in scripture (see Exod 20:5; Luke 12:1-5). Jesus does not seem to buy in to the conventional linkage of sickness and sin, but his explanation is hardly more palatable to modern sensibility. Strangely, Jesus alludes to his coming death. If there is healing work done here, it is done against a background of controversy and contention.

Jesus explicitly proclaims that he is the "light of the world" (John 9:5). The blind man is going to be given light, sight. The miracle is the cause of religious controversy. It is typical for John to depict almost every work that Jesus does as the occasion for controversy and division of opinion.

Is the man's appearance after the healing so drastically changed that the neighbors cannot recognize him? He must say, "I am the man." Perhaps they had so stereotyped him as merely "a blind man" that they cannot conceive of him in his new condition. They conduct their own experiment on him, keep asking him what is going on (9:11). The work of Jesus has caused a large amount of "cognitive dissonance" as sociologists might put it. They can't fix the man's present state within their field of reference. They can't explain, with their conventional categories, just what has happened here.

The man's parents are summoned (9:18-23). They, seeing the controversy the healing has caused, are reluctant to answer. The Pharisees are the religious experts here who feel an authorization to try to sort out just what has happened. But no one wants to give credit to Jesus. No one wants to admit that some new and uncontained power is loose here.

One might have thought that there would be jubilation that a blind man now sees. No. There is controversy and dangerous dissension. The religious authorities, the keepers of revelation, seem to sense that they may be in danger of losing their grip on the movements of God. They can't have some uncredentialed, unaccredited miracle worker roaming about without their authorization!

Thus even the man's parents are reluctant to testify to what has happened. Everyone, even the man, seems reluctant to confess the strange and wonderful healing work of Jesus.

The man himself, despite the wonder that has happened to him, is not yet prepared to make a theological confession about the messianic identity of

Jesus. All he knows is that his once-tragic situation has been dramatically changed.

Moody Smith (in *John*, Abingdon New Testament Commentary [Nashville: Abingdon Press, 1999], 197) believes that, behind this once-blind man's reluctant but nevertheless insightful confession of Jesus lies the controversy within the second-century synagogue. Some Jews felt compelled to confess that something had changed, that something had been revealed to them about Jesus of Nazareth, that he was the Christ. And that confession sparked controversy, perhaps even expulsion of these members from the synagogue.

The man does not yet know everything about Jesus. Yet, on the basis of his experience, he knows that Jesus has dramatically changed his situation. The authority of his own experience now trumps the authority of the religious experts. "All I know is that once I was blind, but now I see."

Jesus is thus depicted as the one who miraculously brings sight to the blind, the one who reveals himself through his compassionate works. But that revelation is not without controversy. Revelation is a challenge to the powers that be. The once-blind man engages in a debate with the religious experts and scholars. They may know more theology than he, but he does have his experience and doggedly clings to what he knows. He doesn't know much Bible, but, "All I know is . . ."

Let us preach this as a parable of what it is sometimes like to be the recipient of divine disclosure.

Proclaiming the text

I've got a friend who is a pastor who taught here at the seminary a number of years ago. Not too long ago, when he came by here for a visit, he told me that he had just had a very difficult experience at his church. The furnace at the parsonage had malfunctioned. Someone came to check it out. The furnace got a clean bill of health, but it was not in good order, as things turned out.

One Saturday in January, my friend awoke early and tried to get out of bed. But he couldn't get fully awake. He thought he was simply tired from the night before, so he went back to sleep. He awoke later and, in a stupor, looked at the alarm clock. It was almost noon! He tried to get up out of bed. His head was throbbing, and he could not move. He couldn't get up, so he fell back in the bed.

At that moment he saw a small child, a little girl, dressed in white. "How did you get in here?" he heard himself ask. "What is a child doing here in my house?"

The little girl gestured toward him, pointing him toward the door. She said something to him like, "You must get up and get out, or you will never get out."

He struggled out of bed at her urging, crawled through the bedroom door and out of the house, and collapsed on the front steps. The child was gone.

Heating experts were called. The house was full of carbon monoxide.

Now, as I said, my friend is a pastor, a theologian. He is not given to flights of fancy. He told me, "I think that 'child' in my room was some sort of angel. I think God sent her to warn me."

I was skeptical, but I kept my skepticism to myself. I told him to be careful to whom he told the story!

"All I know is, a few minutes more, and I'd have been dead."

I hear an echo there of the story that is today's Gospel. Jesus meets a man who has been blind from birth. With some spit and dust, he heals him. Hallelujah! A man who was once blind can now see.

But not so fast. A controversy breaks out. Was this man really healed? How was he healed? If Jesus healed him, what does that say about Jesus?

Fortunately, a group of religious scholars, Pharisees, appears on the scene to help sort things out, religiously speaking.

"Who sinned so that he was born blind, this man or his parents?" they ask (9:2). They, like lots of religious people, want to talk sin, blame, theodicy. Why do bad things happen to good (or in this case) bad people?

Jesus doesn't get caught up in their theological gymnastics. He just heals the man.

The neighbors can't believe it. Isn't this the same blind man who once had to beg to survive?

The religious leaders launch a thorough investigation, get a government research grant, conduct rigorous scientific studies. "All I know," said the man, "is that this man put this stuff on my eyes, and I see. I think he's a prophet."

Though the man is standing right there in front of them, nobody believes it. The man's parents are summoned.

"Is this your son?" the authorities ask.

The parents say, "Looks like our son, but we don't want to get into any big theological controversies. We have no idea how he got his sight back. Ask him."

They call the man back in and say, "This Jesus doesn't have a medical degree, is not on the roll of the AMA. He is a sinner. Now admit that he is a sinner." The surely bewildered blind man says, "I don't know all that much about sin, salvation, sanctification, and all that big religious stuff. All I know is a few days ago I was blind, and now I can see."

"Tell us one more time, from the start, how did he heal you?" religious leaders ask.

"Do I have to go over all this again?" he said. "I have never even seen flowers growing. If you are so interested in explaining all this, why don't you go ask Jesus yourself. Maybe you want to be one of his disciples."

This sends the religion department into a frenzy. They accuse the man of insulting the orthodox faith and throw him out of the synagogue.

On the man's way out, somebody heard him mumbling to himself, "I didn't even want to get into a theological discussion. All I know is that once I was blind, and now I..."

Isn't this a curious story? I know lots of people who think that they are open-minded, intellectual, and curious, that they courageously receive the facts and follow the evidence, no matter where it leads. But sometimes, if the facts or the evidence challenge their settled modern worldview and don't fit their preconceptions of what can and what can't be, well, they simply reject it.

Henry David Thoreau once said that some circumstantial evidence is so strong as to be almost impossible to refute, such as when you find a trout in a pale of milk.

If there is a fact, some obvious and irrefutable piece of evidence, who can ignore or deny the facts?

Almost anybody can, that's who. Each of us lives in an assumptive world, a realm that is bound by certain steadfast convictions of what can and cannot be. When something happens, we rush to fit it into our assumptive world. We have a set of boxes, each one a cause that explains why something happened. When something happens, we rush to file it away in one of those boxes. This caused that, that caused this, and so forth.

Though her surgery was terribly painful, disfiguring, and difficult, she made it through. She found a whole new life for herself and new dignity and a sense of mission. Her recovery was rather miraculous.

In fact, she called it a miracle. "God miraculously gave me the hope and the strength I needed to go on," she said.

I was there when she said that to two friends: "God gave me the hope and the strength to go on."

One friend said, "You have always been a strong person."

The other said, "I don't know anyone who has a stronger sense of self than you."

Isn't it curious how this confession—"God miraculously gave me the hope and strength to go on"—is regarded as a threat?

It is the nature of a miracle to be an intrusion, a dislocation of the expected and the explained. Rather than say, "Wow, that's interesting!" in the face of miraculous claims, we are conditioned to say, "Let's get all the experts together and explain what happened using the conventional, socially acceptable modes of explanation, okay?"

Around a university, sometimes discussions about "the stuff"—debates, methods of research, and procedures for verification—can be a means of avoiding the stuff.

Here was a man who was once blind, and now he can see. And nobody takes time to wonder, to give thanks, to celebrate with him. The whole thing is turned into an intellectual problem. Let's all get together and explain this in such a way that we reassure ourselves that nothing new, nothing that doesn't fit our reassuring modes of explanation has occurred here. Because if something truly new had happened, and if it had happened by the hand of Jesus, then we might have to go back to the drawing board and rethink a few of our cherished assumptions like "if you are sick, you must have sinned," or "there is nothing new under the sun," or "it's up to us to fix the world or the world won't get fixed."

He came to me and said, "After my summer internship in South Africa, I believe that God has called me to give my life in working with the poor."

And I, as a religious expert, a theological scholar who sometimes has to burst the balloon of some of these lay religious fanatics, said to him, "I can understand how you may have gotten on this religious high, but you have no gifts for working with the poor. You are a philosophy major! You're going to Soweto to tell them about Socrates? I know that you feel some guilt after that stuff with what's-her-name your freshman year, but you don't need to go to South Africa to get over that."

And he said, "Well, all I know is that I felt the presence of God in those children. I felt like Jesus touched my life in a way that was undeniable. All I know is that this summer I've felt a joy such as never before."

I wish I had said, "Go ahead. Trust your experience. Clinch your fists and believe. Ignore the narrow-mindedness of the world. Go with what God has given you. Go with what you know."

Relating the text

"Brennan Manning tells the story of a recent convert to Jesus who was approached by an unbelieving friend:

'So you have been converted to Christ?'

'Yes.'

'Then you must know a great deal about Him. Tell me, what country was he born in?'

'I don't know.'

'What was his age when he died?'

'I don't know.'

'How many sermons did he preach?'

'I don't know.'

'You certainly know very little for a man who claims to be converted to Christ.'

'You are right. I am ashamed at how little I know about him. But this much I know: Three years ago I was a drunkard. I was in debt. My family was falling to pieces; they dreaded the sight of me. But now I have given up drink. We are out of debt. Ours is a happy home. My children eagerly await my return home each evening. All this Christ has done for me. This much I know of Christ!'"

—Michael Yaconelli, *Messy Spirituality* (Grand Rapids: Zondervan, 2002), 49

"Some had the experience of God implanted in their hearts. Have you ever gotten up in the morning before the rest of the family, gone out on the back steps with a cup of coffee, and cupped your hands around it against the morning chill? Or, late in the evening, have you ever walked down the back roads and along the rivers of your memory? What do you think about? As an African saying puts it, 'We know somebody walks in the trees at night.' People have had experiences, but we don't often talk about them."

—Fred B. Craddock, *The Cherry Log Sermons* (Louisville: Westminster John Knox, 2001), 55

Fifth Sunday in Lent

Ezekiel 37:1-14

Psalm 130

Roman 8:6-11

John 11:1-45

Amid Sickness and Death—Life

Selected reading

John 11:1-45

Theme

Into our world of fear and death, of endings and beginnings, Jesus comes. Death, our final, greatest fear, is encountered and defeated. Whenever Jesus wades into our fearful, settled arrangements with death, life breaks out. Still does.

Introduction to the readings

Ezekiel 37:1-14

In a vision, Ezekiel sees a valley of dry, dead bones. "Can these bones live again?" (v. 3). A wind from God works a miraculous transformation.

Romans 8:6-11

Paul contrasts the life of the flesh with the life of the Spirit: "the one who raised Christ from the dead will give life to your human bodies," says Paul (v. 11).

John 11:1-45

John tells the story of the sickness of Lazarus, brother of Mary and Martha, and Jesus's visit to Lazarus's tomb.

Prayer

Lord Jesus, into our dying, sick world, you bring life. Your light is determined to shine into our darkness. Your life is insistent on bursting the bonds of our death. Forgive us, Lord Christ, our attempts to secure our lives on our own— to eat right, to live right, to act right, to think right—rather than rest secure in your love and grace.

Disrupt our limited notions of just what can and can't be done in this world. Open our minds to the surprises that you want to work among us. Help us to enjoy your creative determination not to let the cross be the last word on your work. Bring us Easter, even though it is still Lent. Amen.

Encountering the text

The story of Lazarus and Jesus doesn't linger long over Lazarus's fatal illness. Quickly there is a move away from Mary, Martha, and their brother Lazarus to Jesus. Lazarus's illness and death are an opportunity to proclaim the glory of God (John 11:4). Jesus will dramatically demonstrate that his is the life we are seeking in the midst of this death-dealing world.

In the face of death, Jesus proclaims not that "I've come to resurrect someone" but rather that "I am the resurrection and the life." The dramatic story is a study in the various responses of people to Jesus. The story also reveals the various "gods" to which we cling. Mary and Martha are frantic with worry about the death of their brother. They do not ask for resurrection or life; they ask for some temporary respite of their brother's illness.

Jesus's critics witness this wonder of a once-dead man coming out of the tomb and despise Jesus more than ever. In fact, the raising of Lazarus is that point where the resistance to Jesus begins to become murderous. Why are Jesus's critics so enflamed by the raising of Lazarus?

Jesus appears to have upset the accustomed order of things. He has disrupted people's expectations. In the Gospel of John, the accustomed and the expected become de-familiarized. Strange things happen. We are in a new, unexpected, even unsought new world. It is the world now that the Word has become flesh. It is the world after the advent of Jesus.

In John's Gospel "eternal life" is now. Into this world of life and death a savior has come. The Word has become flesh. Heaven has touched down on earth. Therefore, hold on to your hat, when it comes to John's Gospel. Death is not as impressive as we first thought. The boundaries between eternity and today are blurred considerably. In the midst of death, there is life, because Jesus is the Lord of life. Jesus is on his way to the cross, but he will not let the forces of evil and death determine his direction or his life.

Though we are still deep in the season of the cross, Lent, and though Jesus is on his way to die, he stops just long enough in Bethany to resuscitate Lazarus from the dead. Here in Lent is a good time for self-examination, an opportunity to consider our own accommodation to the forces of death, a good time to consider that, if John's testimony is true, as we believe it to be, how then should we live?

Proclaiming the text

It is a very strange story, one of the strangest stories in a very strange Gospel—this story of Jesus raising Lazarus from the dead. Of course, that's the title that we usually give to this Sunday's lesson, "Jesus Raises Lazarus from the Dead." But that is not the title John gives it in John's Gospel. He doesn't give the story a title.

What is this story really about?

An urgent message is sent to Jesus, "the one whom you love is ill" (11:3). Two desperate, frightened sisters—Mary and Martha—send the message to Jesus, expecting that Jesus will rush back to Bethany to heal his sick friend.

As usual, Jesus thwarts expectation. It's the Gospel of John after all. Jesus does not rush to the bedside of Lazarus in Bethany. In fact, John says that Jesus lingered where he was for three more days. He stayed there for three more days? What was he doing? John doesn't say. John doesn't say that he was in the middle of a major theological conference and couldn't leave. John doesn't say that he was healing dozens of sick people who were sicker than Lazarus. John just says that Jesus stayed where he was for three more days.

Of course, by the time that Jesus makes his way to Bethany, it's all over. Martha comes out to tell Jesus the news. No rush now. Lazarus is dead. If only Jesus had come more quickly. Jesus goes out to the cemetery and, though Lazarus has been entombed three days, speaks and raises Lazarus from the dead. "Untie him and let him go!" Jesus says (11:44).

Now it is miraculously wonderful that Jesus has raised Lazarus from the dead, but still the question remains in my mind: Why did Jesus stay where he was for three whole days before rousing himself and going to Bethany at the request of Mary and Martha?

When I go into a church on Sunday morning, in many of the churches I visit, they have something they call "prayer requests." During this time the pastor usually reads out a list of all the people from the congregation who have been hospitalized in the previous week. Sometimes there is extended discussion within the congregation at this time, in which other people in the congregation are added to the list who have become ill over the weekend. Then prayers are offered for those who are sick.

This is what has become of Christian prayer in most of our churches—that is, prayers offered for sick people within the congregation.

Now I am all in favor of praying for the sick. And, as an aging person with increasing health problems, I am all for your praying for me and my health problems.

But don't you think it is rather remarkable that Jesus so rarely prays for sick people? Look at the Lord's Prayer. And there you will find Jesus praying for forgiveness, for daily bread, for the coming kingdom, but he doesn't mention sickness.

Nor does Jesus mention death. I would say that death, or at least the fear of death, tends to be one of our most persistent modern infatuations. Various therapies promise immortality, or at least the closest thing we can get to immortality.

I remember a development officer in the university, whose job it was to raise money for the university, who said that the major reason for his success in raising money for endowed lectureships, endowed chairs, and endowed buildings at the university was immortality. People believe that by endowing this chair, by eating this particular diet, by following this exercise regimen, they can be immortal, or at least close to it. They may not be able to completely give death the slip, but they can certainly avoid death for a long time.

When Jesus received the urgent plea of the sisters, Jesus said to them, "This illness isn't fatal. It's for the glory of God so that God's Son can be glorified through it" (11:4). Jesus lingered a couple more days where he was. Though the sisters suggest that their brother is near death, Jesus refuses to stop everything, to drop everything, and to run to the bedside of Lazarus just because of a little thing like death.

When does this whole episode occur? It occurs when Jesus is on his way to Jerusalem. That is, he is on his way to his death. In the Gospel of John, Jesus's death is spoken of as his "hour of glory." In Jesus's strange, upside-down way of looking at things, death and glory are linked. As Jesus told Mary and

Martha, this illness, this whole episode, in fact his whole earthly ministry that led to his cross, is "for the glory of God" so that Jesus might be thereby "glorified through it."

Jesus refuses to be jerked around by death, by sickness, by those matters that so totally consume us. He does not drop what he is doing and rush right over to Bethany, just on the basis of a little thing like a mortal illness. Maybe this is because Jesus wisely knows that all of us are suffering from a mortal illness.

As St. Augustine said, it is as if when a physician leans over a sick man's bed, shakes his head, and says, "I don't think he will get over this. I don't think he will come out of this alive." So on the very first day of our lives somebody could look over into our crib, shake his head, and say, "I don't think he is going to get over this. I don't think he is going to come out of this alive."

And perhaps Jesus is wise enough to know that there are some things worse than dying. Won't you agree with me when I say that for most of us, the fear of dying is worse than the dying? Most of us hope that our dying will be so quick and painless and unconscious that we will not know that we are actually dying. But most of us will probably be like Lazarus. There will be an illness, for most of us an illness lasting considerably longer than three days, and then we will die. That which we have attempted to deny or avoid will come upon us: the one certain thing about living is our dying. Ready or not, here we come.

So Jesus goes out to the cemetery and stands before the tomb and says, "Lazarus, come out!" (11:43). And Lazarus, bound up in the graveclothes, comes out. And then Jesus heads on up to Jerusalem where he will eventually die and be wrapped in graveclothes himself. So in saying, "Lazarus, come out," Jesus is also saying, "Lazarus, come with me." He is inviting Lazarus to come with him down that path that leads to death. For of course, Lazarus, even though Jesus raised him from the dead after this illness, will die again. Jesus has temporarily resuscitated Lazarus, but not really resurrected Lazarus, not yet. To be resurrected, one has to die.

"Come with me, come toward the death you are avoiding, lay your life into the hands of the living and loving God, and let God give you the life that you cannot earn for yourself. In facing your death, with me, in walking the way of the cross that I walk, you will have eternal life, and that abundantly. But first, we've got to go out to the cemetery."

Sickness is a great challenge in life. And, as we have said, death is one of the most important challenges, one of the most important eventualities that each of us must face. But perhaps, by lingering where he was for three days and not rushing right over to the bedside of his friend Lazarus in Bethany, Jesus was trying to teach us that there are some things that are much more important in the reign of God than our sickness or our dying. Namely, what's more important is the ministry, the service, whatever Jesus was doing that kept him from rushing over to Bethany to the bedside of Lazarus.

I know a woman who suffered from a debilitating illness for many months. She languished in the hospital as doctors tried first one therapy and then another, but still she was in pain and confined to her bed.

During every visit to her in the hospital, I prayed with her, and we prayed each time for healing. But the healing did not come. I prayed, on a number of occasions as I left her room, "Lord, please answer our prayers. Please come into her life and restore her to health so that she can be on her way."

But I remember the conversation we had one afternoon, as I sat by her bedside in the hospital, when she said to me, "Now, preacher, I want you to think with me about what it is that God has in store for me now."

"How do you mean, what God has in store for you now?" I muttered.

"Well, it looks like I am not going to be healed of this illness. But still, here I am. I am in a considerably weakened situation, but here I am. I can still talk. I can still think and care about people. So now I am wondering what God wants me to do now, in this situation. I am sure that, even if I am not healed of this illness, Jesus still expects me to be a disciple."

I think there was a person to whom Jesus came, a person who understood deeply the meaning of this story.

There is no way for us to find some path that is a detour around death. We are human, and all human beings must die. But there is a way to do it. We can walk with Jesus in the way of the cross. We can engage ourselves in those ministries that Jesus gives us in the time that we have.

For most of us there is no way that we can avoid illness. As human beings, from time to time we get sick, sometimes very seriously sick. But what we can do is not to let our normal, predictable frailty jerk us around and determine our destinies and the significance of our lives. Follow Jesus. We can let him lead us to some very different definitions of the abundant life.

Relating the text

A few years ago, someone noted that a couple hundred thousand children are unvaccinated in our state. Why? "Because children don't vote," said a health-care official. "We have decided that it is better politics to put a new kidney in an eighty-year-old than to vaccinate a three-year-old. The great majority of funds expended over a lifetime of health care will be expended in the very last year of a person's life. We have decided that it is more important to keep an aging person alive, in the last years of life, to expend huge resources on holding death at bay for a few months, than to expend on making little children healthy."

Our expenditures for health care—who gets the resources and for what purpose—is an interesting commentary on our values.

William James pointed out that at last two things inform religious faith: a "sense that there is something wrong about us" (an uneasiness) and a sense that "we are saved from the wrongness by making proper connection with the higher powers" (its solution).

—William James, *The Varieties of Religious Experience* (New York: Literary Classics of the United States, 1987), 454

John Calvin shared his age's generalized anxiousness over death. Death was that which rendered all of life, even the best of life, as anxious and unpredictable:

"Innumerable are the evils that beset human life; innumerable, too, the deaths that threaten it. We need not go beyond ourselves: since our body is the receptacle of a thousand diseases—in fact holds within itself and fosters the causes of diseases—a man cannot go about unburdened by many forms of his own destruction, and without drawing out a life enveloped, as it were, with death.... Now, wherever you turn, all things around you not only are hardly to be trusted but almost openly menaced and seem to threaten immediate death."

—John Calvin, *The Institutes of the Christian Religion*, ed. John T. McNeill, trans. Ford Lewis Battles (Philadelphia: Westminster, 1960), 1:223

Passion/Palm Sunday

Liturgy of the Passion

Isaiah 50:4-9a

Psalm 31:9-16

Philippians 2:5-11

Matthew 26:14–27:66 or Matthew 27:11-54

Liturgy of the Palms

Psalm 118:1-2, 19-29

Matthew 21:1-11

Passion/Palm Peculiarity

Selected reading

Matthew 26:14–27:66

Theme

Sometimes we need to be reminded of the strangeness of the gospel. Passion/ Palm Sunday is such a time. The story of our salvation is a story that holds a mirror of truth up to the sinfulness of humanity, as well as a sign of the greatness of our savior who enters Jerusalem on this day. Let us marvel at the glorious peculiarity of salvation in Jesus Christ.

Introduction to the readings

Isaiah 50:4-9a

The prophet Isaiah asks God to help him minister to suffering and weary Israel with some word of comfort.

Philippians 2:5-11

"Though he was in the form of God, he did not consider being equal with God something to exploit. But he emptied himself by taking the form of a slave," Paul proclaims to the Philippians (vv. 6-7).

Matthew 26:14–27:66

On this Sunday we have our longest lesson of the year, the dramatic account of Jesus's arrest, trial, and crucifixion.

Prayer

Lord, even though you knew the praise of the crowd to be fickle and short-lived, even though you knew the fate that surely awaited you on Friday at Calvary, out of love you entered Jerusalem, you went to the temple, you preached your truth, you broke bread with the very disciples who would betray you, and you died before the week was over, forgiving the ones who had crucified you.

Though we are unworthy of such love, we cling to your love. We know it to be our only hope in life and in death, our peculiar comfort. For your sacrifice, for your obedient courage, for your love, for our salvation worked this week before us, we give you thanks. Amen.

Encountering the text

It is a familiar story, the long Gospel that we read on this Passion/Palm Sunday, Matthew's account of Jesus's last week before his death. The story is a rich drama that defies encapsulating in any single sermon. Perhaps we do best, rather than focus on any one part of the story, to focus upon the story as a whole—its general effect.

In a feel-good, sin-denying, death-avoiding world, this story of evil, of sin, of goodness challenged, of divine love, goes against our natural inclination.

Subjects are laid before us that we spend most of our lives avoiding. It is a story that can only be told by a courageous, obedient church.

Let us tell that story today as we meditate upon its peculiarity. Yes, peculiarity. This good news is challenging, truthful, comforting, and peculiar. It is a story that forces us to look at the truth about ourselves. It is a story that forces us to tell the truth about God. God rides in on a donkey, a humble teacher rather than a conquering hero. God takes the blow, endures the suffering, and dies. What a peculiar way for a God to act.

I suggest that on this very special Sunday, that you read the Gospel lesson in a special way. It is a long story, the longest text of the church year. And it is a very good story. Let the sermon, which usually follows the Gospel, precede the Gospel. Preach your sermon, then read the Gospel lesson afterward, ending this Sunday's service in somber reflection upon the events that unfold this holy week.

Proclaiming the text

I've got a friend, a mortician, who claims that I only have about three sermons in my bag of tricks. These three sermons, he claims, I preach in endless repetition, with few variations. One sermon is something to the effect that, "God is large, mysterious, and there is no way I could explain it to someone like you." The other is, "Life is a mess, and there is no way that I can explain it to someone like you."

The third constantly recurring sermon is this: "Christianity is weird, odd, peculiar, and I can't believe you people actually want to be Christians."

Well, as I said, my friend is a mortician. Still, he has a point. Today, you get sermon number three, the peculiarity of being Christian.

And, I don't know about you, but I think the days after September 11, 2001, when we all joined the "9-11 Generation," I really began feeling very peculiar as a Christian.

The peculiarity began here at Duke Chapel, just after September 11. The campus ministers planned to have a prayer service every day at noon, after the tragedy. Every day at noon, here in the chapel, people gathered for prayer. Trouble was, Friday, President Bush declared the "National Day of Prayer." The campus ministers, unaccustomed to having the president tell us to pray, expected about fifty students to show up. They walked in here and there were twelve hundred people prepared to pray. The campus minister leading the service, who was an evangelical, proceeded to lead the gathered congregation in prayer—a prayer of confession. He implied, in his prayer, that we were in trouble as Americans because of our sin, our materialism, our insensitivity to the needs of the rest of the world, our immorality.

Lots and lots of people were deeply offended. People had come for comfort, or celebration, or something, but not for admission and confession of sin.

Now I, as a more compassionate pastor, was offended. I thought this campus minister's timing was terrible. It seemed to me that it was too soon for such honesty. We wanted talk of retribution, justice, comfort, and consolation, not confession.

But I had to admit that he had a point. After all, the very next Sunday we gathered for worship. And what was the first thing—or almost the first thing—we did? We confessed our sin. That's peculiar. We North American Christians are not that much into sin. We like to think that we are basically nice people who are making progress. Thoughts of sin are, well, peculiar.

What's American right now is to feel like a victim, an innocent victim, or maybe a righteous crusader, not a sinner. So, in such a context, church is peculiar because church is where we get everyone together on a weekly basis and teach you that you are a sinner. That's odd.

In today's scripture, Jesus is led away for arrest and crucifixion. But it wasn't just the Roman soldiers who did it. Those words, those terrible words in Matthew 26:56, "Then they all [including his own disciples] forsook him and fled."

Not just Judas, but Jesus's other eleven best friends were also guilty. We will admit as much later in this service when we shout, "Crucify him!" in response to the question, "What should we do with Jesus?"

The same ones who have sung, "Praise him!" are those who shout, "Crucify him!" (Matt 27:23).

Do you have any idea of how odd it is to say that?

A pastor told me about seeing a reporter interviewing a couple who had just lost their adult daughter in the destruction of the World Trade Center. They were in great grief, of course. After talking with them, the reporter seemed to feel the need to say something nice, so he said, "Well, I suppose that when you go to your place of worship this weekend, you will, er, find some comfort."

"We're not going to our church this weekend," the mother said. "You see, our faith teaches forgiveness of enemies, and we're just not ready for that."

There was a person who knew a thing or two about trying to follow a savior who, when he was being arrested for crucifixion, refused to defend himself, refused to let us defend him. (What in God's name is wrong with self-defense?) And then he died (I didn't make this up; it's in this morning's Gospel), forgiving the very ones who crucified him. Odd.

More than one preacher told me of his or her delight at increased church attendance after September 11, 2001. They reported seeing people in church whom they had not seen in a long time. Great!

Alas, a number of these preachers have confirmed that they have had some tough times with these returns and newcomers.

"One person asked why we couldn't have the pledge of allegiance to the flag on Sunday," one of them told me. "And I said, 'How long has it been since you've been in a church? We've got our hands full just trying to be citizens of God's kingdom. We don't have time for any of that patriotic stuff.'" Odd.

In the months after the September 11 tragedy, many of us worked overtime to try to figure out what all this meant. In the days after the tragedy, it became cliché to say things like, "the world as we know it has changed forever," or "this is the most important event in our nation's history."

Lent, any Lent, is a good time to be reminded that Christians are those people, odd as we are, who believe this: The worst thing that was ever done in the long record of human injustice was not what happened to us in the destruction of two great buildings. It was what happened to Jesus on a cross.

Christians believe this: a whole new world began, or the world was changed forever, not on a Tuesday in early morning in Manhattan, but on a Friday at noon at Calvary.

Why would anyone hold such peculiar views? To answer that, you must listen to a strange story, all the more strange because it is true.

[Read today's Gospel from Matthew.]

Relating the text

Great Lutheran preacher and teacher of preachers Paul Scherer began a sermon by saying, "My text is 'God is love!'—not 'love is God!'" And he went on to preach on the cross:

"Let me read the text as it should be read, putting the emphasis where it belongs: not God is *love*, but *God* is love. When you say it that way, you are saying the costliest thing that could be said of God. You are not talking any longer simply of affection, of kindliness, of tender regard. To say as the Bible says, 'God so loved the world, that He gave his only begotten Son,' is precisely in that measure, by all the width of the sky, different from saying that God is either fond of it or mildly amused by it. Its symbol is the cross, where God has come to meet us under the very burden and weight of all our sin and suffering, in order that just there, by paying down on the counter of human life and human history the price of His own coming, He might give us the pledge of victory. That's what genuine love is all about."

—Paul Scherer, "The Love That God Defines!" in *The Word God Sent*
(New York: Harper & Row, 1965), 225–33

What I was told in seminary was something like this: when you preach, you try to lessen the gap between your congregation and the gospel. You start with the Bible over here, and then you reach out—through careful illustration, real-life stories, references to the daily newspaper—to those who are seated over there in the pews.

The preacher is the person who closes the gap, that great divide between contemporary people and today's gospel.

But this Sunday, with Jesus coming into Jerusalem and about to bring out the worst in us, I wonder. Perhaps my best role as a preacher is to widen the gap, to point out the vast difference between Jesus and us. We look at Jesus—God in the flesh—and find him, well, peculiar. This is not exactly what we expected of God and not exactly what we expected God to expect of us.

It's peculiar. And there is just no way to speak truthfully of that peculiarity without sounding a bit, well, peculiar.

Terrifying Friday

Selected reading

John 18:1–19:42

Theme

The story of the crucifixion of Jesus is a violent, terrifying tale of blood, torture, suffering, and death. And yet Christians believe that the events of Good Friday are integral to our salvation. In these terrible events, God is working for our good, bringing all creation into divine embrace. God is with us.

Introduction to the readings

Isaiah 52:13–53:12

Isaiah speaks of the "servant" who "carried the sin of many and pleaded on behalf of those who rebelled" (v. 12).

Hebrews 10:16-25

The Letter to the Hebrews speaks of a covenant that is in their hearts and of forgiveness made possible by the blood of Jesus.

John 18:1–19:42

John tells of the betrayal and denial of Jesus by his own disciples and the trial and terrible crucifixion of Jesus.

Prayer

Almighty God, who for our sakes became human in Jesus Christ, give us the grace to bear the truth that confronts us on this Good Friday. May we, through honest confession of our sin, come to see the ways that we have rebelled against your will for us, despoiled your creation, wasted the opportunities that you have given us, and failed to live up to your loving desires for us.

Grant us the insight to gaze upon your tortured body on the cross and see there the truth of the depth of your love for us, the way that you take upon yourself our sin and bridge the great gap between you and ourselves.

Make this holy day for us a day of truth, your truth. Amen.

Encountering the text

The story that the church tells today is familiar to everyone who will be in church on Good Friday. In a way it is the story that is at the heart of the faith—the passion and death of Christ.

The theological significance of the betrayal and crucifixion of Christ is deep and mysterious, requiring the church's greatest theological reflection down through the centuries. What do we mean when we say, "Christ died for our sin"?

I suggest that you not delve into theological reflection this Good Friday but rather that you simply read the story and reflect upon the self-evident, obvious quality of the passion. It is a horribly violent, terrifying tale.

There are people who think the Christian faith is wrong to form itself around such a violent story. We will say basically two things about the passion: First, it is a story that tells the harsh but real truth about ourselves—that is, we are indeed violent people who tend to crucify our saviors. Second, God does not shrink from entering into the full human condition, even the worst of it, in order to be with us so that God might save us.

Proclaiming the text

We were working our way through some key portions of the Old Testament and I had warned the women's Bible study group that on this Wednesday we would deal with what I called "texts of terror." I got the phrase from a ground-breaking book by Phyllis Tribble (*Texts of Terror: Literary-Feminist Readings of Biblical Narratives* [Minneapolis: Fortress Press, 1984]).

Because it was a women's Bible study, I opened with Jael, who is called "blessed above all women" (Judg 5:24). I told them Jael hammered a tent peg through the skull of sleeping Sisera, an enemy general. There were gasps from a few of the students. Then I told them about Judith, who faked lust for Holofernes, an Assyrian commander, then prayed, "Give me strength today, Lord God of Israel!" (Judith 13:7). She then plunged his own sword into his neck. Oh yes, then there was the wife of the Persian king, who won permission for the Jews throughout her husband's Persian empire to destroy, to kill, and to annihilate as many as seventy-five thousand of their enemies (Esth 9:13-16). Well, the Bible study ended awkwardly with some of the women complaining about my need to "use some discretion in the parts of the Bible you discuss."

By anyone's reckoning, these are indeed "texts of terror." Mostly we ignore these stories (and there are many others) in which there is violence and blood-shed, often in the name of God. I once got into all sorts of trouble for men-tioning that Ananias and Sapphira were struck dead for withholding part of their cash from the early Christian community (Acts 5:1-11). "It's just not an appropriate sort of story for church," I was told.

And yet this day, this Friday we call "Good," we cannot ignore an even more horrifying tale. In reading the story of the passion of Christ, his torture and death, we know that we have left the notion of the Bible as a book filled with exemplary people and a nice, admirable God. Instead, the Bible is revealed, in this story, to be a book about God's relentless determination to love violent, bloody sinners, even if God has to die to do it.

We don't do too well with these terrifying moments of scripture. Who wants to face Elisha cursing a crowd of jeering boys "in the name of the Lord," after which two she-bears appear and maul forty-two of them (2 Kgs 2:23-24)? And God asks Abraham to kill his only child. And in this day, we come to the climactic moment of the whole Jesus story, that ominous event toward which we have been moving steadily each Sunday—God's will puts God's own beloved child on the cross. Many wonder, "How can we believe in a loving God who does or at least allows such unloving things?" How do we believe in a God who evokes such "texts of terror"?

We can try to interpret them in a way that makes them seem less terrible. God sent a ram to take Isaac's place at the last moment. God raised Jesus from the dead. Thus the terrible tales become stories of rescue and resurrection. But that diffuses some of the real terror of worshipping and obeying God and not knowing that there will be rescue, the terror of thinking that you are doing the right thing only to learn later that you did not. That also ignores the terrible truth of the stories in which God sanctions violence: killing every firstborn in Egypt before Passover (Exod 11:5) or ordering Saul to slaughter the Amalekites down to the last woman, child, and donkey (1 Sam 15:3).

It is a great mystery how a loving, generous God somehow gets implicated in all this, just as it is a mystery how God is able to take even the most terrible of terrors of this day on Calvary and weave even this into God's purposes. But there is no mystery that these stories, as terrible as they are, are stories about us.

We like to think that we have at last risen above these terrible events. Of course, we think that from the safety and security of a country that has no war here at home—though we sure know how to make war elsewhere. The violence that we do generally gets done from the vantage point of others. We hire others, somewhere, to slaughter the animals that we consume in gourmet dinners, and we pay the soldiers who must go elsewhere to fight our battles, all the while talking about how good and peaceable we are.

I suppose, like sinners of every time and place, we attempt to take refuge in our presumed righteousness, living under the illusion that if we just behave properly we are terror-exempt. Obey God and avoid ever picking up a sword.

Yet we tolerate a culture in which the murder rate is higher than anywhere in the world. Nearly two million of our citizens are incarcerated in this the freest country of all. The terrors that we work tend to be subtle, but no less terrible for the victims of our legislated, economically induced, urbane terror.

And it might be possible to tell yourself that we have risen above all that Old Testament, primitive terror. We have made progress. We are progressive. We are good. Until this day—this Good Friday and the story that it has to tell. If Jesus had been nailed to the cross by demonstrably, obviously bad people, then we might be able to walk away from this story free of implication. Yet one of his own, Judas, betrayed him. All of his disciples forsook him. A huge crowd, some of whom must have warmly welcomed him into Jerusalem during the first of the week, cried, "Crucify him!"

This is what these texts of terror do for us. They rob us of our presumptions of righteousness, our smug pretentiousness that clings to the lie that we are basically good people who are doing fine after all, that is, people who don't need saving. But we are not such people, today's story tells us. We are members of the fickle, screaming crowd who one Friday marched gaily up a hill outside of town and just happened to crucify God's only Son.

What's to become of us? We have met the most terrifying of enemies and the enemy has our face, the sound of our voice. What's God going to do with us now, the terrible, terrifying mob of humanity? What's God to do with us now?

We must wait until Sunday to find out. But for now, he looks down from the cross to which we nailed him and says, "Brothers and sisters, I love you still. God forgive."

Relating the text

"A person that sees himself ready to sink into hell is ready to strive, some way or other, to lay God under some obligation to him; but he is to be beat off from everything of that nature, though it greatly increases his terror to see himself wholly destitute, on every side, of any refuge, of any thing of his own to lay hold of; as a man that sees himself in danger of drowning is in terror and endeavors to catch hold on every twig within his reach, and he that pulls away those twigs from him increases his terror; yet if they are insufficient to save him, and by being in his way prevent his looking to that which will save him, to pull them away is a necessity to save his life."

—Jonathan Edwards, *Thoughts on the Revival of Religion in New England, 1740: To Which Is Prefixed a Narrative of the Surprising Work of God in Northampton, Mass., 1735* (New York: American Tract Society, n.d.), 247

From the folk I talked to, I heard two reactions to Mel Gibson's film *The Passion of the Christ*. There were those who were deeply moved by the film's depiction of the horrible, intense agony of Christ, though as one of my friends noted, "It took Gibson about two hours to show us what it took Matthew only about five minutes to tell." There were others who were simply repulsed by the sheer violence of the film. One of my friends said, "The film was pornographic in the way it lingered on every horrible moment of the crucifixion. Disgusting."

There is a chance that today's proclamation, following Matthew's story of the passion, may have this same effect upon worshippers in your congregation on this Good Friday.

Imagine being asked to stand before a grand gathering of the good and the wise and being asked to make a speech about goodness, beauty, the meaning of life, the point of history, the nature of Almighty God, or some such high subject and having no material at your disposal but an account of a humiliating, bloody execution at a garbage dump outside a rebellious city in the Middle East. It is your task to argue that this story is the key to everything in life and to all that we know about God. This was precisely the position of Paul in Corinth. Before the populace of this cosmopolitan, sophisticated city of the empire, Paul had to proclaim that this whipped, bloody, scorned, and derided Jew from Nazareth was God with us.

As Paul said, he had his work cut out for him because preaching about the cross "is folly to those who are perishing" (1 Cor 1:18 RSV), foolishness, and stupidity. A cross is no way for a messianic reign to end. Yet what else can this preacher say because, whether it makes sense to us or not, "in God's wisdom, he determined that the world wouldn't come to know him through its wisdom. Instead, God was pleased to save those who believe through the foolishness of preaching" (1 Cor 1:21).

A crucified Messiah? It is an oxymoron, a violation of Israel's high expectations for a messianic liberator.

For God the Father to allow God the Son to be crucified, dead, and buried is for God to be pushed out beyond the limits of human expectation or human help. The cross is the ultimate dead end of any attempt at human self-fulfillment, human betterment, or progress. As Jesus is hanging from the cross, in humiliation and utter defeat, there is nothing to be done to vindicate the work of Jesus or to make the story come out right except "the power of God."

And the cross is also a demonstration of just how far God will go to stand (or, in the case of the cross, hang) with us in solidarity. God is with us.

Good Friday

Isaiah 52:13–53:12

Psalm 22

Hebrews 10:16-25 or Hebrews 4:14-16; 5:7-9

John 18:1–19:42

It Is Finished

Selected reading

John 19:30

Theme

On the cross Jesus did for us that which we could not do for ourselves—paid the price, did the work, atoned for our sin, brought us close to God. Jesus finished for us the work that we attempted but, in our sin and frailty, could not accomplish for ourselves. On the cross, our struggle against God, and our attempts to get to God, were finished by the God who struggled for us and who came to us.

Introduction to the readings

Isaiah 52:13–53:12

These words of prophecy were spoken initially to the Jewish people exiled in Babylon, urging them to return to rebuild Jerusalem. They also apply to God's suffering servant, the Messiah, in his work of redemption.

Hebrews 10:16-25
This passage is an invitation to encourage each other to love and do good, drawing strength in the awareness that Christ knows the hardships we encounter.

John 18:1-19:42
John's account of Christ's suffering and crucifixion lifts up the images of the paschal lamb, the good shepherd, the obedient son, and the king who will establish God's reign of justice and peace.

Prayer

On this day, Lord Jesus, you climbed up Golgotha and suffered death upon the cross, for us.

On this day, you endured the humiliation of the betrayal of your disciples, for us.

On this day, you looked down and saw the crowd, the people you loved, scream "crucify him!" for us.

On this day, you stretched out your arms and, breathing your last, died, for us.

On this day, you cast your fate totally into the hands of your Father and descended to the dead, for us.

We gather this day in great gratitude to thank you for your immeasurable gift, for us. Amen.

Encountering the text

John's Gospel is so rich, so full of symbol and metaphor. It is as if this Gospel cries out for imaginative interpretation, as if there is no way to read this Gospel without allowing it to speak to us at many levels and in many voices.

Wooden, literal readings of John just don't do justice to the richness of the Fourth Gospel.

Therefore, on this Good Friday, it seems justified to focus on just one verse of the Gospel: Jesus's last words from the cross. In this simple phrase, we see a whole world of theology. We will overlay our theology of redemption over this text.

On this day in which our atonement is being worked out by God at a terrible price as Jesus of Nazareth hangs in agony on the cross, our salvation is being accomplished. It is finished. Thanks be to God, it is finished.

Proclaiming the text
"It is finished" (John 19:30 NRSV).

When Jesus says from the cross, "It is finished," it could be read as a word of desperate surrender, of final relenting capitulation: I give up. It could be heard that way. And while it took most victims longer to die on a cross, Jesus has fought quite a battle in his hours hanging in agony. Perhaps these words show that he has finally relented and given in.

There can be virtue in surrender. I heard a stock-market analyst say a while back that it took a courageous investor to sell a losing stock. Most investors, he said, would hold on to a habitually losing stock, rather than sell, because the pain of losing the money was much less than the pain of having to admit that you were dumb to buy that stock in the first place. Only the truly smart, truly courageous, and virtuous investor was able to know when to fold, when to surrender, when to say "I goofed." Is that what Jesus is doing here?

It was a good campaign while it lasted; he gave it his best shot. Perhaps if he had been a bit more critical in his selection of disciples, he might have gotten better disciples. If he had been a bit more conciliatory toward Pilate, perhaps this thing would have gone a bit further. Now, it is finished. The end.

But I am hearing this phrase, "It is finished," in a different way. I am hearing this word as a word of achievement and completion. I am hearing this word as the same word Michelangelo uttered when he put his last touch of paint on the ceiling of the Sistine Chapel. Jesus has fought the good fight; and despite what the soldiers, the politicians, and the howling mob before him think, despite even what his own disciples think, he has succeeded. He has done it. He did not say, "I am finished." He said, "It is finished." His work is done: "He hath poured out his soul unto death: and he was numbered with the transgressors; and he bare the sin of many, and made intercession for the transgressors" (Isa 53:12 KJV). Jesus didn't die as a frustrated, failed revolutionary. His death was the revolution.

"I give up my life for the sheep. . . . No one takes it from me, but I give it up because I want to. I have the right to give it up, and I have the right to take it up again. I received this commandment from my Father" (John 10:15-18).

Though his completing work is invisible to us—all we can see from here is the horror and the blood, the defeat and the death—though we look on his cross and see nothing but the last, the end, the loss, something grand and glorious is being worked out despite us. No need for you to be busy trying desperately to get yourself right with God. Sit there in the silence and just watch what Jesus does as he dies. It is finished.

Earlier, back on the road, when he said, "I have a baptism I must experience. How I am distressed until it's completed" (Luke 12:50), we didn't know what he was talking about. Now we know. He is talking about the accomplishment, the completion, the fulfillment of his work. He is talking about his death. Now, the baptism of his death is accomplished.

Jesus is presented in the Gospels as the most peripatetic, the most frenetic of teachers. He was always on the move, never alighting long in one place. A word here, a story there, then off to elsewhere. Now he is still, at rest.

How did he say, "It is finished"? I think he said it not in defeat—I've done the best I could, now I give up, give in, and die. He said it in victory—I've fought the fight, faced satan down, and now my work is stunningly accomplished. The scapegoat who took on the sins of Israel, driven out into the wilderness to die, has now become the Lamb of God who, driven back to the throne of God, atones for the sins of the whole world.

As Paul says, the only righteous One who knew no sin was made to bear all our sin that we sinners might become the righteous of God (1 Cor 1:30). Don't ask me to explain that thick thought. You are not meant to figure it out; just sit there this day and behold it.

As we once said in the old Communion prayer, "He offered there for us a full, sufficient, and perfect sacrifice for the sins of the whole world." God has now finished the work that God began with us so long ago. God was determined, having created us, having loved us in so many and diverse ways, to get back to us. And now God has. It is finished.

Listen to this, oh ye purpose-driven, upwardly mobile, goal-setting high achievers. He has done what we could not do. Because we could not get up to God, God climbed down to us, got down on our level. And here, in the bloody, unjust crucifixion, we have at last descended to our level. God has finished what God began. It is finished.

What is to be done by us now? Nothing.

What might we learn from the lessons of this day? Nothing.

What are we supposed to do for God before nightfall? Nothing. Did you miss his words? "It is finished."

The letter to the Hebrews tells of that great High Priest in the heavens who, when he had made the full, perfect, final sacrifice, sat down (Heb 10:12). Most priests must be busy, doing good, trotting back and forth from the people to the altar, sacrificing, working, conducting three-hour services on Good Friday, getting ready for Easter, contributing to our relationship with God. But this Great High Priest, when he had done it all, says Hebrews, sat down. He sat down because it was finished. If the world only knew that the cross, that sign of humiliation and defeat, is God's greatest victory, the world would be reconciled to God. And we busy-bee sinners—so busy with our spiritual practices, our religious rites, our purpose-driven churches, our moral achievements (anybody who would come to a three-hour service, and on a Friday, has got to be good at being good!)—in our busy-ness are forced this day to sit down, to be still and know that he is God, to be quiet, and simply to adore the wonder of his completed work on our behalf. This day we come to church planning to get on with the business of getting right with God only to be told by the church to do nothing but to be still, to sit, and to listen.

That business between us and God that began in the garden, in which we first chose our wills over God's will, in which we rebelled and never looked back, this bloody business in which we, down through all the ages, always turned away from God, that is being fixed, finished this decisive day. So all you frenetic spiritual busybodies and anxious, purpose-driven do-gooders hear this: the sad dealings between us and God can only be finished by God. We've run up debts that can't be covered by us. The good news is that the battle is done. The war is won. The debt is paid. It is finished.

Relating the text

Years ago I wrote a book on burnout among clergy. I interviewed scores of clergy who had called it quits. One pastor said he found that one of the most debilitating aspects of parish ministry was that "it's never finished." There is always one more sermon to be written, one more book to be read, one more hurting person to be visited and counseled.

"God, how I envy housepainters!" another ex-pastor said. "They can actually see the results of their work. They get done!" What a joy it is to have an ending, to be able to say that it is over and done with. That was one of the things I loved most about the academic life: commencement. No matter how bad the year had been, no matter how many disappointing students I had taught or lousy lectures I had delivered, there was always that day in May when it was over.

Today a work is being done, a work that Jesus did not at first enthusiastically undertake. He prayed in Gethsemane that this cup might pass. He did not want to die. And yet, when it became clear to him that this was indeed the Father's will, the Son who was one with the Father and the Spirit went to the cross. He endured it all without shirking any of it, he received directly the blows that were set upon him, and now all of that is finished. Shortly, there will be the long silence. The preacher's sermon, that challenged so many, will end.

That business between us and God—that unpleasantness begun in the garden, that tendency to be gods unto ourselves, our rebellion, our clinch-fisted, violent pride, that sin—is about to be addressed, not with words, but with a deed. Jesus is about to do for us that which we cannot do—have shown time and again we cannot do—for ourselves. We are about to learn that discipleship is not a matter of our doing something for God, but rather is a matter of having something done for us by God.

I recall C. S. Lewis's story, in *The Great Divorce*, in which the bishop (!) dies and finds himself getting off a bus in some unknown place. "Welcome to heaven," someone says to him. The bishop promptly presents himself to the person who seems to be in charge. "Where will we be gathering for the meeting?" he asks. (Bishops are addicted to meetings.) There is no meeting, he is told. "Well, there must be a meeting. There is work to be done, good to be accomplished, problems to be addressed. We are responsible people who have responsibilities. When is the meeting?"

No meeting. No work to be done. No responsibilities to be met. It's done. Over. Finished. God has done it all for us.

The story ends with the bishop boarding a bus bound for hell, eager to get there and get busy. Heaven is a place of blessed rest; hell is where the work is never done.

The theologian Karl Barth said that we must always remember that the name *Israel* does not mean "struggle for God" or "struggle with God" but rather "struggle against God."

Once there was One who came to us, who touched the untouchables, turned his back upon the world's bright baubles, loved even unto death, and never turned his eyes away from God. And we hated him for it. He came to us with wide-open hands in gracious invitation, seeking us, both patient with us and hotly pursuing us. And thereby he brought out the very worst in us.

We figured that things between us and God were not all that bad, but when he spoke to us of God, and ourselves, and rubbed our noses in the filthy rags of our presumed righteousness, well, we thought we were good until we met him. He called upon us to attempt great moral feats, then watched as we fell flat on our faces. He invited us to join up with God's reign, then he set God's reign's demands so high that when it came time for us to stand up and show what we were made of, we fled, slithering into the darkness. He said, "Come to me. Take on my yoke." And we with one voice cried, "Crucify him!"

Well, after all the struggle and all the blood and gore, after all our betrayals and our murderous determination to have God on our terms, all that is now over. This day, it is finished.

Easter Day

Acts 10:34-43 or Jeremiah 31:1-6
Psalm 118:1-2, 14-24
Colossians 3:1-4 or Acts 10:34-43
John 20:1-18 or Matthew 28:1-10

Having Not Seen

Selected reading
John 20:1-18

Theme
Faith in the resurrection of Jesus comes to some of us, not through reasoned consideration of the evidence, not by some tangible proof, but rather through trust—trust in the power of the risen Christ working in us. We each come to the mystery of the resurrection through our own path, for God reveals such a mystery to us in various ways, according to our need and ability.

Introduction to the readings

Acts 10:34-43
Peter, when asked to testify to his faith, testifies to the story of the death and resurrection of Jesus.

Colossians 3:1-4
The power of Christ to defeat death is proclaimed to the early Christians.

John 20:1-18

On Sunday, Mary Magdalene, Peter, and the beloved disciple come out to the tomb of Jesus. What they find there, or, more accurately, do not find there, astounds them.

Prayer

Lord God of power and glory,

In the rising of the sun you raised Jesus from the dead.

You delivered him from the dominion of death and defeat, you vindicated his ministry and work; you raised him up.

We praise you this day for all the gifts of new life that you bring us. Especially do we praise you for all the signs of Easter that we see among us,

for all our daily victories over sin and death,

for the sustaining love of friends and family who enable us to go on, even when life is difficult,

for the springtime renewal of nature,

for the triumph of peace over war, justice over injustice, right over wrong,

for the continuing conviction, instilled in us at Easter, that you are Lord, that you intend to bring all things unto yourself, that life will triumph over death, and that ultimately, your purposes for the world will not be defeated. Amen.

Encountering the text

Forgive us preachers if we search a familiar biblical text hoping for some new insight, some weird discovery, some detail we missed in earlier readings. After all, many of us have been at this preaching business for some time now. Not only must we interest our hearers in the sermon, but also we must interest ourselves!

John's story of the resurrection is vivid, rich, full of fascinating detail. In John, the details are often pregnant with meaning. John renders a world in which, when Jesus appears, everything bursts open with meaning, therefore it seems fair for us to treat the details of John's narrative in some, well, detail.

Tom Long, great interpreter of the word, called my attention to an interesting detail in John's Easter. Everyone was busy running. The tempo has picked up in this Gospel. After a long series of monologues by Jesus in which he bids farewell to his disciples, after a bloody crucifixion in which things moved terribly, tragically, slowly, Easter bursts in upon us and everyone begins to run.

The race of the "beloved disciple" will concern us most in today's sermon. He is surely meant to be the center of our focus. He is the one who, though he does not see, though he has no conversation with the risen Christ, believes. And so will we.

Proclaiming the text

I wonder how you have come here this morning. In my pastoral experience, church crowds are always larger on Easter, so that means there may be a greater diversity than usual in the congregation.

I expect that some of you have come here because you are always here, even when it's not Easter. Others of you may have come because, though you are not usually here on Sundays, it's Easter. Still, others of you have come because someone invited you or someone forced you, or you simply came out of curiosity.

I watched you arriving this Easter and I noted that, though you came by automobile or lumbering up the sidewalk, none of you came running. None of you ran toward Easter, which, notes Tom Long, is curious because, according to John's Easter Gospel, there was a great deal of dashing about on the first Easter.

First, according to John, Mary Magdalene came (John 20:2) and she, seeing the stone rolled away and the tomb empty, started running. Not that she believed in resurrection at this point, for that would come later (20:11-18). For now, in the predawn darkness, she just begins running back to tell the rest of the disciples that Jesus's body is gone.

On her sprint back to town, she meets Peter and the beloved disciple. In her shock and fear, she reminds me of a boy in my high school chemistry class. During some chemistry experiment gone wrong, there was an explosion in the back of the class. Nothing serious, just a loud bang. And he, seated at the front, bolted out the door, ran down the hall, and was not heard from again that day.

"What on earth were you thinking about?" the teacher asked the next day.

"I wasn't thinking about anything," he said. "I was just running. I didn't know what to do, so I ran."

Mary Magdalene, in her grief, ran. Jesus was crucified, dead, and buried. Now someone had taken his body. So she ran.

On her way back, she met two disciples. When she tells them what she saw, or didn't see, they break out into a run. She ran from the empty tomb, but they ran toward it.

Tom Long called my attention to an interesting detail. John says these two disciples didn't just run together toward the tomb; they ran against each other toward the tomb. They get in some sort of race, rushing—now one gaining on the other, then falling behind, gaining again—toward what?

Why did they run against each other? What did they think they were running toward? Mary Magdalene interpreted the empty tomb as further tragedy. Not only had they killed Jesus, but also someone had stolen his body. Perhaps they were running toward that awful, terrible, last insult.

"There's been a bad accident on the school ground," someone told the mothers at coffee. Every one of them jumped up and started running toward the school. Why run? Why run toward the tragic? If it is not your child who is hurt, then some other mother's child is hurt. We run toward both good news and bad. We must know, and quickly, if the news is for us.

Perhaps they ran as rivals, says Tom Long. Throughout John's Gospel, it's Peter who is the leader of the disciples, the one with a ready word on most occasions.

But it was this "beloved disciple," whoever he was, who seemed closest to the heart of Jesus. They ran to see which one of them—Peter the leader or the disciple who was beloved—would arrive first.

A group of kids are walking down the sidewalk arm-in-arm. Someone shouts from down the street, "There's free ice cream being given out down at the corner store," and watch them become rivals in a race to the corner. They want to see if the good news is true, if this be good news for them.

As these two disciples run, surely there was something in them telling them that, in this strange event, they were running toward some strange, new, possibly terrifying future. Someone says to us, "Come! Look at this!" and we come, we run, toward exactly what we do not know. But we run.

Perhaps that describes you this Easter. You have come here. But when I ask you, "Why have you come?" you have no ready answer. Perhaps you do not know why you have come here. You have no clear picture of what you think you'll see or experience here.

I think John says that these two sprinting disciples came to Jesus's tomb just like that, not knowing, running toward some new, strange event that they instinctively knew meant a change in their world. John says that the beloved disciple outran Peter, won the race, got there first (20:4). That may seem a small detail, but isn't it interesting John mentions that the beloved disciple got there first? Not only that, John says that he was the first one to peer into the empty tomb and believe. The beloved disciple was the first to believe in Easter.

I think, like Tom Long, that John wanted to tell us not only that the beloved disciple got there first but also the way he got there. Others came to Easter in different ways. Mary will not believe until she stands face-to-face with the risen Christ and hears him call her name, "Mary!" Thomas doesn't believe until the risen Christ offers to let Thomas touch his pierced hands and wounded side.

But the beloved disciple comes to Easter another way. He believes without seeing. He doesn't hear Jesus. He doesn't see the risen Christ. All he does is come, peer into the dark, empty tomb, and he believes. Long says that "the beloved disciple, unlike the others, believes in the resurrection in the light of Jesus' absence." There is nothing there, no evidence. No Shroud of Turin, no photos, just an empty place. But, "He saw and believed" (20:8).

Now can you see why John probably went into all that about the footrace? The very first believer in the resurrection, the first to believe in the triumph of God, came there by the same path that you and I do by not seeing the risen Christ. To almost no one here, I suspect, has the risen Christ personally appeared in a garden and called you by name as he did to Mary. No one here has touched his wounds and believed. We have believed on the basis of the words, "He is not here."

"Blessed are those who have not seen," says Jesus, which means all of us here, "and yet have come to believe" (20:29 NRSV).

How did the beloved disciple come to faith in Easter on that first Easter? Trust. The beloved disciple knew his beloved Jesus. Thus, when he saw the empty tomb he did not think abandonment, defeat, death. He thought freedom, victory, life. In a moment he sensed that Jesus had taken their relationship to a new, unexpected, and more wonderful area.

– 238 –

Erik Erikson said that a child develops trust in the first six months of life. The infant learns that, when it cries out, momentarily a voice will be heard saying, "There, there, what's wrong?" or a loving face will soon appear. The infant learns thereby that parents care, that the world is a trustworthy place.

Eventually, the infant will tolerate long absences of the parent. The infant does not need the parent physically present every moment of the day, clearly in sight, because the young child has learned that, even though the parent is not right there in view, the parent is nearby; the parent will come when called. Trust.

The beloved disciple did not have "proof," as we call something proof. He had no legal certification of the resurrection. Yet he had his relationship with Jesus, and that was enough. He believed.

And so have you. Blessed are those who, having not seen, believe. Blessed are you.

Relating the text

One Easter I found out the hard way that Easter lilies, which blossom in such profusion on church altars this Sunday, are very fragile flowers. They don't look fragile, all large and white and substantial appearing. But they are very fragile. Touch an Easter lily, even a light brush against the flower, and it almost immediately turns brown.

I tried to move the lilies, so the choir could have more room for their anthem, and ended up defacing most of them.

"Some flower of Easter," I thought to myself, watching them turn brown, "some symbol of life and resurrection."

But then I thought. Life really is fragile, as fragile as those lilies. Life is short, brief, and insubstantial. We are all on our way toward death and the deface-ment that comes with mortality.

How much more wonderful then the claims of Easter. Nothing lasts in this world, in this life. Everything is busy decaying. Almost nothing is as substantial and resilient as it first appears.

Into this scenario of death and decay comes something from the outside. An act of God. God bringing life out of death. Easter!

"How I wish I could have been there on that first Easter," he said, "Wouldn't it have been great to have seen it for yourself, an eyewitness?"

He assumed that his problem with the resurrection was that he was two thousand years away from it. If he could have run to the empty tomb himself, he thinks that belief would be easier.

Yet such a view denies the way the Gospels tell about the first Easter. Was it easy for those who were eyewitnesses? Not really. They saw an empty tomb, but what did that mean? It might just as well have meant that someone had stolen the body of Jesus.

The Gospels report the first Easter as an occasion for fear, disbelief, and astonishment. There was joy, but the joy came after the more understandable emotions of disbelief and incomprehension.

Easter is like that. What we have here is not so much a problem of history, the gap between our time and the time of the first Easter. What we have here is a problem of faith. Not faith as blind belief in something, but rather faith as the ability to trust even that which we do not have the equipment to comprehend. The problem is not one of time, a gap between our modern time and their premodern time. The problem is faith in God's ability to work life from death.

"How did you like the sermon this Easter?" I asked.

"Fine," she said. "Fine, yet I confess that the sermon is rarely the main thing for me on Easter," she said.

"What is the main thing for you on Easter?" I persisted.

"I always find music a bit more to the point of Easter," she responded. "Easter strikes me as something not to be argued, reasoned out, demonstrated. It's something to be experienced, enjoyed, wondered at. Therefore, on Easter, the music seems most to the point."

Even I, as preacher, had to agree.

It is asking a great deal of people like us to conceive of something so wondrous as resurrection. Most of us think on the basis of our experience. When we see something, we try to fit it within our past experience in order to make sense of it. Yet how will we make sense of the resurrection, since there is almost nothing within the range of our experience that prepares us for so great a mystery?

We will have to wait, to wonder, to be willing to receive it as a gift. The resurrection will have to be something God gives us, not something we attain through our earnest efforts to think clearly. It is a gift. We do not understand it. We stand under it.

I heard someone say that the most comforting aspect of Sunday service was when the gathered congregation rose and with one voice repeated the words of the Nicene Creed. He noted what a comfort it was that the congregation did not say, "I believe." Rather, the congregation said, "We believe."

Sometimes, in saying the creed, we are affirming the faith for those in the congregation who, at that moment cannot affirm the faith. We are believing for them, affirming the faith during a time which, for them, may be a time where faith is unsteady. At other times, there is the graciousness that occurs when they affirm the faith for us.

Through Closed Doors

Selected reading

John 20:1-18 (illuminated by John 21:3-14)

Theme

The risen Christ moved through closed doors in order to get close to his disciples. The power of the resurrection is a promise that there is no force on earth, including the forces of our own doubts and unfaithfulness that can keep the risen Christ from us.

Introduction to the readings

Acts 10:34-43

Peter tells the story of Jesus's crucifixion and resurrection—how God raised him on the third day.

Colossians 3:1-4

"If you were raised with Christ," Paul tells the Colossians, "your life is hidden with Christ in God" (vv. 1, 3).

John 20:1-18
John tells the story of the resurrection appearance of the risen Christ.

Prayer

Lord Jesus, on this grand day you gave death the slip and rose to new life. The tomb could not hold you. Nor could our limited lives and truncated imaginations. You not only rose from the dead but also came back to us. You not only kicked open the door of your tomb but also forced open the closed doors of our cold hearts. You came back to us, spoke to us, and empowered us to be witnesses of your resurrection.

This is our only hope, in life and in death, that you will continue to overcome our cowardice and reservations, that you will keep kicking open our locked doors, and that you will come to us and show us your glory, making every dull day of our lives an Easter. Alleluia! Amen.

Encountering the text

There is something about this forever-reaching God that is determined to draw us into his loving embrace. It would be one thing to preach about Christ, but "we preach Christ crucified" (1 Cor 1:23) and resurrected. We do not preach ideas, precepts, or principles, but a person Jesus Christ raised up before us, pursuing us. At the beginning of his influential textbook on preaching, H. Grady Davis says that "The truth we preach is not an abstract thing. The truth is a Person" (*Design for Preaching* [Philadelphia: Fortress, 1958], 19).

Our challenge as Easter preachers is well represented by the movements of Christ in John 20. It is "the first day of the week," that is the first day of the Jewish workweek, the first day when Israel, including the disciples of Jesus, is attempting to get back to normal after a particularly bloody weekend. This is not to be. Our deadly yearning to get back to business will be disrupted by the resurrection.

Mary Magdalene comes to the tomb "while it was still dark" (John 20:1), that threatening time when Jesus performed some of his most notorious wonders. Mary is literally in the dark. Note that the story begins with a woman who boldly ventures forth, even in the darkness. Mary Magdalene notices that the stone has been taken from the tomb and apparently assumes that the body has been stolen (20:2). This will be the first in a long series of misapprehensions and incorrect interpretive conclusions by the disciples after Easter. Whatever has happened here in the darkness will be difficult for them to understand.

We, the readers, know what has happened, due to our previous encounters with the text. Our knowledge and their lack of knowledge is both a warning and an encouragement to us. It is a warning in that these first witnesses failed to understand, so we also might misunderstand. It is an encouragement in that those who were historically the closest to Jesus did not understand whereas we who are far removed from these events understand. They did not see whereas we, hearing their story, see and understand. By the grace of the living God there is a sense in which we know more about the truth of what's what than even the very first witnesses. Our God is of the living and not the dead. Apparently history is not our problem with these narratives, so we do well to be suspicious of any who would hand these narratives over to the historians.

Now the men arrive at the tomb, after a breathless run. Simon Peter is the first to dare enter the darkness of the tomb, and there he sees the linen cloths carefully folded and placed by themselves. The careful placement of the cloths is an interesting narrative detail and, especially in John's Gospel but throughout all biblical literature, details are important. Perhaps these carefully folded cloths are proof that the body has not been stolen. Perhaps they are an indication of the careful, deliberate way in which Christ is raised. Who knows? To work with such literature or to allow such literature to work with us, we must have a high tolerance for ambiguity and a willingness to suspend our desire for sure and immediate comprehension.

When the second disciple follows Peter into the tomb and sees the circumstantial evidence, he also "saw and believed" (20:8), but what he "believed" is ambiguous for he seems to believe that the body has been stolen because he "didn't yet understand the scripture that Jesus must rise from the dead" (20:9). Visible evidence in the world is interesting but not too informative without the gift of revelation.

"Then the disciples returned to the place where they were staying" (20:10). Back to their homes! They "believe" but go back to business as usual, back to the sweet, anesthetizing reassurance of the mundane and the everyday, the predictable and the stable. If there is a resurrection it is obviously not some projection or wish fulfillment on the part of the grieving disciples. They are quite content to chalk all of this up to the power of death. The stealing of the body is simply one final indignity worked upon crucified Jesus and his grieving followers.

But Mary stayed, weeping, and stooped to look in the tomb. Mary remained, in grief, but still daring to linger, to stoop, and to look. To Mary is given the vision of two angels. The angels have no message for her, only a question about her grief. Unlike some of the other angelic visitations in scripture, these angels are ambiguous messengers who do not directly proclaim resurrection. Mary turns around and sees someone standing there, someone whom she does not know. Seeing is not yet believing until the figure speaks to her. Even when the risen Christ speaks to her, she does not yet know. Revelation, even that which comes through hearing, is hardly ever self-evident, immediate, at least from our point of view. She thinks the speaker is the gardener.

Then Jesus calls her by her name, "Mary." That is all he says. He does not tell her about his resurrection; he simply calls her. Yet at that moment of vocation, she hears, she sees, she understands. She calls calls him "Teacher," which may be a term of endearment, and of course Jesus is a teacher, but this may also indicate that Mary is yet on the way to a full recognition of Jesus's identity, moving from teacher to "Lord" (20:18).

Jesus says, "Don't hold on to me" (20:17). The risen Christ is on the move, ascending, restlessly eluding our grasp. He is not to be held, even by those who love him. Perhaps this is a great Johannine warning for those of us who are called to talk about the risen Christ, the great command of the living Lord, "Do not hold on to me!" We must find a way to talk about Jesus that is faithful to the encounter that does not attempt to secure, fix, restrain, or limit his movements among us and his movements beyond us.

The risen Christ is on the move, and now Mary must be on the move. She goes back to the unbelieving and unseeing disciples and preaches to them, "I've seen the Lord." Then "she told them what he said to her" (20:18). In John's Gospel, this woman is the first evangelist, the first preacher. This faith is birthed through the testimony of women, the first who are given the gift of witnessing to the resurrection. Is this not a summary of all good Christian preaching, the two-point sermon: "I have seen the Lord," and "here is what the Lord has told me to tell you"?

For Mary, seeing is believing, but only when seeing is accompanied by speaking. For Mary, a vision of the risen Christ is also a commission, a vocation, an assignment from the risen Christ to go and tell.

Note that Mary must go to the disciples and preach to them what they do not believe. Preaching is always concerned with unbelief and the first "unbelievers" who need the good news are Jesus's own disciples (the church) who, in their belief, are the first to disbelieve and the most in need of evangelization.

Note also that John does not report the response of the disciples to Mary's "sermon." We are told what Mary the first "preacher" did and said, but nothing of how the congregation reacted to her words. Presumably their response is not Mary's concern. Presumably their silence is indicative of their disbelief. We learn in the next story, where the risen Christ must kick through the locked doors of the disciples (church), that they did not believe Mary for they were cowering behind locked doors "for fear" (20:19-23). So the risen Christ did for the disciples what Mary alone could not: he came and stood among them and spoke. He breathed on them and gave them great power. The risen Christ passes through closed doors. The risen Christ overcomes all barriers to get to his disciples.

Proclaiming the text

In a poem titled "Men at Forty," the poet Donald Justice writes of how wisdom has often brought them to "Learn to close softly / The doors to rooms." This is true. I'm well past forty, and I can testify that the longer you live, the more you learn to be careful upon closing a door. Be careful when you slam the door in someone's face saying, "I'm done with you! It's over!"

Someday you might have to go back, open that door, and try to resume the relationship that you thought you had sealed shut. "I've closed a door on that part of my life," she said. She's growing up or at least thinks she's growing up and has put her youthful past behind her. But we'll see. Perhaps the future is less in her control than she thinks. Maybe it isn't over until someone else says it's over.

True, part of growing up, becoming wise, is learning when to close a door. Sometimes we keep coming back again and again, going over the same old script, trying to make the unworkable work. It is wisdom to know when to close the door firmly and move on into another room. You've got to know when to risk and put down your bet, and you've got to know when to fold, when to cut your losses, and when to close the door on the game.

Thus we find the disciples of Jesus. For about three years they have trooped along behind him on the Galilean highways and byways. They have tried to understand his teaching, which hasn't been easy, considering this is the Gospel of John! They have heard him speak of himself as the Christ, the Messiah, and the Holy One of God who is one with the Father.

But all of that seems distant to them now—only a dream after the horrible nightmare of the past week. Can you imagine the trauma of seeing the one whom you thought to be the savior of the world terribly beaten, whipped, and crucified? Now Jesus has been sealed in the tomb for three days. Pilate has shut the door on the King of the Jews once and for all.

John says that the disciples gathered that night on the first day of the week. The events of the past week have plunged them all into darkness, and now they are cowering together, filled with fear. The same authorities who had killed Jesus may now be after Jesus's followers. And the doors are shut.

John says that the doors were shut and locked "from fear." And they had much for which to be fearful. But some of them may have been filled with grief also. And well they should grieve, for in the death of Jesus they had suffered a great loss—shut the doors.

Those of you who have gone through some grief recently know how important it is in the aftermath of death to close some doors. A woman in my church lost her husband to a heart attack on Christmas Eve. I stopped by her house for a visit in late January and was aghast to see a still-decorated tree, unopened packages around the room, and everything still in place as if her husband was going to walk in at any minute.

I told her, "You've got to face facts and close this door on your past. You have got to find a way to move on."

That's what the disciples had done. They had closed the doors on their past with Jesus, and they were adjusting to the facts. It's over. It was good while it lasted. Close the door.

And then, at their lowest, in the dead of night, the risen Christ appeared before them. He said, "Peace," to them. He breathed on them. He bestowed on them the power to forgive the sins of others. In short, he gave them all the power and all the Spirit that so empowered his ministry.

But perhaps most amazing of all, Christ came through their locked doors. The dark tomb could not hold him, nor could the dark despair and resignation of his followers. He came back to them, even through their locked doors.

Here is Easter hope. The resurrection doesn't simply mean that Jesus rose to eternal life. It doesn't simply mean that we hope to see our loved ones when we die. It also means that the very first thing that the risen Christ does is return to the same cowardly and misunderstanding disciples who had so disappointed and forsaken him. He came through their locked doors.

I say that is the Easter hope because we gather today, just as those first disciples gathered, as those who are cowardly in our commitment to the way of Jesus and misunderstand much of his teaching. We also gather behind locked doors. The fire marshal won't let us lock exit doors in many buildings, but there are still locked doors. There are the locked doors of our hearts that hold despair—"God has disappointed me before, and I won't trust God again" or "He is hopeless. He will never get over this addiction" or "I'm dying and I'm dying alone."

A woman I know woke up one morning and discovered that her husband lying next to her was dead. She was crushed, vowing she would remain a widow, alone for the rest of her life.

Then one spring day I got her call. "Guess what? I'm in love again. It's possible for me to fall in love with two men." I did the wedding two months later.

There is great good news here, Easter news. I know that many of you have trouble believing. You are filled with doubts, and some of those doubts are mixed with fear. You have failed in your attempts to be a faithful follower of Jesus. You don't know what tomorrow holds for you, and that scares you.

Well, here's the good news: the risen Christ can come through locked doors. There is no security system that's been devised that can keep you safe from his incursions. He came to his first disciples and promises to keep coming back to us, keep intruding among us, keep pressing in upon us, and keep opening the door that we don't know how to unlock. Even in the dark door of our deaths, Christ promises not to forsake us, to keep coming back for us, keep talking to us, and breathing upon us.

Your faith is based on this Easter miracle. Your relationship to God, thank God, is not based on what you can feel or believe or think. It's based upon the fact that the risen Christ came to you, moved through whatever locked door you were hiding behind, breathed his life-giving breath upon you, and raised you up toward himself.

I know someone who for forty tortuous, tumultuous, wasted years fled from the summons of God. He tried everything to silence the address of God, always fleeing in the other direction whenever he feared that God was calling his name.

The week he came back to church, after a twenty-year hiatus, he explained his return to us in three terse words: God got me. Christ is risen! He is risen indeed! He has opened, is opening, will open your door. Amen!

Relating the text

We were discussing the weakness of historical criticism of scripture, the way that historians have a way of so dissecting and eviscerating the biblical text, turning it into an object of historical investigation, that they sometimes kill the Bible for us preachers.

A pastor responded, "I think that the question, when reading scripture, ought to rarely be the historical 'when,' but rather ought to be the location question, 'where.' Not, 'when did Christ do this' but rather 'where does Christ do this?'"

I thought he said it just about right. Where is the risen Christ? Wherever there are locked doors trying to keep him out, there is Christ, miraculously breaking in.

Second Sunday of Easter

Acts 2:14a, 22-32

Psalm 16

1 Peter 1:3-9

John 20:19-31

Resurrection of the Body

Selected reading

John 20:19-31

Theme

Christianity is founded upon a fact, an astounding, unexpected, but nevertheless real event: the resurrection of Jesus Christ from the dead. Christians are those who see all human history, all human destiny, in the light of this event. This is the core, founding, irreducible event upon which our faith rests. We believe in the resurrection of the body.

Introduction to the readings

Acts 2:14a, 22-32

Peter joyfully proclaims the message of the resurrection of Jesus.

1 Peter 1:3-9

You are receiving the salvation of your souls, proclaims the First Letter of Peter to a suffering church.

John 20:19-31

Thomas is moved from doubt to faith in the presence of the risen Christ.

Prayer

Lord Jesus, we have been surprised by your resurrection, caught off guard by your lively return to us, astounded by your power to defeat death. We have doubts. Do not reject us in our doubts. Come to us, heal us of our reservations, our timidity, and our unwillingness to believe that which the scriptures so boldly proclaim. Give us the imagination and the courage, the vitality and the boldness to proclaim with the saints, "He has risen! He has risen indeed!" Then help us to live each day in the light of that proclamation. Amen.

Encountering the text

On this Sunday, the second Sunday of Easter, it is our custom to read the story of the doubts of Thomas. Thomas is the patron saint of all those who have difficulty conceiving of and believing in the resurrection. Yet, the story of Thomas is not only a story of doubt but also a story of the way that the risen Christ ministers to doubt. From this vivid story we learn at least two core truths: First, doubt of the resurrection was present among the disciples from the very start (we are not the first generation of believers to have difficulty assimilating the fact of the resurrection). Second, Jesus reassures our doubts by his loving presence (belief in the resurrection is a gift of the risen Christ).

Now that we are in the time after Easter, on this "Low Sunday" as it is traditionally known, this is a good time for the church to take stock of what has happened among us. This is a good opportunity for a teaching sermon on the centrality of our belief in the resurrection.

Belief in the resurrection has been challenged by some biblical scholars and theologians (what else is new?). This Sunday is our opportunity to counter those challenges with a strong, informed affirmation of the resurrection. We have the stories of resurrection, but now we must step back and reflect upon the meaning of those narratives. We must take some time to do some theology. In so doing, our sermons will be not only pedagogical but also pastoral, reassuring our people in their doubts, even as the risen Christ reassured doubting Thomas.

Proclaiming the text

A Christian is someone who believes that God raised Jesus from the dead. Never was this belief not in contention. When the Apostle Paul, on Mars Hill, preached Jesus's resurrection from the dead (Acts 17) he was greeted with hoots of derision. The pagan world still derides this central Christian belief. Even in this morning's Gospel, we find Jesus's own disciples having doubts. Thomas said that he would not believe unless the risen Christ stood before him. The risen Christ did just that. Thomas believed. I want you to believe.

No historian doubts that without the belief in the resurrection, there would be no Gospels, no Christians.

Yet the story of doubting Thomas is a reminder of the patent absurdity of such a thing happening in time and space. First-century people may not have been scientists, but they all knew that dead men don't rise to new life. In every age, belief in the resurrection of Jesus must overcome a strong prior prejudice against the possibility of such a thing happening, because it runs counter to our expectation based on everyday experience.

The resurrection is a jolt to anybody's imagination, even if they are not doubting Thomases: "Overcome with terror and dread, they fled from the tomb. They said nothing to anyone, because they were afraid" (Mark 16:8).

Here I want to assert before you a few core, central, absolutely trustworthy facts about the resurrection. Here is our Easter faith: we believe, against our natural tendencies to disbelieve, in the resurrection of Jesus as a bodily resurrection. In the Apostles' Creed we confess that we believe in "the resurrection of the body." The ground of this confession is the prior belief in the bodily resurrection of Jesus. We hold this belief against two common tendencies. The first is to physicalize the event, to reduce it to a resuscitation or revivification of a corpse, like what happened to Lazarus when Jesus resuscitated him. The second is to spiritualize the event, as though his Spirit or soul was raised like a ghost, leaving his body behind.

For Paul the resurrection meant new life in a new body, not the return of the same old life in a perishable physical body. Paul's picture is that of a seed growing into a plant. It is Jesus's earthly mortal body that is transformed into an immortal spiritual body. Everything is new, yet there is continuity between the crucified body of Jesus and his risen body.

It is not an exaggeration to say that the entire structure of the Christian faith stands or falls upon the fact of Jesus being raised by God from the dead. Who is God? What is God up to in the world? Who are we as children of God? What are we supposed to be up to? All these questions are answered through the resurrection. God is the one who "raised Christ from the dead" (Rom 8:11), "gives life to the dead and calls things that don't exist into existence" (4:17). Christians have no other God than the one who creates new "life from the dead" (11:15).

Likewise, the resurrection says who we are. This world, for all of its goodness, is not the end, not the ultimate destination of human life: "On account of his vast mercy, [God] has given us new birth. You have been born anew into a living hope through the resurrection of Jesus Christ from the dead" (1 Pet 1:3).

The resurrection is also a summons to mission. The risen Christ tells his followers to go and tell the whole world that Jesus Christ is both crucified and risen.

At the present time there is uncertainty in the churches whether it is imperative to preach the gospel to people of other faiths. Do not all religions say the same thing, only in different idioms? Isn't it arrogant of us to think that we have "the truth"? The church has a peculiar truth to preach and we must preach it, that Jesus's death and resurrection is God's way of reconciling the whole world unto himself, that this is God's self-appointed means of salvation for all.

Without the resurrection, we are without hope. With the resurrection, through all the difficulties of life, we can go on because we know the end of the story. That end is in the hands of the God who raised crucified Jesus from the dead. Without the resurrection, we have nothing to say to a hurting, unsteady world. With the resurrection, we have good news. Say that good news in all that you do; become an embodiment of the hope and new life that Easter offers. What has been said to us, I say to you, so that you might say it to all: "The Lord is risen! He is risen indeed!"

Relating the text

"This was once a good church," said the district superintendent to her as he appointed her to the decaying, inner-city church. "But it has declined terribly. You go there and just try to keep them comfortable. That's about the best you can do when a church is dying."

When she got there, she found that the church had more possibility and potential than she had been led to believe. Things began to happen. New members showed up. Programs were started. Fifty new members joined in the first year. Good news!

Not necessarily. She was moved to another church within the next year.

"It's just not the same church," some of the older members complained.

"She has changed everything," said another. "We liked our church the way it was."

Question: Do we really want resurrection of the dead?

"I'm cancer free," she said.

"Wonderful!" I said. Having been her pastor through months of difficult treatments, I was delighted to be there to celebrate with her. The one who was once considered "terminally ill" had now been fully restored to health.

"Yes, wonderful, but also a bit disconcerting," she said.

"How do you mean that?"

"Well, I took the doctors at their word. They said I was terminal, that there was little chance that the therapy would be successful. So I planned to live for about a year and then die. That was what they told me to expect. Now, to be told that I have many more years to live, that I have a future, well, it's just a bit disconcerting. I've got to go ahead and live despite my plans to die!"

One reason why people find the resurrection difficult to believe is that it is demanding!

Two Sundays before Easter, Jesus went out to the cemetery and, with a loud voice, raised dead Lazarus. It's not the right time for such a miracle, during the season of Lent when we are more apt to sing, "Lord, have mercy," than "Alleluia!"

Now, in the afterglow of the resurrection, a Sunday after Easter, we say that we want Easter. Do we?

Robert W. Funk tells about how he once formulated the proposition "The resurrection was an event in the life of Jesus" and presented it to members of the Jesus Seminar. He writes:

"My proposition was received with hilarity by several Fellows. One suggested that it was an oxymoron.... Others alleged that the formulation was meaningless, since we all assume, they said, that Jesus' life ended with his crucifixion and death. I was surprised by this response.

"I shouldn't have been. After all, John Dominic Crossan has confessed, 'I do not think that anyone, anywhere, at any time brings dead people back to life.' That's fairly blunt. But it squares with what we really know, as distinguished from what many want to believe. Sheehan is even blunter: 'Jesus, regardless of where his corpse ended up, is dead and remains dead.'"

—Robert W. Funk, *Honest to Jesus* (New York: Harper Collins, 1996), 258

Disbelief in the fact of the resurrection has taken many forms, all of them creative, if misguided, attempts to deal with the resurrection through the conventional categories of modern thought. These attempts are all bound to fail, for the resurrection, by its very nature, is an exploding of conventional categories, the ultimate disruption of our world, including the thought patterns of our world. Still, people try to make sense out of the resurrection through our conventional, limited, Western ways of making sense.

Gerd Lüdemann calls for Peter's belief in the resurrection "to be interpreted psychologically as failed mourning and the overcoming of a severe guilt complex. He had sinned against Jesus by denying him" (*What Really Happened to Jesus* [Louisville: Westminster John Knox Press, 1996], 129).

Robert Funk says, "To claim that Jesus rose from the dead is a way of confessing that Jesus revealed what the world was really like, that he caught a glimpse of eternity. Affirmations of Jesus' resurrection should send his devotees searching through his parables and aphorisms for traces of that glimpse" (*Honest to Jesus* [San Francisco: Harper San Francisco, 1997], 313).

For Bishop Spong, the essence of the resurrection was Peter's experience of seeing Jesus as "the inbreaking reality of God" (John Shelby Spong, *Resurrection: Myth or Reality?* [San Francisco: Harper Collins, 1995], 277).

The story of Thomas and the risen Christ ought to remind these scholars that their work is not that original!

We were having a discussion of "difficult Christian beliefs." In due time, someone mentioned the difficulty of believing in the bodily resurrection of Christ. Many found this a rather farfetched possibility. Life from death? A dead body risen from the tomb? How can that be credible?

A woman spoke up, "Well, I do believe in the resurrection. I've seen it. I've lived it. When my husband walked out on me, I could have died. I did die. My life was over. Dead end.

"But then, by the grace of God, and with the coaxing of good friends, I came back. I came to life. I got a whole new life. It was a miracle.

"I believe in the resurrection. I've lived it."

Third Sunday of Easter

Acts 2:14a, 36-41

Psalm 116:1-4, 12-19

1 Peter 1:17-23

Luke 24:13-35

If Easter Is True

Selected reading

Luke 24:13-35 (related to the first and second lessons for today)

Theme

If Easter is true, if indeed the crucified Jesus has been miraculously raised from the dead and vindicated as the Messiah, how then should we live? If this central affirmation of the Christian faith is true—that the once-dead Jesus has been raised into eternal life, that Jesus's way has been vindicated and affirmed by God as God's way—then we must adjust our lives accordingly. Easter is a revelation of who God really is and what God really wants out of us and the world. If Easter is true, then God is the one who raised crucified Jesus from the dead.

Introduction to the readings

Acts 2:14a, 36-41

Peter concludes his speech to the scoffing crowd at Pentecost with an appeal to the crowd to repent and be baptized.

1 Peter 1:17-23

The First Letter of Peter exhorts an early congregation to live their lives in the light of the sacrifice of Christ.

Luke 24:13-35

On the afternoon of the first Easter, two disciples are walking to the village of Emmaus. On their way they are joined by a mysterious stranger.

Prayer

Lord Jesus, you have opened the doors to life. In your resurrection you revealed to us the scope of your love, the depth of your determination to reach us and have us.

Give us the grace to see the implications of your resurrection: your presence with us, your victory to encourage us, your summons to empower us. Then, in your grace, give us the courage to follow you where you lead us. Enlist us on the side of life against the powers of death. Lead us to live in the light of your victory. Make us your vital Easter people. Amen.

Encountering the text

Here, in the aftermath of the resurrection, we are still trying to figure out the world now that Jesus Christ has been risen from the dead. Appropriately, all of our lessons this Sunday deal with the various responses to Easter. In Acts 2, Peter calls for response to his testimony to the resurrection. It is not enough simply to believe in the truth of the resurrection; repentance and baptism are required.

First Peter tells an early congregation that "you have been born anew." The implication of that truth is: "love each other deeply from the heart."

Even the Gospel shows two disciples, not simply encountered by the risen Christ, but also walking with him, sharing food with him, then racing back to Jerusalem to tell the others, "The Lord has risen indeed."

One of the reasons why we preach is to say upfront what we believe, to testify to the faith of the church. Another reason for preaching is to ponder the implications of our beliefs.

In his earthly ministry Jesus called people to active discipleship, to put into practice their beliefs. Today's lessons stress that the risen Christ is the same as the crucified Jesus. The challenges that Jesus places before us are intensified, given new life by the resurrected One.

One of the reasons why we read and interpret scripture is to link us with our tradition, to be instructed by the saints of the past. And yet, in the light of Easter, a major reason why we do business with God's word, scripture, is that we truly believe that God speaks to us through the reading and interpreting of scripture, here and now.

We believe that Easter is true.

Proclaiming the text

Somewhere I recall a theologian who said that one reason why people find it difficult to believe in Easter, to have faith that the resurrection of Jesus Christ is true, is that if the resurrection is true, then their lives would have to change. They would be living in a whole new world and would have to adjust their lives accordingly, if Easter is true.

Christians believe that Easter is true. We believe that God, in an amazing act of divine vindication, raised crucified Jesus from the dead. In so doing God definitively acted in the world. God revealed who God really is and what God is really up to in the world. God—Father, Son, and Holy Spirit—is the one who wins victories through suffering, who lifts up the downtrodden and the oppressed, who will not allow the victims of evil and injustice ultimately to be crushed. In the end, no matter what evil is done, God will get God's way with the world. Easter is true.

And if Easter is true, as we believe it to be, how then should we live? That is the question before us this Third Sunday of Easter. Appropriately, all of this Sunday's lessons show believers attempting to adjust themselves to the fact that Easter is true.

In Acts 2, Peter, questioned by a mocking crowd after the Spirit's descent at Pentecost, responds with a short sermon. This Jesus "whom you crucified" has now been shown, through the resurrection, to be "both Lord and Christ" (Acts 2:36). Quickly the crowd gets the point. Upon hearing of the resurrection they respond, "What should we do?"

Peter tells them to repent and be baptized, and they, too, will receive the Holy Spirit, for "this promise is for you, your children, and for all who are far away" (Acts 2:39). If Easter is true, it's a whole new world in which those who were once, in their sin, far from God, are brought near, gifted with the Holy Spirit, promised a share in God's reign. Easter is an invitation to exchange citizenship and join up in that new reign.

A couple of Sundays ago, when I stood and proclaimed, "Jesus Christ is risen, he has risen indeed!" as I recall, you responded with "Alleluia," with songs of praise, and that's right. But if Easter is true, then it's also appropriate to ask, "What should we now do?" now that Easter is true.

First Peter proclaims to a struggling early congregation that in the resurrection Jesus is "revealed at the end of time. This was done for you" so that you were liberated (1 Pet 1:20). Easter is true! Then, love each other deeply from the heart. You have been born anew. It's like the resurrection of Jesus is new birth for all of us old, dying sinners, so that we are made into different kinds of people who are able now to love each other "from the heart," if Easter is true.

And then in today's Gospel we find this wonderful story of the walk to Emmaus. They didn't know the stranger who walked with them on the road, who opened the scriptures to them? The women had run back from the cemetery, saying that Jesus had been raised, but they did not believe the testimony of the women. That is, they didn't know that Easter was true. Then, at the table that evening, when Jesus broke the bread, their eyes were opened, and they saw the Lord. They ran all the way back to Jerusalem saying, "the Lord really has risen!" (Luke 24:34). Easter is true.

They thought that the Jesus movement had ended; it was just beginning. They thought that night was coming when it was really the dawn of a new day. Easter is true.

Easter is true. Of course, that's what Christians believe. But if Easter is true, how then should we live? If Easter is true, then it means that Jesus Christ is not just a wonderful teacher, an inspiring person, a notable historical figure. Jesus Christ is none other than the full revelation of God. He is Messiah. He is Lord. Now, we know who God is, what God looks like, what God wills for us and the world, if Easter is true.

If Easter is true, then never again are we permitted to lose heart, to despair, to give up. If God transformed the evil, bloody crucifixion into a grand triumph, well, who knows what God can do with our setbacks, dead ends, failures, and frustrations? No place is beyond the reach of God's redeeming grace, if Easter is true.

If Easter is true, then it's a lie that death is the last word, the final act, the end. If Easter is true, then it isn't over until God says it's over. If Easter is true, then our end is really our beginning. At the end, when this life is over, we are given not oblivion, darkness, and despair but a future, a new birth, a new beginning, if Easter is true.

If Easter is true, then we are not left alone. The risen Christ came back to the very disciples who disappointed and betrayed him. The risen Christ gathered these depressed, despairing, and bereft individuals and formed them into a new family, a community, the church. We—who are taught by our culture to think of ourselves as competitive, lonely, contentious individuals, each looking after ourselves, each seeking our own self-interest—are the church, Christ's body, the visible presence of the risen Christ in the world, if Easter is true.

If Easter is true, then you don't have to climb up to God, and you don't have to think hard and go through all sorts of mental gymnastics in order to be close to God. In bread and wine, God comes close to you. You come here to church on a Sunday morning, thinking that you are getting up, getting dressed, and coming to church to seek God only to be surprised that here, in worship with fellow Christians, in the Lord's body and blood, in the singing and scripture reading, maybe even in the sermon, the resurrected, living Christ is reaching out to you, if Easter is true.

Easter is true! How then should we live?

Relating the text

Easter is more than simply "Jesus has been raised from the dead, so now we will get to see our loved ones when we die." Easter is about a whole new world, not someday, but today. Not somewhere in eternity, but now. Of course, that whole new world is not completely here, not in its fullness. But it is sure on the way. That vision enabled Martin Luther King Jr. to keep working, keep marching, and not lose hope. It is the vision of Easter, the vision that is the most powerful motivation for Christian action in this world. We know a secret about the world and the direction in which the world is moving—Jesus Christ is risen! He has risen indeed.

If we pray "Thy will be done on earth as it is in heaven," then we will want to work to arrange the world to resemble as closely that world in which we fully expect to inhabit in eternity. We want the world here, today, to look very much like the world we long to inhabit for an inestimably long period of time. Our final destiny, the goal of it all, where our world is heading, is subsumed in a word, *heaven*. Eternity, according to John's Gospel, and maybe the other Gospels as well, begins now. Or as Catherine of Sienna put it, "all the way to heaven is heaven."

Eugene Peterson speaks eloquently of the nature of what happens at the "Lord's table" in the Eucharist. We offer our bread and wine and our lives to Jesus, but then the risen Christ offers us something in return:

"Then Jesus gives back what we bring to him, who we are. But it is no longer what we brought. Who we are, this self that we offer to him at the 'table,' is changed into what God gives, what we sing of as 'Amazing Grace.' Transformation takes place at the table as we eat and drink the consecrated body and blood of Jesus. A resurrection meal. 'Christ in me.'

"We initiate the practice of resurrection at the eucharistic table, but it doesn't end there. We continue the identical practice at every meal we sit down to. For the Christian, every meal derives from and extends the eucharistic meal into our daily eating and drinking, tables at which the risen Lord is present as host.

"All the elements of formation-by-resurrection are present every time we sit down to a meal and invoke Jesus as host. It's a wonderful thing, really, that one of the most common actions of our lives is also the setting in which the most profound transactions take place. The fusion of natural and supernatural that we witness and engage in the shape of the liturgy continues—or can continue—at your kitchen table.

"'Supper's ready—come and get it.'

"'Please pass the bread.'

"'Grandmother, let's not have any Godtalk, okay? Let's just get on with life.'"

—Eugene Peterson, *Living the Resurrection* (Colorado Springs: NavPress, 2006), 56–58

This prayer from Lancelot Andrewes certainly encapsulates the active, engaging, practical way that we are expected to walk with the risen Christ:

"Lord Jesus, I give you my hands to do your work. I give you my feet to go your way. I give you my eyes to see as you do. I give you my tongue to speak your words. I give you my mind that you may think in me. I give you my spirit that you may pray in me. Above all, I give you my heart that you may love in me. . . . I give you my whole self that you may grow in me, so that it is you, Lord Jesus, who live and work and pray in me."

—Quoted by James Howell, *Yours Are the Hands of Christ*
(Nashville: Upper Room, 1998), 120

"Our speaker is a pastor in the Christian tradition," said the person who introduced me at the civic club. True, I do try to practice my faith within a tradition that is Christian. Yet "Christian tradition" sounds suspiciously like something that is old, that is past, that is, well, dead. Do they mean "church"? Christians are, of necessity, traditionalists, and we honor the past. But we must be clear that our God is not chained to the past, not locked and sealed shut in the tradition.

Christ is risen, he is risen indeed!

A friend of mine is a member of a church that claims for its clergy "apostolic succession." They claim a ministry that goes all the way back, through the laying-on-of-hands, to the apostles, thus linking their ministry to the earliest ministers of the church.

Yet my friend takes little comfort in this claim of "apostolic succession." He says that it can be a way of putting too much stress upon the past and not enough stress on the future. "What we need," he says, is "apostolic progression—progressing forward into the future with the apostles, living the faith rather than relegating the faith to the past."

Fourth Sunday of Easter

Acts 2:42-47
Psalm 23
1 Peter 2:19-25
John 10:1-10

The Door

Selected reading

John 10:1-10

Theme

Jesus Christ is the gate, the door that leads us to God. Jesus is both the passage to God and God's gracious passage toward us. Jesus is thus the unique means whereby we encounter the truth about God. He is the door.

Introduction to the readings

Acts 2:42-47

The Acts of the Apostles pictures the church as a very different sort of human gathering, a group of people who live in the light of Easter.

1 Peter 2:19-25

The First Letter of Peter seeks to console a struggling congregation with words of hope.

John 10:1-10

Jesus speaks of himself as a door, a door that leads to God.

Prayer

Lord Jesus, in your resurrection you returned to us, you sought us out, spoke to us, opened yourself up to us. You became for us a door, a gate to God. Give us the grace to enter that door, to move closer to the God who, in your love, has moved close to us. Amen.

Encountering the text

Today's assigned text is very typical of the Gospel of John. It is full of metaphors and images, whereby Christ is represented to his followers. Jesus speaks of himself as the shepherd who has the best interest of the sheep in mind. The sheep are in the sheepfold and are beset by various threats, including "robbers and bandits." They crawl in to work mischief among the sheep. Others take the legitimate entrance, the gate, or in other translations, "the door."

In calling himself the shepherd, John says that Jesus is using a figure of speech. We will use one of Jesus's figures of speech—the door—to reflect upon Jesus's significance for our lives today. We will do this by noting the ways that Jesus as a door illuminates our relationship with Christ.

Proclaiming the text

"The most important part of a church is the front door." So declared a distinguished church architect. I thought he was going to say the sanctuary, the baptistery, the pulpit, or even the fellowship hall. No, what he said was the most important part of a church is the front door.

The front door is the first thing that newcomers encounter about a church. A banker told me that, when banks changed their front doors, it was a signal of a fundamental shift in the business of banking. In the early days of the last century, he said banks were built to look like impregnable fortresses. Their front doors tended to be thick, impenetrable, solid, secure, and all the other things that people wanted to believe about a bank. You put your money in here, was the promise, and we will make sure that nobody can get to it but you.

Then, in the mid-twentieth century, banks became more "user friendly." They attempted to attract customers, to put a warm and friendly face on banking. Gone were the big, thick, impenetrable doors, and glass doors were installed. Now you could look into the bank and see activity going on in there. You felt more welcome. The bank became accessible.

What do our church doors say about our church? At my place, Duke Chapel, we have great big neo-Gothic–style doors to go with our great big neo-Gothic–style building. The doors are about seven inches thick and solid oak. The oak planks are held together with huge, hand-wrought iron nails. We have learned the hard way that on a winter day, when the wind is blowing and those doors are open, if a strong wind gets hold of them, it slams you against the wall with great force. I would guess each of those doors weighs something like a thousand pounds. What do those doors say about our church?

A door should be fit not only to the size of the opening into the building but also to the life that goes on within the building. I remember the gangster movies that depicted the speakeasies of the roaring 1920s. Someone would come up to the door and give the appointed secret knock. A little slide window would open in the door and a voice from the inside would say, "What's the password?"

If the right password were given, something like "Joe sent me," then the door would open and the entrant would be admitted to all of the illicit excitement that was going on inside.

I can still remember the door into the principal's office in the elementary school that I attended. Half of the door had a window, which, as we have said, lends light, vision, and accessibility. But somehow it didn't function like that on the principal's door. On that door, the half window of the door had printed, in large gold letters, "PRINCIPAL." But inside you could see this ancient, austere man, sitting behind a desk, just waiting to deal out punishment, floggings, fines, and calls to your parents. There was no way to go through that door without your knees shaking and your hands trembling!

Some of the most interesting doors that I encounter as a pastor are the doors into hospital rooms. When I walk up to the door of a patient's room, to visit a parishioner of mine, I'm always somewhat relieved when the door is open. That means that the patient not only is probably awake but also may not be terribly sick. When the door is closed, it might mean that some procedure is being performed on the patient and I will have to wait, or that the patient is so sick that visits are inappropriate.

I stand there before the closed door. I read the chart that the doctors and nurses leave on the front of the door, searching for some clue of the patient's status. I gingerly open the door, perhaps lightly tapping it, wondering in what sort of state I will find the person who is ill.

On my pastoral visits, when I come up to the front door of a house, I knock and listen. Often I hear movement inside and a series of locks being turned and unlocked, and then as the door is opened slightly, I hear a voice asking, "Who is it?"

I understand the need for security, but this is not a very auspicious beginning for a visit. It doesn't feel very hospitable from the other side.

What is the chief function of the door? Is it a means of entering or a means of exit? Are doors built mainly for the benefit of those on the outside, or are they designed mostly to the specifications of those on the inside? Is the purpose of the door to keep people out or to welcome people in?

In today's Gospel, Jesus says that he is the door. It is an interesting figure of speech. "I am a door."

You get this sort of thing throughout the Gospel of John. John has a highly figurative, deeply metaphorical, symbolic presentation of Jesus. It is in John's

Gospel that you get images such as, "I am the way, the truth, and the life," or, "I am the good shepherd," or, "I am the vine and you are the branches." And now this Sunday, "I am the door."

Our Gospel lesson begins with Jesus saying that he is a shepherd, a favorite designation for Jesus in the Gospel of John. He is not only the shepherd but also the good shepherd. He is not only the good shepherd but also the shepherd who is so good that he is willing even to lay down his life for the sheep.

Then Jesus talks about those who refuse to go through the door of the sheepfold, those robbers, bandits, and mischief-makers who try to sneak over the wall and wreak havoc among the flock. Only a thief, a burglar, or a bandit would jump over a fence and climb in through a window, rather than come through the door.

And then Jesus moves from this reflection about doors, and the sort of people who refuse to use them, to the direct statement, "I am the door."

What does it mean for Jesus to say directly to us, "I am the door"?

Looked at one way, when Jesus says, "I am the door," he is using a rather humble image for himself. Jesus is the door that leads to God. The door is not the house, not the dwelling place, not the goal; a door is a passageway into the house, a means of getting to a destination. Thus, when Jesus says, "I am the door," it is similar to Jesus calling himself "the way." He is the way to God, the way to abundant life, the path to true freedom. Jesus is the means whereby we get to God. Or maybe the traffic is moving in the other direction, with Jesus. Maybe Jesus is better thought of as the way God gets to us.

Do you remember one of the most famous of all religious paintings, by the nineteenth-century English painter Holman Hunt? I've seen that painting at Kebel College, Oxford. Jesus stands there in the darkness holding a lamp in his hand, knocking on the door. It is a beautiful image of Jesus, the light of the world, knocking on our door, attempting to bring us light.

But this scripture does not talk about that. It does not talk about "Behold, I stand at the door and knock" (Rev 3:20 RSV). Rather, here Jesus says simply, "I am the door." He is the way, the path.

This is who Christians are. We are people who think that, of all the possible ways that one might get to God, the best way, the surest way, the only way, is Jesus. In this Jew from Nazareth who lived briefly, died violently, and rose unexpectedly, we have the surest way to God.

As I said, this strikes me as a rather humble image of Jesus to apply to himself. If he is the door, he is not the destination, the end result, but the way to that end. And yet, as we have said before, doors are important. A door tells you a great deal about the character of the house and what goes on inside. When we look at Jesus, we believe that we have seen as much of God as we ever hope to see. Here is not only a door into the house, but a door that is part of the house, a door that tells us much about the house.

In his parabolic speech in this passage, Jesus condemns those bandits who refuse to use the door, who try to sneak over the wall and steal or harm the sheep. He does say, in another passage in John, "I am the way, the truth, and the life. No one comes to the Father except through me" (14:6). Perhaps he is saying something similar here. He is the door, the way to God, the only way.

You can take such language a number of ways. From our mouths as Christians, such talk may sound arrogant, unbearably exclusivist. There is no possible way to God except by Jesus. Of course, we do believe that. And yet the way we believe that is with a certain amount of humility. That is, we cannot imagine that people like us would have any way to God except through Jesus. He has been for us that door, that opening, that way, that window, by which we have done something that is very difficult for people like us to do—namely, to be close to God.

We are also simply confessing that we cannot imagine any means of being with God, the true and living God, except by the way of Jesus. That is, we cannot imagine being in the presence of God that was not in the loving, compassionate, suffering, self-sacrificial way that was the way of Jesus.

There were saviors who attempted to save by raising an army, by starting a revolution, by overthrowing the government, by the worldly wisdom of coercion, or violence, and military might.

Jesus does what he does through words, through preaching and teaching, through action, through self-sacrificial love, by dying. This is the way, the door, the only door, that leads to God.

A while back I was in a discussion with a group of people in church concerning our "war on terrorism." Most of the people in the room thought the war was necessary, justifiable, and right. They had numerous reasons why they thought this to be true. The terrorists had committed a great wrong against us, and we were the innocent victims in this situation. As a nation we must defend ourselves, rid the world of the menace of terrorists, and so on.

A few people in the room thought the war was not a good idea. They doubted that it would be effective, that there were other means of neutralizing the terrorist threat. They worried that we would end up doing more damage than good.

Then someone in the room said, "What would Jesus do? We're Christians. That means that all of these good reasons, either for the war or against the war, may be beside the point. Is there anything that Jesus teaches us, anything that Jesus shows us that can help us decide this issue?"

I thought that she had it just about right. As Christians debate these issues, we ought not necessarily be oppressed by simply, "what works?" Or simply by, "what do the majority of Americans believe?" We believe Jesus is the door. We believe that there is no way for us to get to God or for God to get to us except through this door, this door named Jesus. Therefore it behooves us as those who are trying to move through this door, to use him as the criterion for our behavior, the model for our actions. He is the door—the only way.

I am saying all of this to you because you are those who are gathered here in church today. This means, in light of today's scripture from the Gospel of John, that you know what I am talking about. You are those who have gathered here in the house of God. How did you get here? You had to come through the door. That door is Jesus.

You grasped the handle, opened the door. Or, maybe more to the point, that door has miraculously, graciously opened to you, and you walked through the threshold and came inside.

That is why, historically, the baptisteries are usually in the very front of the church. One had to get around it in order to get into the sanctuary. This was a good reminder that baptism is the door through which we get into the church. Or more to the point of the scripture, baptism is a sign of Jesus, the way that we get to God through him, the entryway, the front door.

This means that when Jesus said, "I am the door," when he asserts, "I am the door that leads to eternal life," many of you sitting here today can say, "Amen!" In your own life, you have demonstrated the truths of this passage of scripture. Jesus has been for you the door, the way to life eternal. That's why you are here. For you, this scripture is not so much an exhortation to do something that you have not done, but a confirmation of what you have already done, something that you have found to be true in your own experience.

He is the door. Amen.

Relating the text

Church-growth experts, those who study the growth and decline of churches, speak of the "back door syndrome." They say that churches do a good enough job of attracting people, even of receiving new members. In other words, we do a great job of managing our front door. But we don't do as good a job of managing our back door.

We get people to join our church, but we never really integrate them into the church, and they leave through the back door. We fortunately get a lot of people who come in through our front door, but we lose far too many through the back door.

Then there are the revolving doors. I once read a history of skyscrapers. It said that one of the most important, absolutely necessary inventions for the skyscraper was the revolving door. When a building is more than a few stories high, the interior drafts in the building increase the air pressure and make it impossible to open the front door. When the drafts are working, the air sweeps in the front door, slamming the door shut, making it difficult to open.

Thus, the revolving door was invented, which enables us to enter and exit a building while controlling the updraft within the building. Of course, a revolving door can be somewhat of a challenge. With a revolving door, one has to know when to let go, and get in the building, without being pushed out!

Are there those who, like those bandits whom Jesus criticized in today's scripture, try to get into the sheepfold without going through the door? They hope that they can have a part in Christ's body, without taking up the disciplines of Christ, without bending their lives to the will of Christ.

Fifth Sunday of Easter

Acts 7:55-60
Psalm 31:1-5, 15-16
1 Peter 2:2-10
John 14:1-14

Power Surge

Selected reading

John 14:1-14 (with reference to 1 Peter 2:2-10)

Theme

Jesus promises us that he will empower us, even us, to bring light to the world. Jesus is reported to have done some spectacularly good works in the Gospels, and yet Jesus promises us that we will do even greater works because of him. To follow Jesus is to have faith that he empowers us to do his work in the world, to have confidence that Jesus is saving the world through us.

Introduction to the readings

Acts 7:55-60

As Stephen is martyred for his faith, he looks up to heaven, and, filled with the Holy Spirit, he has a vision of Christ seated at the right hand of God.

1 Peter 2:2-10

An early Christian congregation is told, "you are a chosen race, a royal priesthood, a holy nation, a people who are God's own possession. You have become this people so that you may speak of the wonderful acts of the one who called you out of darkness into his amazing light" (v. 9).

John 14:1-14

Jesus reassures his anxious disciples, telling them not only that "whoever has seen me has seen the Father" but also that they "will do even greater works than these" (vv. 9, 12).

Prayer

Lord Jesus, though you ascended to your Father, reigning there as God, with God, you did not desert us. Rather you were with us in a whole new way. You have empowered us, even us, with your Holy Spirit. You have commissioned us, even us, to do the work of your kingdom. You have sent us, even us, as your emissaries in the world, your hands and feet, your heart for the world.

Give us the courage to see your power at work in us, even us. Embolden us to believe in ourselves as much as you believe in us. Amen.

Encountering the text

In today's Gospel, Jesus is preparing his disciples for his imminent departure. This prompts anxious questions from his followers that center around the anxiety of "what is to become of us?" All their power has come from their proximity to Jesus. Now that Jesus is going away, what about them?

Jesus at first reassures them, telling them to not be "troubled" (John 14:1). He tells them that he and "the Father" are one (14:9-11). As proof of that oneness with the Father, Jesus points to the manifestations of God's power that they have witnessed (14:12-14).

But then Jesus moves from talk about his unique relationship to the Father to some rather astounding statements about his disciples: "Whoever believes in me will do the works that I do. They will do even greater works than these because I am going to the Father" (14:12); those who pray in the name of Jesus enjoy part of Jesus's very special relationship to the Father: "ask me for anything in my name, I will do it" (14:14). Jesus's people do the very same work that Jesus does. To these fearful, often inadequate disciples Jesus promises that they will perform even greater miracles than he has worked.

Wow. Sweeping claims are being made by John not only for the divinity of Jesus but also for the power of his followers. Jesus has a particular, powerful relationship to the Father. But that is not the only truth of today's Gospel: Jesus gives a particularly powerful relationship to his followers.

Proclaiming the text

In this morning's Gospel, from chapter 14 of John's Gospel, Jesus gathers with his disciples to prepare them for the somber events that are to come. When his disciples express anxiety about Jesus's departure, an exasperated Jesus asks, "Have you been with me so long and still you don't know me?" He makes an astounding claim for himself: he and the Father are one, so much are they one that the "father who dwells in me does his works" (14:10). Jesus is able to do that which only God can do.

But then there is more. Jesus prepares his followers by empowering them, reassuring them that they are going to do greater things than Jesus has done. Greater things than even Jesus has done? How can that be? Jesus has done some amazing feats by this point in the Gospel of John. You have heard about the healings, the changing of water to wine, the restoring of sight to the blind, the raising of Lazarus from the dead, as we have preached our way through much of the Gospel of John this year.

And yet Jesus boldly predicts: you will do even greater marvels than he has done, implying that these disciples, so filled with dread and anxiety, are also being filled with a miraculous power because of their relationship with Jesus. Even as Jesus has glorified the Father through his powerful works, so will we glorify the Father, through Jesus, by the works that we will do.

As Jesus leaves his disciples he promises them a divine power surge.

When you look at our church, you may think warmth, friendliness, or maybe even joy, but do you feel power? There are so many aspects of modern life that make us feel powerless. We live our lives under the watchful—well, mostly watchful—eye of the modern bureaucratic state where we are reduced to a number, not a name. We feel a dissipation of the power of the individual in the vast homogenizing tendencies of our world.

The promise was that in a democracy each of us would feel empowered to help shape the direction of our society. But in the last election, as you voted, did you feel power surge through your veins? I doubt it.

"What's the use of trying to change things? I'm just one person," was how one young adult explained why she was totally inactive in politics.

Earlier in John's Gospel it is said that Jesus, the light of the world, came into the darkness. And there was great resistance on the part of the world's darkness to Jesus's light but "the darkness doesn't extinguish the light." The light, the world's true Light, will eventually, powerfully triumph. And we believe that. But this morning John's Gospel would have us to believe even more: the triumph of God also comes through us.

Here is Jesus's astounding promise: "I assure you that whoever believes in me will do the works that I do. They will do even greater works than these because I am going to the Father" (14:12). Jesus is returning to the Father. He returns, not as an able assistant of God the Father, but as God's Son, one with God. Now Jesus empowers us.

Here were a bunch of fearful, self-centered, anxious disciples, huddled together and asking only one question: "Oh Jesus, what is to become of us?"

And it was to these that Jesus promised, "Those of you who believe in me will do even greater work than I have done."

Do you believe it? Do you believe that our church, for all its faults (and if you have been at all active in our congregation you know that we have faults), is empowered to do even greater works than the works done by Jesus?

How did this Gospel of John begin to tell the story of Jesus? It began in much the same way as all the Gospels began: with Jesus calling a group of ordinary people to be his disciples.

That's the way Jesus works. In fact, the Gospel of John itself, written by some early follower of Jesus, is itself a fulfillment of Jesus's promise. Jesus preached some powerful sermons, did some mighty acts, but we would have known about none of it had it not been for the eloquent testimony of the writer of this Gospel. Jesus empowered some ordinary person to give an extraordinary divine witness to Jesus.

As your pastor, if I had the time in this sermon, I could testify to the truth of Jesus's promise: you will do even greater works than I. As evidence for that claim I would point to some of the people sitting here in this congregation this morning.

Jesus raised the dead. I have seen you raise up from your heart-rending divorce and start a whole new life. Jesus healed the blind. I have seen you open the eyes of some despairing person to the vision of a new world simply by loving that person, by standing with that person and giving hope when there was no hope to be seen. Jesus turned water into wine. I have seen you transform what could be a dull, watered-down Bible study into a spirit-filled imbibing of the new wine of God's presence, just by the way you taught the lesson.

I could go on. Sure it takes a great deal of faith to believe that Jesus is who he says he is in today's Gospel: Jesus and the Father are one. When we've seen Jesus, we've seen God. But it also takes some faith to believe what Jesus says about us: God is doing ever greater works through not-so-great people like us!

By the way, in today's epistle, 1 Peter 2:2-10, the writer says to a struggling early Christian congregation, "You are a chosen race, a royal priesthood, a holy nation, a people who are God's own possession" (v. 9). What an astounding thing to say to this little group of early believers, hanging on by their fingernails in the face of imperial persecution and scoffing! The word *priest* is rarely used in the New Testament. When the title *priest* is used, such as in the letter to the Hebrews, it is always applied just to Jesus.

Yet here the case is different. Here *priest* is applied to these ordinary Christians, these laity who are living out the faith in their time and place. They are called "a chosen race"; they are the "royal priesthood," the main preachers who tell the world about the ultimate triumph of God in Jesus Christ.

It's a great deal to claim for ordinary people like you and like me. We are God's great answer to what's wrong with the world. We are God's great, spirit-induced power surge into the world.

Now let's go live like it!

Relating the text

Jesus says in today's Gospel that he is the way to God. Jesus is the way to God because Jesus is one with the Father. That means not only that Jesus is our way to God but also that Jesus is God's way to us. That means when we look at Jesus and see his boundary-breaking love, his far-flung compassion for the downtrodden and the sick, his gracious way with sinners, then we see God. We're not looking at an imitation of God, or even some mirror image of God. We are seeing God. We couldn't make a way to God so, in Jesus, God graciously made a way to us.

And by implication in today's Gospel, Jesus, the Way, says that by working through us, his followers, God is also making a way to the world through us.

In my present job, I've been doing things that I'd never done before. Last year a pastor asked me to come out to his little, rural church and baptize a twelve-year-old boy whom he had been instructing in the faith. I was happy to oblige until the pastor said, "He very much wants to be immersed. Can you do that?"

"Er, uh, sure I can do that," unwilling to admit that I had never baptized anyone by immersion.

I arrived at the church that Sunday morning and, sure enough, there was the pastor standing on the front steps of the little church with a small boy.

"Jeremy, this is the bishop," the pastor said proudly. "It's an honor for you to be baptized by the bishop."

Young Jeremy looked me over and said only, "They tell me you've never done one of these before. I'd feel better if we had a run-through beforehand."

"That was just what I was going to suggest," I said.

We went into the church's fellowship hall, where the pastor showed me their newly purchased font, dressed up by a carpenter in the congregation, surrounded by pots of flowers. Jeremy said, "After you say the words, then you take my hand and lead me up these steps, and do you want me to take off my socks?"

"Er, uh, you can leave them on if you want," I said.

Well, we had a wonderful service that Sunday. I preached on baptism, the choir sang a baptismal anthem, then the whole congregation recessed into the fellowship hall and gathered around the font. I went through the baptismal ritual. Then I asked Jeremy if he had anything to say to the congregation before his baptism.

"Yes, I do. I just want to say to all of you that I'm here today because of you. When my parents got divorced, I thought my world was over. But you stood by me. You told me the stories about Jesus. And I just want to say to you today, thanks for what you did for me. I intend to make you proud as I'm going to try to live my life the way Jesus wants."

Though I was weeping profusely (Jeremy asked, as I led him up the steps into the pool, "Are you going to be okay?"), I baptized Jeremy, and the church sang a great "Hallelujah!"

It was for me one of the most potent experiences of the power of God made manifest, surging through the church, to claim new life for Christ's mission.

"In all of our thinking and living it is important to keep the negative and positive counterparts together. Both are good. It is good never to retaliate, because if we repay evil for evil, we double the evil, adding a second evil to the first, and so increasing the work of evil in the world. It is even better to be positive, to bless, to do good, to seek peace, and to serve and convert our enemy, because if we thus repay good for evil, we reduce the tally of evil in the world, while at the same time increasing the tally of good. To repay evil for evil is to be overcome by it; to repay good for evil is to overcome evil with good. This is the way of the cross."

—John Stott, *The Message of Romans: God's Good News for the World,*
The Bible Speaks Today (Downer's Grove, IL:
InterVarsity, 2014), ch 20

Sixth Sunday of Easter

Acts 17:22-31

Psalm 66:8-20

1 Peter 3:13-22

John 14:15-21

Thinking after Easter

Selected reading

Acts 17:22-31

Theme

Easter is a disruption in our accustomed, predictable, assumed world. After Easter, we are forced to go back and rethink so much of what we once thought to be true and possible. Easter demands a whole new way of thinking about the world, a way of thought based upon the gracious revelation of God in Christ.

Introduction to the readings

Acts 17:22-31

Paul speaks in Athens, telling the story of Jesus.

1 Peter 3:13-22

The First Letter of Peter gives practical advice to an early congregation, advice based upon the resurrection of Jesus.

John 14:15-21
Jesus urges his disciples to love one another.

Prayer

Lord, help us to understand your truth. Enable us to lay aside our doubts, to cast away our preconceptions, and to think of you with open minds, willing hearts, and an eagerness for your word to us.

By the power of your Holy Spirit, reveal to us those things that we could not have known had you not loved us enough to show them to us.

For your grace in speaking to us, in coming to us, in giving us new life in the resurrection of Jesus, we give you thanks. Amen.

Encountering the text

The Acts of the Apostles might better be named the Acts of Paul because, for some time now in Acts, the journeys of Paul have been center stage. He has been traveling throughout the eastern Mediterranean. Now Luke, the writer of Acts, takes Paul to Athens, the center of classical Greco-Roman culture.

Luke takes him before the gospel's cultured despisers in Athens. Paul confronts them using the best of his classical rhetorical skills.

Paul begins by citing evidence for his claims within common human experience of nature. All goes well for him until he cites beliefs for which there is little evidence; namely, the resurrection of Christ and the last judgment. It is here that Paul's speech ends and the audience has had enough. The audience divides into those who mock and deride Paul's words and those who are interested in possibly hearing more. Only a few are baptized.

Paul's speech demonstrates the difficulty of thinking about Easter, the tough work of rethinking the world after Easter. We will want to ponder that difficulty in today's sermon on Acts 17, as well as to note that the congregation represents those who have had the truth of Easter revealed to them. That's why they're here this Sunday. That's why they are thinking about Easter.

Proclaiming the text

We had been having a discussion about morality. Is God necessary for good deeds?

A graduate student in biology spoke up. "It all boils down to genetics. We are learning that there's a genetic tendency toward certain behavior that is developmentally beneficial."

This seemed to me the strangest, silliest thing I had ever heard. Then I remembered, he is living in a world of cause-and-effect, biological determinism. And so what he thinks makes sense, if one grants the reality of his "world."

I could imagine two undergraduates walking hand-in-hand in May. One looks into the eyes of the other and says, "I feel a certain evolutionary propensity to propagate the species through you."

His response seems to me one of the dumbest things I've ever heard. Then I remember: he's been indoctrinated into a cause and effect, in that everything can be explained genetically that enables him to think certain things and not other things.

As a preacher, I get you in here and want to help you think about God. But that's not easy. Because immediately, as I begin to talk and you begin to think, you think while you are standing somewhere. You come here with certain convictions about what can and can't be, what it is reasonable to expect in the world.

They told us in seminary preaching classes, "Always begin where your hearers are." Start with something your congregation knows and understands before you attempt to move them toward anything new or unfamiliar.

"People don't come to church," said Harry E. Fosdick to us preachers, "burning to know whatever happened to the biblical Jebusites."

No! They want help with everyday problems. So, start with everyday problems, then move to Scripture to seek answers to their modern questions. Begin where your hearers are.

But what if the good news is good because it is news—that is, it isn't something you have come up with but something that has come to you? What if my job is more than simply to devise some answers to your questions, but rather to give you different questions?

What if my task, as preacher, is not simply to help you think about the world in a new way, but rather to show you a new world, thereby to convince you that you don't yet know how to think?

In today's scripture Paul has been traveling all over the Mediterranean, preaching. He's had a good bit of success. But can the good news of Jesus make its way in a university town? Among sophisticated-thinking people? Will it play in the town with the highest percentage of Ph.D.s in the whole Mediterranean?

Luke, writer of the book of Acts, takes Paul to Athens, which is the cradle and pinnacle of classical civilization. Frankly, Paul is unimpressed. He looks on the Parthenon, the Erechtheion, the Apollo Belvedere, and the Elgin Marbles and sees "the city was flooded with idols" (Acts 17:16). Good Jew that he is, Paul sees this capital of classical art as a wasteland of idolatry. So Paul does a very Jewish thing. He argues in the synagogue, and then he argues out in the street, down in the marketplace, everywhere he can start a fight with anybody.

Some hear Paul and scoff, "What is this babbler saying?" That's a somewhat typical academic put-down for anything that has been excluded from academia—mocking, derision. The Greek name for anybody who didn't speak Greek was *barbarian* because that's how they sounded when they spoke another language, like "ba, ba, barbarian."

Others, more liberal, more open-minded, say, "He seems to be about a proclaimer of foreign gods" (7:18). We are not narrow-minded. Life has its spiritual side. "Let's have a discussion about the spiritual." So they bring him to the Areopagus, where they had their big philosophical debates, and they ask Paul, "What is this new teaching?" (17:19).

Paul stands up and gives the most marvelously crafted pagan oration. This is Aristotle's perfect classical speech. First, begin by flattering your hearers: "People of Athens, I see that you are very religious in every way" (17:22).

Or is he beginning with Jewish condemnation of their pagan idolatry?

Paul seems to say, "People of Athens, you have never met a god you couldn't worship."

He tries to relate to them a little natural theology. They at least have experience in nature. "From one ancestor" he tells them that we have common human origins. He speaks of the change of seasons. "In God we live, move, and exist" (17:28), Paul quotes from contemporary poets.

Then he says, "God overlooks ignorance of these things" and has fixed a day we will be judged by a standard higher than that of our own devising (17:30). God has proved all this by raising Jesus from the dead.

And with that, school is out. When they heard of the resurrection, some mocked. Such a typical, intellectual response. Others say, "This is awfully interesting. We really ought to get together and discuss all this again sometime."

I take this to be a story about thinking after Easter. We think through analogies. Something strange intrudes, "Well, it's like this." But how do you think about things that have no analogy in our experience?

In this world, I am the center and source of all judgments. Don't worry about Bible people or other people, because "it seems right to me" and "who are you to question me?"

In this world, what lives and what dies stays that way. How am I to think of God's victory over death and defeat in the resurrection of Jesus?

As a preacher, I want so badly to be heard, to be understood, for you to understand. But it's hard to understand when the matter for understanding is Easter.

I, like Paul, try to take you as far as I can down the road toward comprehension: I connect with your experience; I grope for analogy, correlation.

But then we get to a point where past experience and present modes of conceptualization just break down. I must proclaim that for which there are few analogical allies in this world: judgment of God and resurrection of Jesus.

Reason can take us just so far, said Aquinas. Then faith is required—a gift, grace—to enable comprehension.

Almost everybody that day didn't get it. But some did. Dionysius got it, and a woman named Damaris. They came forward to be disciples.

And the great thing about this is: that's you. You are only a small percentage of the folk in this town. If this stuff is true, why aren't there more people here on Sunday?

If this stuff is true, it's sort of amazing that we get this many people here on Sunday. Faith is not the result of a savvy application of your intellect to certain problems. It's a gift. Grace.

What is the proof of Easter? In one sense, you are. Despite all evidence to the contrary, despite all the officially sanctioned means to keep you from saying yes, from getting it, you got it. It's a gift. And you got it.

Relating the text

St. Thomas Aquinas wrote that there is a great difference between experiential knowledge that a chaste person has of chastity even if he has never thought about it intellectually, and the abstract, theoretical knowledge of the concept of chastity that a theologian has. He says that there is a "knowledge by connaturality." It is a knowledge that comes by living and doing and receiving, even before that knowledge is put into words.

Perhaps, as we think about things, we think in a desiccated, abstracted, detached fashion that precludes thinking about some of the most important things in life.

Since education seen as transformation is not a magical, mystical moment, repentance is required. Repentance is the process by which our thoughts are reshaped and our actions informed by a new perception of the nature of the world.

"The Greek word *metanoia*, 'repentance,' literally means an 'afterthought.' In this sense metanoia is a change of mind about some ideal or attitude previously held to be true. The change of mind represented by the term involves emotional as well as cognitive dimensions. The change in perception is related to a parallel alternation in our mood or feeling; it implies a change in behavior as well. When one examines the usage of the term in the New Testament, it is apparent that metanoia is basic to the proclamation of the gospel. For example, Jesus is depicted in Mark as entering Galilee to proclaim: 'The time has come; the kingdom of God is upon you; repent, and believe the gospel' (Mark 1:15 NEB). In the preaching and teaching of Jesus, faith is seen as growing out of repentance, and turning to God is understood as the beginning point of a process of transformation" (Malcolm L. Warford, "Metanoia: A Way of Thinking About Christian Education," *New Conversations*, no. 2 [Fall 1977]: 7).

Later in Paul's letters, the idea of metanoia is interpreted as a complete refashioning of the individual's nature and destiny. Paul describes this transformation: "Don't be conformed to the patterns of this world, but be transformed by the renewing of your minds so that you can figure out what God's will is—what is good and pleasing and mature" (Rom 12:2).

Seventh Sunday of Easter

Acts 1:6-14
Psalm 68:1-10, 32-35
1 Peter 4:12-14; 5:6-11
John 17:1-11

An Antisocial Faith

Selected reading

1 Peter 4:12-14; 5:6-11

Theme

Though suffering for our faith is not common among Western Christians, those who bear God's light to the world can expect two things: to meet social resistance to the Gospel message and to be blessed for their bold discipleship.

Introduction to the readings

Acts 1:6-14

The eleven remaining disciples accompany the risen Jesus to Mount Olivet where they receive his promise of the Holy Spirit. Then, when he is taken up into a cloud, two angels appear to promise his return.

1 Peter 4:12-14; 5:6-11

As Peter draws his letter to a close, he assures his readers that their "fiery ordeal" (v. 12 NRSV) is a test of faith and an opportunity to share in Christ's suffering. He also assures them of God's grace to restore and strengthen them.

John 17:1-11

In this, his "high priestly prayer," Jesus glorifies God and then prays for his disciples that they may be protected and kept in unity of faith.

Prayer

God of strength and unity, Jesus prayed fervently for his disciples that they be protected in faith. Peter spoke to his people of the blessings that would sustain them in the face of their suffering. Even though most of us have not known the kind of fiery ordeals that fell to the early believers, we do face a world that is largely hostile to your word of truth. Give us strength to proclaim Christ boldly and to let the light of his love shine in dark arenas. If we face challenges or persecution, let the power of your Spirit work through us, turning our feebleness to effectiveness. And sustain us, O God, with the nourishment that comes from feasting on your word and the life that flows through your sacramental means of grace. Amen.

Encountering the text

Peter is addressing a dire concern. For it is evidently the persecution of Christians initiated by Nero that his readers are facing. It will be remembered that Nero, upon causing the great fire in Rome in 64 CE, found a scapegoat among the followers of Christ. Blaming them for the crime, he undertook a vengeful persecution. Tacitus, the Roman historian, reports that those who confessed to believe in Christ were made subject of sport, being covered with animal skins and attacked by dogs, nailed to crosses, set on fire, even burned at night for the illumination of Nero's garden parties.

Yet, in the face of this, Peter speaks with hope. The use of the term *fiery ordeal* is a way of casting the people's suffering in terms of the purification of gold and silver. Faith is refined when put to such tests. Moreover, to suffer for the name of Christ is to be united with him in his suffering. Those who suffer such persecutions are blessed, says Peter, because the glory and the Spirit of God rest upon them.

As the lection skips ahead from chapter 4 to 5:6-11, Peter gives some straightforward, profound instructions: humble yourselves to face whatever fate comes your way, for God will finally exalt you; in the meantime, cast your anxieties on God and trust in his care; be disciplined and alert to the evils afoot in the world; and remain steadfast in faith, knowing that believers everywhere are facing the same persecutions.

The crowning word of hope in light of such bleak circumstances is Peter's promise that after the suffering has ended, God will restore his people. While suffering people would take some immediate comfort in the idea that they would be strengthened and restored to health if they survived the persecution, Peter has his eye on a more far-reaching promise. God has called the faithful to an "eternal glory in Christ Jesus" (1 Pet 5:10). His concluding doxology underscores the infinite nature of his point: "to him be power forever and always" (5:11).

Proclaiming the text

We hear occasional stories today of people suffering for their faith. A Liberian pastor of my acquaintance returned from study leave in America and was met at the airport by local authorities and placed immediately in prison for the anticipated crime of proclaiming the gospel.

Stories such as this indicate that there are still places in the world where people are persecuted for their faith. But in most of the world today the kinds of suffering Christians face are milder than imprisonment and are far from the terrifying ordeals of those who fell prey to the devouring lion named Nero.

Dealing with passages like this one is a challenge because it would be a gross misreading of the text and an inexcusable dishonoring of the martyrs' faith for us to try to equate the petty persecutions of our comfortable world with those persecutions of Peter's day. If we choose to give up certain activities because of our convictions, what pain is there in that? If we are shunned or ridiculed by people who cannot understand our quaint Christian ways, that is little enough to complain of. Nonetheless, we must try to find a way to come to terms with this word from Peter, for it is certainly a word for us.

Perhaps the way to address it is not to ask what are the ways you have suffered persecution for your faith, but to ask the question, will we one day be asked to suffer for our faith? Will God call us to a place or a ministry where our lives will be placed on the line for what we believe? This we can hardly know. But we should be "clearheaded" and "alert" (5:8) to the possibility that we will one day face increasing levels of persecution from the world we live in. We do live in a society that is still largely hostile to the faith we proclaim and the way of life it engenders. Even free societies, like those throughout the Western world, are increasingly opposed to the message of Christ and the lifestyle of faithful Christians. If society consists of the sum of prevailing opinions and practices in our culture, then it is clear that living a life of faith is an antisocial way of behaving. It is to act in ways that are contrary, even offensive, to the norm of society.

It is not difficult to catalog examples that demonstrate this truth. Here is the place where Karl Barth's old dictum about preaching with the newspaper in one hand is useful. Just read aloud the local issues having to do with drug use, violence, sexual abuse, family violence, and crime. Every preacher will have a fresh supply of convincing illustrations regarding the state of local affairs. You will find it difficult, however, to locate many reported instances of wholesome behavior and godly activity. It's not that believers are inactive in the world but that such things are rarely reported as news. When the social norm is to highlight and even celebrate depravity, Christian behavior is strictly antisocial.

That is the way of the world. Human society is largely a dark place. When human nature runs free, it usually runs amok.

Into this darkness, a light is needed to shine so that society is challenged, changed, redirected. Society needs something antisocial to lift it to new possibilities. Sometimes that positive, antisocial behavior erupts spontaneously, as when a disaster releases the compassion of even the stone-hearted. We have seen that happen occasionally, following terrorist attacks, hurricanes, and tsunamis. But there are some people devoted to the light during the less dramatic days.

Who should bring this light to the world? Perhaps it should be the people who live by a higher standard of behavior than the rest of society; the people who have a different morality; those who seek to do the right thing when the news camera is off; those who have a solid sense of rightness and goodness, a truly trained moral compass; and those who have a good book to guide them and keep them on track. Who should bring this light to the world? The children know the answer. They love to raise their little index fingers and sing: "This little light of mine, I'm gonna let it shine...All around the neighborhood, I'm gonna let it shine."

Do we suffer for our faith? Yes, perhaps some of us do. But if we take our call as believers seriously, perhaps many more of us will. If you let your little light shine, sooner or later you are going to get your finger burned. The reason is that our "hoods" don't really want to be transformed and there aren't that many who want to hear the message of Jesus. The world is in the grip of an adversary that prowls around looking for someone to devour. Taking prey from the mouth of a lion is a good way to get your hand chewed off. If you stand against such a world, if you act antisocially, you are going to meet resistance. It may not be as profound as it was in Peter's day, but it will challenge us.

Therefore, insofar as we face resistance and meet persecution for the sake of the name of Christ, then Peter's words of comfort apply for us. "You are blessed, for the Spirit of glory—indeed, the Spirit of God—rests on you" (4:14).

Relating the text

Cartoonist Johnny Hart, creator of the *B.C.* comic strip, is well-known for being a Christian. The *Los Angeles Times* once censored three of Hart's cartoons because his message of hope and faith was too blatant. The problem, the publisher complained, was that the cartoons subjected newspaper readers to a point of view that they did not solicit. Reporting on the sexual exploits of Hollywood stars no doubt continued unabated.

The Soviet persecution of Christians is now only a historical memory. Yet, its effects still linger. On a trip to St. Petersburg, Russia, a number of years ago, I became acquainted with the granddaughter of the former pastor of St. Peter's Lutheran Church. It was once a magnificent Gothic church, but the Soviets took it over and stripped it bare. They removed all vestiges of the faith, dug a huge hole in the floor, poured massive concrete bleachers around the periphery, and erected a thirty-meter diving platform. The church was converted into an Olympic diving pool. As for the pastor, his granddaughter recounted how he had been arrested at night and executed behind the church. The church officials were sent off to Siberia. Later, when the Soviet Union fell apart, the church was returned to the remnant of believers who then faced the enormous challenge of restoring it to a place of worship.

A martyr's death comes still to some. Here are words about faith and suffering spoken by Archbishop Oscar Romero the moment before he was shot to death in church:

"We have just heard in the gospel that those who surrender to the service of people through love of Christ will live like the grain of wheat that dies. This hope comforts us as Christians. We know that every effort to improve society, above all when society is so full of injustice and sin, is an effort that God blesses, that God wants, that God demands of us. We have the security of knowing that what we plant, if nourished with Christian hope, will never fail. This holy Mass, this eucharist, is clearly an act of faith. This body broken and blood shed for human beings encourages us to give our body and blood up to suffering and pain, as Christ did—not for self, but to bring justice and peace to our people. Let us be intimately united in faith and hope at this moment."

At this point, the guns rang out in the sanctuary, ending his life.

Those who have suffered for the sake of Christ are the ones to learn from, people like Dietrich Bonhoeffer:

"God is weak and powerless in the world, and that is precisely the way, the only way, in which he is with us and helps us. Only the suffering God can help.

"To endure the cross is not a tragedy; it is the suffering which is the fruit of an exclusive allegiance to Jesus Christ.

"A Christian is someone who shares the sufferings of God in the world."

"Jesus has many who love his kingdom in heaven, but few who bear his cross. He has many who desire comfort, but few who desire suffering. He finds many to share his feast, but few his fasting. All desire to rejoice with him, but few are willing to suffer for his sake. Many follow Jesus to the breaking of bread, but few to the drinking of the cup of his passion. Many admire the miracles but few follow him to the humiliation of the cross. Many love Jesus as long as no hardship touches them."

—Thomas à Kempis, *Imitation of Christ,* chapter 36

Scripture Index

Page numbers in bold indicate the passages that are the selected readings for each week.

CPSIA information can be obtained
at www.ICGtesting.com
Printed in the USA
LVHW080743240120
644626LV00001B/1